Markus Messling
Universality after Universalism

Beyond Universalism
Partager l'universel

—

Studies on the Contemporary
Études sur le contemporain

Edited by / Édité par
Markus Messling

Volume 4

Markus Messling

Universality after Universalism

—

On Francophone Literatures of the Present

Translated from the German by
Michael Thomas Taylor

DE GRUYTER

This project has received funding from the European Research Council (ERC) under the European Union's Horizon 2020 Research and Innovation programme – Grant Agreement Number 819931

European Research Council
Established by the European Commission

ISBN 978-3-11-221518-0
e-ISBN (PDF) 978-3-11-112830-6
e-ISBN (EPUB) 978-3-11-112961-7
ISSN 2700-1156
DOI https://doi.org/10.1515/9783111128306

Library of Congress Control Number: 2023940029

Bibliographic information published by the Deutsche Nationalbibliothek
The Deutsche Nationalbibliothek lists this publication in the Deutsche Nationalbibliografie; detailed bibliographic data are available on the internet at http://dnb.dnb.de.

Cover image: based on an original idea by Hannes Brischke
Typesetting: Integra Software Services Pvt. Ltd.
Printing and binding: CPI books GmbH, Leck

www.degruyter.com

Acknowledgements

This book was first published in German in 2019, with a French translation in early 2023,[1] and the acknowledgments in these editions convey my gratitude toward interlocutors and intellectual settings that were essential for its creation. Since the German edition was published, I have also been able to discuss my ideas in a number of international contexts; here, I would like to mention those which were especially beneficial for the present version of the book.

One crucial context has been my work with the team of the ERC grant "Minor Universality: Narrative World Productions after Western Universalism," based at Saarland University. Together with Elsie Cohen, Azyza Deiab, Franck Hofmann, Mario Laarmann, Clément Ndé Fongang, Hélène Thiérard, Maria-Anna Schiffers, Laurens Schlicht, and Carla Seemann, we organized events such as the conference "Histoire/histoires: Le concret et l'universel dans les SHS" or the summer school "Restitution, Reparations, Reparation: Towards a New Global Society" at the Villa Vigoni, the Italo-German Center for European Dialogue at Lago di Como. At the series of Minor Universality Lectures at Saarland University we discussed problems of universality after universalism with René Aguigah, Omri Boehm, Julia Christ, Ibou Coulibaly Diop, Laurent Demanze, Souleymane Bachir Diagne, Alexandre Gefen, Ananya Jahanara Kabir, Soumaya Mestiri, Olivier Remaud, and Camille de Toledo. This was also the setting for the growing series of interviews with Arjun Appadurai, Leyla Dakhli, Souleymane Bachir Diagne, Giovanni Levi, Gisèle Sapiro, Adania Shibli, and Maria Stavrinaki.[2]

Leyla Dakhli and Mohamed Kerrou were partners in organizing the symposium "Universalismes, hégémonies et identités" at the Académie tunisiennes des sciences, des lettres et des arts (Beït al-Hikma) in March 2022, which took place amid the backdrop of political and social pressures weighing heavily on Tunisian society in its struggle for a new universality, for a life lived in dignity, between two great universalistic camps and their claims (namely, republicanism and Islamism). I am grateful to Sihem Sidaoui for conversations about the role of recent literature and postrevolutionary cinema in imagining a new society in Tunisia.

One encounter that was central for the book's theoretical questions was the exchange held at the Nobel Symposium in Stockholm in August 2022, organized by Stefan Helgesson, on the theme "(World) Literature and the Problem of the

---

1 *Universalität nach dem Universalismus: Über frankophone Literaturen der Gegenwart* (Berlin: Matthes & Seitz, 2019); *L'universel après l'universalisme: Des littératures francophones du contemporain*, foreword by Souleymane Bachir Diagne, trans. Olivier Mannoni (Paris: Presses universitaires de France, 2023).

2 https://www.youtube.com/@ercminoruniversality4876/videos.

Universal: Philosophical and Philological Approaches." For stimulating conversations in Lidingö and Stockholm about philology, textual and cultural theory, world literature, sociology of literature, and much else, I thank Rosinka Chaudhuri, Debjani Ganguly, Christina Kullberg, John K. Noyes, Francesca Orsini, David Scott, Galin Tihanov, Piet Vemeulen, and Helena Wulff.

In October 2022, I traveled with the ERC team to Mexico City, where we joined Sergio Ugalde Quintana in organizing the multilingual conference "Universality after Universalism: Questions of Philology, Translation, and Intellectual Biographies" at the Colegio de México. The conversations with partners including Humberto Beck, Rafael Mondragón, Daliri Oropeza, Shadi Rohana, and—again and again—with Sergio in Mexico, Teotihuacán, and Puebla were important for me in differentiating the historically violent implications of Christian universalism and tracing their concrete expression in forms of cultural power and subversion in the position and transformation of the baroque in Mexico's past and present.

In January 2023, I was privileged to give a lecture-cum-seminar in the Experimental Critical Theory Program at UCLA, under that year's framework of "Narrative Thinking." I am enormously grateful to Zrinka Stahuljak and Giulia Sissa for this invitation, which led to exciting discussions with colleagues across disciplines on the question of historical narrative and the politics of public memory and the importance of aesthetics as a means of establishing community.

For ongoing conversation about the possibilities of unfolding the ideal of humanity from narrative forms, I am grateful to Albrecht Buschmann, Leyla Dakhli, Franck Hofmann, Giovanni Levi, Olivier Remaud, Gisèle Sapiro, Christiane Solte-Gresser, Camille de Toledo, and Souleymane Bachir Diagne, who also graciously allowed his foreword to the French edition to be included in this version of the book.

Finally, the translation of the book itself leads to the question of a new universality that Souleymane Bachir Diagne has called the "lateral universality of translation." Michael Thomas Taylor has masterfully translated my writing, strongly influenced by francophone debates and framed in a German-language tradition of "world poetics," into an anglophone discussion that at times hegemonically forgets its own particularity. I am grateful to Michael not only for his translation, but also for the extended and illuminating conversations about traditions of discourse and scholarship, the power of language, and the desire to let idiosyncrasies of thought and language shine through.

I would like to thank Andreas Rötzer and Loan Nguyen of Matthes und Seitz and Paul Garapon of Presses universitaires de France for their generosity and for granting the rights for this edition. I also owe special thanks to Ulrike Krauß and Gabrielle Cornefert for providing a home for this book at De Gruyter.

Foreword
Souleymane Bachir Diagne

Today, Markus Messling writes, European universalism is coming to an end. This statement, expressed in the tone of a simple observation, forms the major premise of the present book. It is also the thesis of Immanuel Wallerstein's work *European Universalism: The Rhetoric of Power*.[1] Wallerstein argues that the time in which "European humanity" (to use Edmund Husserl's phrase) believed it could impose upon "others" its own narrative of itself as the natural bearer of universality—and consequently, the time of a "civilizing mission" and the responsibility it took upon itself (the famous "White Man's burden")—is the time of a world that is no more: a world in which *the West* is the self-proclaimed center and *the Rest*, its periphery.

Just as the revolution of modern science once dislodged the earth from the center of a closed world by envisioning it as one planet among many within the *apeiron* of an infinite universe, Europe now appears in the guise suggested by geography, or to quote Jean-Paul Sartre, as "the peninsula that Asia pushes up to the edge of the Atlantic."[2] There is perhaps no better way to describe the postcolonial world than as a "provincialization of Europe," as one region among the many regions of the earth, just as what has happened with decolonization in its many forms is quite simply that the plurality of a world of languages and human cultures has proven irreducible to the centrality—the one universality—claimed by Europe.

A certain European consciousness might continue to inhabit this postcolonial state of affairs in a state of sadness and melancholy. And this is the astute reading that Markus Messling proposes here of the work of writer Michel Houellebecq— as the paramount symbol, within the world of French letters, of such an unhappy consciousness and of "the melancholy of the White man." Yet Messling's book makes another essential claim, which is that the end of European universalism is not in fact the end of universality but perhaps its beginning.

In his book *European Universalism*, Immanuel Wallerstein sketches out the course we must take: to begin constructing a universality that would be truly universal, and not merely the product of the European imperialist "rhetoric of power" named in the book's subtitle. Markus Messling's book goes further. Messling is not content to invoke the promise of a universality inscribed within the

---

1 Immanuel Wallerstein, *European Universalism: The Rhetoric of Power* (New York: New Press, 2006).
2 As quoted in Léopold Sédar Senghor, *Anthologie de la nouvelle poésie nègre et malgache de langue française*, précédée de *Orphée noir*, ed. Jean-Paul Sartre (Paris: Puf, 1969), x.

plurality and diversity of the world. He shows instead how this universality manifests itself as something that can be intuited and thought within the sphere of *littérature-monde,* and in particular in literature written in French.

French certainly holds an important place in the invention of European universalism. For as Markus Messling reminds us, it played an essential role in the narrative that France constructed about itself—one built upon the idea that this country, as well as the language that it has claimed as the very principle of its identity, maintains a particular relationship to universality. Messling's book rightly points out the importance of attending to the singular character of French universalism in discussions that speak, perhaps too generally, of European or Western universalism. The untranslatable French word "laïcité" is a sign of this singularity.

This is why the "Francophonie" and its literatures, as well as the problems posed by the word itself, constitute a privileged field for examining the question of universality from a position rooted within the plurality of the world, from a universality after pluralism. The unique value of Messling's books lies in its method of pursuing such an investigation through readings of "francophone" authors as diverse as Mathias Énard, Léonora Miano, Kossi Efoui, Camille de Toledo, and Wajdi Mouawad.

All these readings speak, in their own way, against the idea that the only response lies in "submitting" to a "melancholy" opening toward nothingness. They suggest instead that at the end of European universalism we find the task of turning this "nostalgia" into a "resource for the future," as one of the book's chapters calls it. The book argues, in other words, against the pretension of an imperialist universalism. It seeks to know how one might employ the ability to construct and compare multiple perspectives, along with the decolonizing power that this brings—yet without becoming ensconced in a relativism that would translate nothing but a confining conception of cultural identities.

Between the "emaciated universalism" named by Aimé Césaire in his "Letter to Maurice Thorez,"[3] and a relativism that closes off the possibility of any "commonality" so necessary in our world, in which planetary emergencies compel us to find a common humanity to ensure that we may inhabit the earth together, there is in fact space for a "lateral universality" of encounter and translation.[4]

---

3 Aimé Césaire, "Letter to Maurice Thorez" (October 24, 1956), in *Écrits politiques (1935–1956),* ed. Édouard de Lépine, preface by Marc Césaire (Paris: Jean-Michel Place, 2016), 387–394, on 393.
4 It is the philosopher Maurice Merleau-Ponty who contrasts a "universalism from above" to a "lateral universality" (in *Signes,* Paris: Gallimard, 1960, 193). This concept is at the center of my work, and Markus Messling shows here the convergence with his own research.

This is a space of encounter because it is continuously born and reborn from the work of horizontally expounding relations between the cultures and languages of the world. And it is a space of translation precisely because learning to speak the same language—amid our post-Babel plurality of languages—means nothing else.

This book by Markus Messling is both an invitation and an aid to think about this (multi)lateral universality whose time is now.

Translated from the French by Michael Thomas Taylor

Translator's Note

Works originally appearing in languages other than English have been cited from published translations wherever possible; where none existed, I have translated the sources. As a general rule, I refer only to the published translations in the footnotes and bibliography, except for the novels and other primary literary sources discussed in the book. For these literary texts, the bibliography provides the original publication information, while the footnotes indicate the first date of appearance.

Contents

Universality after Universalism

We are witnessing an epoch in which a new consciousness of the world is taking shape. However far back in human history we might trace the material processes of globalization, there is general agreement today that its dynamic has rapidly accelerated since the nineteenth century, giving rise to an awareness of living under the specific conditions of a "globalized world."[1] We can hardly think of the world today without simultaneously being cognizant of its global interconnectedness. And yet the circulation and interweaving of people, data, and goods of all kinds have not necessarily generated a universalistic consciousness—this much has been made unmistakably clear by the pushbacks against universalism that have come from relativistic and identitarian impulses worldwide. In his book *Necropolitics*, the Cameroonian historian and philosopher Achille Mbembe has shown that Western democracies throughout history have consistently contravened their own claims, structurally co-creating a "dark body" that has been oppressed and exploited as a part of humanity lacking the very right to have rights. He argues that colonialism is as much part of the history of democratic modernity as are the policies of isolation that emerged from it and still have an effect today:

> Today we see the principle of equality being undone by the laws of autochthony and common origin, as well as by divisions within citizenship . . . Confronted with the perilous situations so characteristic of the age, the question, at least in appearance, is no longer to know how to reconcile the exercise of life and freedom with the knowledge of truth and solicitude for those different from oneself. From now on, it is to know how, in a sort of primitive outpouring, to actualize the will to power by means that are half-cruel, half-virtuous.[2]

---

1 See also, from a range of perspectives: Jürgen Osterhammel, *The Transformation of the World: A Global History of the Nineteenth Century* (Princeton: Princeton University Press, 2014), "Introduction to the First German Edition," xiv–xxii; Ottmar Ette, "European Literature(s) in the Global Context," in *Literature for Europe?*, ed. Theo D'haen and Iannis Goerlandt (Amsterdam: Rodopi, 2009), 123–160; Arjun Appadurai, *The Future as Cultural Fact: Essays on the Global Condition* (New York: Verso Books, 2013); Sebastian Conrad, *Globalgeschichte: Eine Einführung* (Munich: C.H. Beck, 2013); Samuel Moyn and Andrew Sartori, "Approaches to Global Intellectual History," in *Global Intellectual History*, ed. Samuel Moyn and Andrew Sartori (New York: Columbia University Press, 2013), 3–30; Lynn Hunt, *Writing History in the Global Era* (New York: W.W. Norton and Company, 2014), especially 44–77.
2 Achille Mbembe, *Necropolitics*, trans. Steven Corcoran (Durham: Duke University Press, 2019), 3. See also Immanuel Wallerstein, "The Ideological Tensions of Capitalism: Universalism versus Racism and Sexism," in *Race, Nation, Class: Ambiguous Identities*, ed. Étienne Balibar and Immanuel Wallerstein (New York: Verso, 1991), 29–36.

Global thinking and a consciousness of humanity are by no means one and the same.[3] Here, we clearly see the limits of exclusively economic notions of globalization, which have often neglected cultural consciousness as a supposedly idealistic superstructural phenomenon.[4] Pressured by a latent historical sense of guilt, Western democracies appear increasingly unable to articulate a new consciousness of what it means to be human in the face of identitarian spasms and paranoid defensive positions. And at the same time, it is no coincidence that intellectuals such as Souleymane Bachir Diagne,[5] Mondher Kilani,[6] Chimamanda Ngozi Adichie,[7] Felwine Sarr,[8] or, here too, Achille Mbembe, are insistently formulating proposals for such an awareness. These are thinkers whose colonial experience has always made them part of a history of relating to Europe's consciousness of the world. It is not enough to imagine that the goals, forms, and practices of living together have been essentially completed by Western progress, to be copied by others, writes Felwine Sarr, a Senegalese economist and cultural theorist, in his book *Afrotopia*. "This kind of mimicry is anesthetizing and deadly. It marks the end of *poïesis* (creativity). It's a veritable amputation of the generic function of the human as creator."[9] The question being raised by thinkers such as Sarr or Mbembe of what place formerly colonized societies—in this case, in Africa—have within world society thus goes beyond exploring the scope of possible futures available to these writers' society of origin.[10] It entails a demand for the repair of human

---

3 Consider, for instance, Mbembe's analysis of a world that appears to be increasingly connected via global digitalization, yet with rifts that are being deepened by the technology sector: "Le droit universel à la respiration," *Analyse Opinion Critique*, April 6, 2020, https://aoc.media/opinion/2020/04/05/le-droit-universel-a-la-respiration/, accessed May 2, 2021.

4 This point was made by Ottmar Ette in *TransArea: Eine literarische Globalisierungsgeschichte* (Berlin: De Gruyter, 2012).

5 Souleymane Bachir Diagne and Jean-Loup Amselle, *En quête d'Afrique(s): Universalisme et pensée décoloniale* (Paris: Albin Michel, 2018).

6 Mondher Kilani, *Pour un universalisme critique: Essai d'anthropologie du contemporain* (Paris: La Découverte, 2014).

7 See, for instance, Chimamanda Ngozi Adichie's lecture "The Danger of a Single Story" at the TED Global Talks 2009, www.ted.com/talks/chimamanda_adichie_the_danger_of_a_single_ story/details, accessed August 18, 2020.

8 Felwine Sarr, *Afrotopia*, trans. Drew S. Burk (Minneapolis: University of Minnesota Press, 2019).

9 Sarr, *Afrotopia*, 97.

10 On this point, see Susanne Gehrmann, "Afropolitanism and Afro/euro/peanism: New Identity Concepts in the Era of Globalization," *Ibadan Journal of Humanistic Studies* 26, no. 2 (2016): 177–191, and Gerhmann, "Cosmopolitanism with African Roots: Afropolitanism's Ambivalent Mobilities," *Journal of African Cultural Studies* 28, no. 1 (2016): 61–72.

relations in and to the world in general.[11] Achille Mbembe builds here on the critique of colonialism by the first generation of the *négritude*, on Aimé Césaire and above all on Frantz Fanon, who sought to establish not only a counter-discourse to colonialism but also a new consciousness of humanity:

> In general fashion, whether with Césaire or Fanon, or with Senghor or Glissant, the question of repudiating the idea of "man" as such once and for all never arises. More often the concern is to point up the dead ends of the Western discourse on "man" with the aim of amending it. The point then amounts either to insisting on the fact that the human is less a name than a praxis and a becoming (Wynter), or else to appeal to a new, more "planetary" humanity (Gilroy), to a poetics of the Earth, and to a world made of the flesh of All (Glissant), within which each human subject could once more be the bearer of his speech, his name, his acts, and his desires.[12]

Meeting this demand is the great challenge Europe faces today. We must narrate ourselves in a new way.

In one of his last masterpieces, the 2010 *Film Socialisme: La liberté coûte cher,* Jean-Luc Godard displaces European society onto the Mediterranean Sea.[13] Here, it is a cruise ship and its passengers that represent the old continent. On board, we find a web of history: Nazi criminals, French philosophy, a police agent from Moscow, an American singer—the shadow side of Europe's grand narrative, contradictory and labyrinthine, absurd and abysmal. The sea is rough, waves crash against the ship's bow, and the stormy wind swallows the voices of the characters on deck. What is being said remains unintelligible. In Godard's view, the process of communicating with the world, of coming to an understanding, is in crisis. Europe no longer understands itself. Like a ship tossed back and forth by the waves, the old continent is weary for a tranquil place in the world. The irony of coincidence has it that Godard's film was shot on the Costa Concordia, the ship that was later run aground so dramatically off the Italian island of Giglio by its captain's arrogance.[14]

Then the film makes a cut. The second part of Godard's video montage is tellingly titled: "Quo vadis Europa." Where *is* Europe going? One sequence in the film is set at a gas station in France. In a series of montage scenes, the owner's

---

11 See the video "Rhinoceros Asks . . . Souleymane Bachir Diagne: What Is Reparation?," https://www.rhinozeros-projekt.de/zeitschrift/das-projekt, accessed March 29, 2021.
12 See Mbembe, *Necropolitics*, 160.
13 Jean-Luc Godard, *Film Socialisme: La liberté coûte cher* (Paris 2010), https://www.imdb.com/title/tt1438535/.
14 The question of the Méditerranée as an "empty center" of European self-reflection is something I have pursued with Franck Hofmann in two books: *Leeres Zentrum: Das Mittelmeer und die literarische Moderne, Eine Anthologie*, ed. Franck Hofmann and Markus Messling (Berlin: Kulturverlag Kadmos, 2015); *Fluchtpunkt: Das Mittelmeer und die europäische Krise*, ed. Franck Hofmann and Markus Messling (Berlin: Kulturverlag Kadmos, 2017).

children express moral doubts about their parents, whose fundamental republican principles—*liberté, égalité, fraternité*—have come to hold hardly any validity at all. It is not only that the violence engulfing the world has torn apart these emancipatory ideals: they have themselves in fact too often been deployed to legitimize oppression and violence. The parents are enjoined to justify this reality, in a sequence staged as an intergenerational tribunal in which the culture that emerged from the Enlightenment, Europe itself, pleads its own defense. The banality of the location reveals just how quotidian, just how far-reaching, this loss of certainty and legitimacy have become. A young woman stands next to the gas pump reading Honoré de Balzac's serial novel *Lost Illusions*.

And then—the entrance of a Peruvian llama. Or to be more precise, the llama is simply there. Within this culturally charged scene, creatureliness enters the stage. And yet the animal, left behind by a circus, is more than a bizarre object of amazement. Read as an ironic quotation, it marks the appearance of the world itself. Like the world-famous rhinoceros drawn by Albrecht Dürer, which tragically died in a shipwreck in the Gulf of La Spezia, or the stranded stingray that the party of revelers stumbles upon at the end of Fellini's *La Dolce Vita*, the llama joins the ranks of tropical animals that have been imprinted into our collective memory as placeholders for a terra incognita. Godard's llama enters the stage as a metaphor calling for the violent appropriation of a "new world" that has been repressed into the subconscious and now refuses to release its grip on Europe. The final monologue delivered by the gas station owner, a true apologia in which he tries to justify himself to his son, is quietly stretched in this scene to reach back into that world-historical situation produced by the universalism of European modernity. The conclusion of the father's speech is anything but reassuring: "Wars everywhere, for the last fifty years. We see ourselves in these wars as if reflected in a mirror . . ."

Europe has paid far too little heed to the Christian values it loudly claims for itself, to the idea of enlightened reason or the ideals of 1789 that it likes to proclaim to the world, for there to be any doubt that its demand for civilizing progress has essentially served to assert its own interests. Its constantly repeated insistence on human rights and democracy rings hollow in the face of the devastation wrought by the two Iraq wars of 1990/91 and 2003—both of which were waged under the banner of enforcing international legal norms, and in the second case at least, absurdly so. "Does the end justify the means? That is possible. But what will justify the end?" Albert Camus asks in *The Rebel*. "To that question, which historical thought leaves pending, rebellion replies: the means."[15]

---

15 Albert Camus, *The Rebel: An Essay on Man in Revolt*, trans. Anthony Bower (New York: Vintage Books: 1991), 292.

European universalism has always fought for its positions with arguments that have too easily been used to water down its claims of universality and deny to certain groups the force of its ideals. One need only recall, for example, the theological dispute that unfolded in Valladolid, Spain, in 1550/51 on the question of whether America's "Indians," as they were called in the debate, were to be treated as Christians. The result—despite Bartolomé de Las Casas's objections—was that claims of Christian universality were sacrificed in practice in order to further the ruling interests of the Spanish crown and its vassals. Or the modern era's transatlantic slave trade, which was legitimized contrary to the idea of universal natural law by theories of race that degraded Africans to livestock. Here, the Enlightenment's discovery of "human nature" paradoxically served to emphasize biological differences all the more insistently. There are many such examples. Taken together, however, they have revealed throughout history that European universalism was not universal—that it rather sought to universalize its own beliefs, epistemic assumptions, and norms, and that it did so through power and violence.[16] In 1914, at the height of European imperialism, Europe had assimilated the world and moreover installed a regime of standardization and subjugation, exploitation and murder, whose demarcations and conflicts still dominate our times.

Today, European universalism is coming to an end—ending, too, a model of appropriating the world that has been symbolically centered on Paris since the French Revolution. More than any other country, France has not only committed itself to the ideals of 1789 but made universalism the very principle of the state—internally, in policies enforcing harmonization and centralization; and externally, in the sense of a *mission civilisatrice* that has been practically identical with France's imperial mission since the revolution. If Hegel articulated the concept of European universalism as the coming-to-itself of spirit, Paris is its site and figure. In serving as the "capital of the nineteenth century," to cite Walter Benjamin's dictum, Paris also paradigmatically represented the universalizing claims of European modernity. The immaterial, rationalist core of this claim was the notion of French as the *langue de la clarté*, the language of clear thought and reason, which was

---

16 For a systematic critique, see Immanuel Wallerstein, *European Universalism: The Rhetoric of Power* (New York: New Press, 2006), 1–29, and Souleymane Bachir Diagne, "Penser l'universel avec Étienne Balibar," *Raison publique* 19, no. 2 (2014): 15–21; for a historical approach, see the contributions in *The Epoch of Universalism/L'époque de l'universalisme (1769–1989)*, ed. Franck Hofmann and Markus Messling (Berlin: De Gruyter, 2021). And, of course, for an account of the violence immanent in European rationalism, see the ever-pertinent Max Horkheimer and Theodor W. Adorno, *Dialectic of the Enlightenment: Philosophical Fragments*, trans. Edmund Jephcott (Stanford: Stanford University Press, 2002).

elevated to the measure of civilizing progress.[17] This claim to culture has always demonstrated to colonial subjects both equality and hierarchy, both the possibility of integration into modernity and the impossibility of participating outside the center. The almost mythical inner dichotomy in France of province and metropolis is reflected in the outer dichotomy of France and the French-speaking world.

This historical background, this enormous tension between a universalist program and the constriction of its norms, is why today's francophone community has a very particular awareness of the problem posed by the dissolution of European legitimacy.[18] Compared to other postcolonial contexts, the francophone world stands out in that the question of how to justify the idea of humanity always remains inscribed within the very language of French. Simply because of the language itself, this tension remains present and unresolved. Writing in French always raises the question of a universality capable of transcending the claims the center makes to impose its norms.

Criticisms of French universalism have raged ever since its assertion as a political mission by the French Revolution. Since the early twentieth century, the critique has swelled into a crisis[19]—especially in intellectual processes of decolonization in which French universalism stands as a model for a humanistic undergirding of European power. Frantz Fanon summed up this charge in his 1961 book *The Wretched of the Earth*:

> In its narcissistic monologue the colonialist bourgeoisie, by way of its academics, had implanted in the minds of the colonized that the essential values—meaning Western values—remain eternal despite all errors attributable to man.[20]

During decolonization, discourses of rejection and counteridentity flourished that remain powerful today. Yet elsewhere, too, such as in the French feminist debate of the 1990s, various discursive positions have drawn their strength from the question of how they relate to republican universalism. "It is surely disturbing," writes Naomi Schor, "that to this day there is no example of a universalism that is all-inclusive. *Parité* may save French universalism, but the future of universalism as anything but an illusion at worst, or at best a noble ideal with unsurpassed

---

17 See Naomi Schor, "The Crisis of French Universalism," *Yale French Studies* 100 (2001): 43–64, on 44–46.
18 See the broad overview of historical backgrounds and positions within the francophone spectrum in *Postcolonial Thought in the French Speaking World*, ed. Charles Forsdick and David Murphy (Liverpool: Liverpool University Press, 2009).
19 See Schor, "The Crisis of French Universalism," 55–56.
20 Frantz Fanon, *The Wretched of the Earth*, trans. Richard Philcox (New York: Grove Press, 2005), 11.

emancipatory potential, remains in doubt."[21] This question of just representation implies a connection to the postcolonial context. But today a new self-awareness is emerging on the part of speakers of French who possess nationalities beyond that of France that no longer centers on Europe, but rather on a global intellectual development:

> Is it France's fear of its own reflection or simply the eternal comfort of academic immobility that, in the long run, will eventually atrophy and marginalize French thought and literature on an international level, where the French imagination is increasingly represented by creators and thinkers from elsewhere?[22]

All postmigrant societies of the West are today navigating in this field of tension. But the French Republic's universalistic self-image has resulted in a particular urgency in the need to find a "solution" to the problems generated by the contradictions of its own universalism. Recently, this has resulted in the remarkable reports to the French president, Emmanuel Macron, on looted art,[23] as well as the report on the memory of the Algerian war[24]—an event uniquely burdened by the question of a guilt that French society is examining only with hesitance.[25] This very debate being carried out by France as the "nation universaliste" thus essentially shows that the universalism the nation proclaims would first have to be reestablished, or even concretely constructed, through reparative acts. It is in this sense that Souleymane Bachir Diagne has sought to resolve the contradiction between postcolonial critique and universalism and to turn it toward the future.[26] This means seeing that the global condition of our times consists above all in the challenge of shaping the consequences of centuries of colonialism and the collapse of the European claim to interpret the world—and not only strategically in terms of power, but also materially,

---

21 Schor, "The Crisis of French Universalism," 64.

22 Alain Mabanckou, "Introduction: Labourer de nouvelles terres," in *Penser et écrire l'Afrique aujourd'hui*, ed. Alain Mabanckou (Paris: Éditions du Seuil, 2017), 9.

23 Felwine Sarr and Bénédicte Savoy, "Rapport sur la restitution du patrimoine culturel africain: Vers une nouvelle éthique relationnelle," November 2018, https://www.vie-publique.fr/sites/default/files/rapport/pdf/194000291.pdf, accessed May 2, 2021. The report has also been published in book form: Felwine Sarr and Bénédicte Savoy, *Restituer le patrimoine africain* (Paris: Philippe Rey/ Édition du Seuil, 2018).

24 Benjamin Stora, "Les questions mémorielles portant sur la colonization et la guerre d'Algérie," Januar 2021, https://www.elysee.fr/admin/upload/default/0001/09/0586b6b0ef1c2fc2540589c6 d56a1ae63a65d97c.pdf, accessed May 2, 2021.

25 See Raphaëlle Branche, *Papa, qu'as-tu fait en Algérie?* (Paris: La Découverte, 2020).

26 See the discussion by Souleymane Bachir Diagne, "On the Postcolonial and the Universal?," *Rue Descartes* (Collège international de Philosophie) 78, no. 2 (2013): 7–18.

as a politics of memory, and therapeutically.[27] Hence in turning to France, the present book seeks a perspective that analyzes a general condition of the world in which we live rather than exonerating any one particular standpoint. And in this sense, its reading of literature written in French is a reading of a contemporary constellation of symptoms.

When it comes to using literary texts to understand the symptoms of historical constellations, Walter Benjamin's book *Charles Baudelaire* remains unsurpassed.[28] Benjamin prepared his study of a "lyric poet in the age of high capitalism," as the book is subtitled, out of excerpts from his work on the Paris arcades; the book itself remained a fragment. In this project, Benjamin brings together the revolution of 1848, the Paris Commune, and Blanqui's anarchism with Baudelaire's thought and writing—not, of course, by programmatically deriving Baudelaire's work from these other moments (the Paris Commune, for instance, took place after Baudelaire's death in 1867). Rather, Benjamin argues that both Baudelaire's work and these other historical moments were part of an earthquake in the experience of society and the world engendered by the revolution of 1789. Benjamin dissects a subcutaneous link connecting the rage and barricades of 1848 and 1870/71 with Baudelaire's furious poetry. "Baudelaire's poetry," Benjamin writes, pointing to the radical rejection of the arrangement that the French bourgeoisie made with the Bourbon Restoration, and to the power of this uprising, "has preserved in words the strength that made such a thing possible."[29] One need not accept Benjamin's premises for his philosophy of history to understand the power of a literary history that focuses on the

---

27 "Shaping" here no longer means simply determining how the old relationships constituting the world are transformed into new ones, but also listening and drawing conclusions from those emancipatory movements of the formerly colonized world that emphasize the aspect of dignity, self-respect, and empowerment as conditions for entering into horizontal relationships in the field of politics. For a foundational account of the problem of alienated consciousness, see Frantz Fanon, *Black Skin, White Masks* (London: Penguin Classics, 2020); on the therapeutic dimension of (post)colonial relations see Achille Mbembe, *Sortir de la Grande Nuit* (Paris: La Découverte, 2010), translated by Daniela Ginsburg as *Out of the Dark Night: Essays on Decolonization* (New York: Columbia University Press, 2019), as well as Felwine Sarr, *Afrotopia*, and in particular the chapter "Healing Oneself, Naming Oneself," 62–69. See also Elsa Dorlin's account of how the militancy of oppressed social groups in North America developed from political strategies of revenge to those of empowerment, in *Se défendre: Une philosophie de la violence* (Paris: La Découverte, 2017), 139–156.

28 Benjamin, Walter, *Charles Baudelaire: Ein Lyriker im Zeitalter des Hochkapitalismus* (Frankfurt am Main: Suhrkamp, 1974); translated by Harry Zohn as *Charles Baudelaire: A Lyric Poet in the Era of High Capitalism*, in *Walter Benjamin: Selected Writings* (London: Verso, 1997), and as "The Paris of the Second Empire in Baudelaire," in *Selected Writings*, vol. 4, 1938–1940, ed. Howard Eiland and Michael W. Jennings (Cambridge, MA: Belknap Press, 2003), 3–92.

29 Benjamin, "The Paris of the Second Empire in Baudelaire," 63.

perception of epistemic upheavals. By describing the restructuring of approaches to reality, such a method attempts to grasp the emotional, psychological, and social conditions and costs of radical political ruptures. And in this sense, such an approach can make present a dimension of history that is all too easily forgotten when history is represented only in terms of what has asserted itself as factual reality.

In turning toward reality, francophone literatures all over the world are today posing the question of appropriating the world anew. Yet they remain tied, at least implicitly, to France as their point of reference, just as French literature itself remains tied to global critique. With the end of European universalism, a new type of writing has recently emerged in France that has turned away from the introspections of postmodernism.[30] French literature, and of course especially the novel, has returned its attention to the question of reality, bringing into play the energies that today haunt Europe: insecurity, anger, a longing for ideals, melancholy. This literature nevertheless serves a function that is not merely compensatory: it offers an opening to a world of globalization that far exceeds France. In francophone literatures, in other words, the question of Europe encounters a form of universalism that is reflected back toward Europe. In these literatures, a new realism and a new claim to appropriating the world belong together. This combination inherently poses the question of how to generate a new universality. And it is this historical constellation that the present book attempts to grasp.

Since the beginning of the French Empire, the rationalistic and idealistic premises of the European model have come to be questioned, and their hegemonic implications have been precisely analyzed by work in postcolonial studies.[31] The boundless violence of the modern period, together with the social and ecological cost it has exacted, have largely invalidated Europe's claim to paradigmatically shape and interpret the world.[32] One result is a "provincialization" of Europe: its claim to knowledge of the world is today increasingly being driven back into its

---

30 See also Dominique Viart and Bruno Vercier, *La littérature française au présent: Héritage, modernité, mutations,* 2nd ed. (Paris: Bordas, 2008), 15–21 and 211–213.

31 The field of critical and/or postcolonial studies is so vast that it makes no sense to try and reflect it in this book's bibliography. Salient recent positions include Françoise Lionnet and Shu-mei Shih, eds., *The Creolization of Theory* (Durham: Duke University Press, 2011); Rajiv Malhotra, *Being Different: An Indian Challenge to Western Universalism* (Noida: HarperCollins Publishers India, 2011); Samuel Moyn, *Christian Human Rights* (Philadelphia: University of Pennsylvania Press, 2015); Achille Mbembe, *Critique of Black Reason,* trans. Laurent Dubois (Durham: Duke University Press, 2017).

32 See also the chapter "Lost Legitimacy" in Amin Maalouf, *Disordered World: Setting a New Course for the Twenty-First Century* (London: Bloomsbury, 2011), 69–152, especially 145–151.

own world.[33] This is painful and unsettling. "Should we say: that was our child-hood? / Or further still, the memory / of an age of thought that lives on in us? / An age of equilibrium, of reason. / A memory of what the spirit of humanism / has carried as its conscience and hope," writes Camille de Toledo, a writer and cultural theorist, in *L'inquiétude d'être au monde*, of the unease of being-in-the-world. "Rest-lessness is the name / that we give to this new century."[34] A crack has opened up in the self-confidence of the West. Europe has become melancholic.

The caesura of 1989 may have seemed to some to be the sign of an intellectual situation in which there was no alternative to Western universalism.[35] But this per-spective resulted from a narcissistic error in judgment. Even at that time, the liter-atures of the world painted a different picture of their contemporary moment by highlighting a diverse group of oppositions and a world characterized by the simul-taneity of difference.[36] They thus stand in an emancipatory tradition of relativism, which acts against imperial claims and processes of standardization by rightly weighing local situatedness and the cultural particularity of life. Since the Romantic period, however, this tradition has been radicalized again and again by positions that have overemphasized and essentialized what they claim as their own. Today, we live in a time of openly declared Kulturkampf and the global dominance of identitarian conceptions of culture. Our present is marked by a contrast between the mutual global dependence of states and identitarian assertions directed against the universal claim of modernity. This is a return to old constellations.

Nationalism, pan-Arabism, Islamism, *négritude*, isolationism, or China as the other civilization—these are but some of the historical movements that have served to relativize European universalism and construct a strong counter-identity. But relativism is also a historical principle that is dialectically inherent in European modernity itself: in Europe, too, a rejection of the ideology of prog-ress has led to countermovements that characterize the claims of modernity as foreign and hegemonic in opposition to these movements' own claims for au-thentic belonging. Seen from a slight remove, the return of ethnonationalist concep-tions of society and culture in our present day is not so far from the problems of modern fundamentalism: "And ultimately it is the same rejection of modernity, rea-son, and enlightenment that has today become so fashionable and blossomed on

---

33 See Dipesh Chakrabarty, *Europa als Provinz: Perspektiven globaler Geschichtsschreibung* (Frankfurt am Main: Campus Verlag, 2010).
34 Camille de Toledo, *L'inquiétude d'être au monde* (Lagrasse: Verdier, 2010), 12–13, on 13.
35 Francis Fukuyama, *The End of History and the Last Man* (New York: Free Press, 1992).
36 See Bill Ashcroft, Gareth Griffiths, and Helen Tiffin, eds., *The Empire Writes Back: Theory and Practice in Post-colonial Literatures* (London: Routledge, 2002).

both sides of our shared Mediterranean," wrote the Syrian philosopher Sadik al-Azm shortly before his death. He continues:

> On my side of the sea, the Islamists developed and spread the doctrine of the twentieth century as a century of complete "jahiliyyah"—an age of idolatry, ignorance, and paganism that repeats the fallen *conditio* of Arabia before the Koran was revealed. And as for the other side of the Mediterranean, I wonder if the fundamentalist Islamist doctrine of the complete "jahiliyyah" of the twentieth century and of modernity is different in any way from, say, T. S. Eliot's condemnation of the twentieth century (and of modernity) as a "wasteland" full of "hollow men" or "stuffed men" and women who "come and go / Talking of Michelangelo."[37]

Nothing is pure about the two principles of the philosophy of history, namely universalism and relativism. Their relationship is complex. The identity asserted in relativism tends to universalize itself, that is, to elevate itself to the norm for the nation, for larger contexts, or even for the world. And although this may certainly be an ambition pursued by many societies, it is the modern European view of the world, with its rationalistic concept of the subject and the resulting functionalist concepts of nature, society, and the state, that has been particularly successful in this universalization.[38] This viewpoint has given itself a name, appearing as a universalism that historically has always been driven by its own economic interest and by an interest in power, and that has always pursued policies for its self-realization. We can see how universalism was able in this process to absorb discourses that had themselves been derived from antimodern, antiuniversalist positions, for example, in the civilizing notion of the "German spirit" as a means for the "world to recover and heal" in the age of imperialism—a notion that was itself, at least in part, a product of the Romantic rebellion against the French *mission civilisatrice.*

   Today, we thus find ourselves in a dilemma: the universalist arguments for *liberté, égalité,* and *fraternité* that are based on a notion of shared humanity are the strongest we have to counter the emergence of ethnic and racist political strategies and to defend human rights. And yet in view of the dialectic characterizing the universal claim these arguments make, we can no longer wield them without qualification. As the French philosopher and sinologist François Jullien writes: "if each era thus has its own form of resistance, let us declare ours to be this—to resist tenaciously, at every step, the twin threats of uniformity and identitarianism. And to open

---

37 Sadik al-Azm, "What's in a name? 'Naher Osten,' 'Vorderasien' und die Macht der Bezeichnung," in Hofmann and Messing, *Fluchtpunkt*, 27–35, on 35.
38 See Felwine Sarr, *Afrotopia*, 13 and 17.

up a new path, supported by the formidable power of difference, toward a profoundly shared commonality."[39]

Faced with this difficult political task, it helps to recall the plea made by the
Chicago historian Dipesh Chakrabarty: that we distinguish between Europe's "hyper-
rational" claim to represent universality and the rational claim that there is universality. If the first position is a rejection of European dominance, the second is an
assertion of those "weapons of criticism" that Chakrabarty identifies as the truly universal achievement of the European Enlightenment: Marxist critique and political liberalism.[40] This kind of critique, which dialectically turns European universalism
against itself, which negates universalism with its own arguments, has functioned as
an engine of history.

This criticism upholds the principles of universalism with aims that include
defending these principles against the hegemony claimed for European civilization. Susan Buck-Morss has described one such dialectical moment, in which a
European universalist history of philosophy transforms into a consciousness of a
shared humanity, as exemplary for the Haitian Revolution: the moment in which
the army of freed slaves sings the "Marseillaise" in marching to face the—equally
revolutionary!—French occupying troops.[41] It is precisely in this early period of
European imperialism and its universalist *mission civilisatrice* that we find other
telling examples: Jean-François Champollion, for instance, who had become famous during his own lifetime for deciphering Egyptian hieroglyphics, was a driving force as a curator at the Louvre in Paris in acquiring colonial collections.
Faced with the destruction of cultural artifacts and cultural sites on the Nile resulting in part from his own efforts to create an encyclopedic museum, which he
also saw with his own eyes during his journey to Egypt in 1828/29, he concluded
that the universalist aspiration of Europe had derailed. In 1829, he wrote a "Note"
to the Egyptian Viceroy Mehmet Ali Pasha that can be regarded as the birth of the
idea for the international protection of cultural assets.[42] Or consider the most

---

39 François Jullien, *Il n'y a pas d'identité culturelle* (Paris: L'Herne, 2017), 93.
40 See Chakrabarty, *Europa als Provinz*, 12—which is not a translation of *Provincializing Europe:
Postcolonial Thought and Historical Difference* (Princeton: Princeton University Press, 2000) but a
separate compilation of texts by Dipesh Chakrabarty. The preface to the German volume uses the
phrase "Waffen der Kritik," but this text was originally written in English, where the phrase is
"weapons of criticism." I would like to thank the program director Judith Wilke-Primavesi of
Campus Verlag and translator Robin Cackett for this philological information.
41 See Susan Buck-Morss, "Hegel and Haiti," *Critical Inquiry* 26, no. 4 (2000): 821–865; Buck
Morss, *Hegel, Haiti, and Universal History* (Pittsburgh: University of Pittsburgh Press, 2009).
42 Markus Messling, *Philology and the Appropriation of the World: Champollion's Hieroglyphs*,
trans. Michael Thomas Taylor and Marko Pajević, with the collaboration of Karina Berger (Cham:
Palgram Macmillan/Springer, 2023).

famous scientist of the nineteenth century, Alexander von Humboldt. Humboldt's diaries and writings reveal how he sought throughout his life to free himself from the premises of a scientific model of knowledge that, beginning with his journey to the Americas, had prompted him to remove the bones of native American ancestors from their grave sites and ship them to Europe—against the will of local populations and his own Indigenous guides. To him, this desecration of human dignity appeared to be a stigma left by his own claims to enlightenment.[43] These early testimonies spring from a guilty conscience, but they stand for more. They express an understanding of the conflict that European universalism has mostly been unable to "hear." In this history, the world itself stands in the way of an unlimited belief in progress, refusing to be sublated, which makes constellations of this kind central for understanding imperialism.

The recourse of universalist thinking to itself has recently led to critiques of the discourse of human rights, specifically pertaining to their normative, cultural, and gender-specific preconditions. These critiques have highlighted, for instance, how these rights have only had partial validity for certain groups of people. It has been asked whether human rights need not be adjusted to fit different cultural or religious contexts in order to give equal validity to different understandings of humanity.[44] This last problem has been especially salient in anthropology. Time after time, observations of the world's cultures have led to relativistic arguments that have fundamentally questioned the idea of universality.[45] Yet an important

---

43 Ottmar Ette, *Weltbewußtsein: Alexander von Humboldt und das unvollendete Projekt einer anderen Moderne* (Weilerswist: Velbrück, 2002).

44 For an account of the many positions in this debate, see, for example, Michael Walzer, "Two Kinds of Universalism," in Walzer, *Nation and Universe: The Tanner Lectures on Human Values*, delivered at Brasenose College, Oxford University, May 1 and 8, 1989, 509–532, www.tannerlectures.utah.edu/_documents/a-to-z/w/walzer90.pdf, accessed August 31, 2020; Jürgen Habermas, "Der interkultureller Diskurs über Menschenrechte," in *Recht auf Menschenrechte: Menschenrechte, Demokratie und internationale Politik*, ed. Hauke Brunkhorst, Wolfgang R. Köhler, and Matthias Lutz Bachmann (Frankfurt am Main: Suhrkamp, 1999), 216–227; Charles Taylor, "Conditions on an Unforced Consensus on Human Rights," in *The East Asian Challenge for Human Rights*, ed. Joanne R. Bauer and Daniel A. Bell (Cambridge: Cambridge University Press, 1999), 124–144; Martha Nussbaum, *Women and Human Development: The Capabilities Approach* (Cambridge: Cambridge University Press, 2000); Samuel Moyn, *The Last Utopia: Human Rights in History* (Cambridge, MA: Harvard University Press, 2012); Shereen El Feki, *Sex and the Citadel: Intimate Life in a Changing Arab World* (New York: Pantheon Books, 2012); Chimamanda Ngozi Adichie, *We Should All Be Feminists* (New York: Anchor Books, 2014). For an overview, see Christoph Menke and Arnd Pollmann, *Philosophie der Menschenrechte* (Hamburg: Junius, 2007).

45 The paradigmatic account of this position is still Comte de Gobineau, *Essai sur l'inégalité des races humaines*, in *Oeuvres I*, ed. J. Gaulmier (Paris: Gallimard, 1987), 133–1174. On Gobineau, see Markus Messling, "Von der Adelsranküne zur Rassentheorie: Gobineaus Sprach- und

tradition of anthropology since Claude Lévi-Strauss has responded with the structuralist thesis that human beings are essentially the same, inasmuch as they always and everywhere create culture in an effort to satisfy certain basic principles of coexistence. In this view, cultures differ only in the way they do this, which also opens up differing ways of understanding the world.[46] Philippe Descola has called these different images of the world, which are at once epistemic regimes and ontologies, "dispositions of being."[47] Two aspects play a part in this anthropological view. On the one hand, the universalist idea that there is one right way of knowing the world is undermined by a reference to the rationality or meaningfulness of different human forms of expression. This argument thus structurally integrates occidental culture into the general human process of symbolization, a "kind of syntax for the composition of the world."[48] And on the other hand, the mediation of these different dispositions of being always aims toward a universality that would make it possible to transcend cultural diversity.[49] This mediation consequently contains a moment in which hierarchies are dissolved and conflicts tamed.

Hence the end of universalism entails problems that are not only ethical but epistemological[50]—because of course the question immediately arises as to the standpoint from which it would be possible to recognize and describe the gap between images of the world. In the case of Philippe Descola, this is unmistakably a

---

Kulturanthropologie," in *Rassedenken in der Sprach- und Textreflexion: Kommentierte Grundlagentexte des langen 19. Jahrhundert*, ed. Philipp Krämer, Markus A. Lenz, and Markus Messling (Paderborn: Fink, 2015), 189–209.

46 Claude Lévi-Strauss, *Race and History* (Paris: UNESCO, 1952); Philippe Descola, *Beyond Nature and Culture*, trans. Janet Lloyd (Chicago: University of Chicago Press, 2013); Gérard Lenclud, *L'Universalisme ou le pari de la raison: Anthropologie, Histoire, Psychologie* (Paris: Gallimard, 2013).

47 Descola, *Beyond Nature and Culture*, 128–244.

48 Descola, *Beyond Nature and Culture*, 125.

49 On Philippe Descola as well as the models proposed by Dipesh Chakrabarty, Gayatri Chakravorty Spivak, and Sheldon Pollock, which also builds on notions of postuniversalistic universality, see chapter 5.2 in Markus Messling, *Gebeugter Geist: Rassismus und Erkenntnis in der modernen europäischen Philologie* (Göttingen: Wallstein Verlag, 2016), 437–455.

50 This insight also informs David Scott's book on the post-1989 upheavals, *Refashioning Futures: Criticism after Postcoloniality* (Princeton: Princeton University Press, 1999), which draws from a critical universalist, namely anticolonial Marxist-influenced thinking, in which he speaks of a "Gramscian interregnum," a "transitional moment that I shall characterize as 'after postcoloniality'" (10). The task, he argues, is to take the step "from a politics of theory to a theory of politics" (19). The need to reconceptualize the world also from the perspective of the Global South is formulated by Scott as an epistemological problem in *Conscripts of Modernity: The Tragedy of Colonial Enlightenment* (Durham: Duke University Press, 2004): "What are the critical conceptual resources needed for this exercise? There is today no clear answer to this question" (Prologue, 1).

Parisian standpoint, bound to a structuralist tradition of the Collège de France that in no ways claims the ability to simply leave behind our European epistemological framework and the ways it has been shaped by the epistemic regime that Descola has called "naturalism." This standpoint relativizes itself, while thereby elevating itself once again, in terms of its claims to knowledge, to become a measure of understanding. An epistemic regime that claims to have a total perspective of the world results precisely from a distancing that is produced by the European view of the world. This measure, however, must always be communicated to the other epistemic regimes; it must make itself plausible. A gap thus arises between the form of universalism that has declared itself to be the only true epistemic regime, and a stance bound to a certain standpoint that seeks to generate universality in the first place. The more this stance succeeds in universalizing itself, that is, in plausibly refuting objections and expanding the scope of recognition for its validity, the greater its claim to universality. If our aim is to avoid positing a speculative concept of reality as absolute, then such universalizing processes are central to our ability to acquire knowledge.[51] Without them, we would have no defense against any form of subjective assertions or "fake news."

If, for Hegel, history is "progress of the consciousness of freedom,"[52] if the unfolding of reason to(ward) itself generates an identity between the concepts of truth and freedom, then the end of universalism calls both into question. In what we might call a "cosmopolitan turn," some strands of Western science have pursued a purification that attempts to internalize both their own boundedness to a specific location and the epistemological preconditions of others, in order to strive toward a new global understanding of the planet.[53] This has provoked skepticism. For even forms of cosmopolitics—that is, political strategies of global citizens who seek liberation from the universalist heritage these strategies themselves carry—always have the tendency to focus so much on themselves that they reestablish centrality and fail to adequately attend to globalization's social margins. The political consequences of universalism, however, mean that these margins are precisely where an ethical perspective requires us to direct our focus.[54] From a normative

---

51 Isabelle Thomas-Fogiel, *Le Lieu de l'universel: Impasses du réalisme dans la philosophie contemporaine* (Paris: Édition du Seuil, 2015).
52 Georg Friedrich Hegel, *Lectures on the Philosophy of World History*, trans. H. B. Nisbet (Cambridge: Cambridge University Press, 1975), 54.
53 See Ulrich Beck and Edgar Grande, eds., "Varieties of Second Modernity: Extra-European and European Experiences and Perspectives," special issue, *The British Journal of Sociology* 61, no. 3 (2010): 409–638.
54 See Paul Gilroy, "Planetarity and Cosmopolitics," *The British Journal of Sociology* 61, no. 3 (2010): 620–626.

point of view, it has therefore been emphasized that cultural particularity must no longer be sublated into a narrative of progress,[55] that instead we must always contextualize claims to universality.[56] Does this mean that we are ultimately faced with a plurality of universalistic claims that can no longer be transcended in a movement toward universality? How can something like universal validity be thought at all if there is no longer any overriding standpoint that could authenticate this claim?

We stand faced with the paradox of needing to give reasons for universality, because it is the basis for deriving legitimacies in a global society, even as we can no longer formulate its claims conceptually but must concretely produce them from the ground up.[57] Of course, literature cannot solve this problem in the guise generated by philosophical critique. Literature does not formulate anything conceptually; on the contrary, it narratively unfolds and reveals the problem in a way that makes it accessible to experience. This also means, however, that it can make visible the problems characterizing the process of negotiation that come with the melting together of universalism and the search for a new universality. Through narration, literature can make it possible to experience fears of loss together with hopes. And in this way, literature already participates in producing a new consciousness of the world. What its analysis can illustrate is the emergence of a new *consciousness* of universality.

The process of negotiating between the individual and the general is a generic characteristic of literature. Literature aims for a universality of the human being and its fate, and yet it must continually endow this universality with a form taken from a concrete historical context. In this process, it not only employs mythological, rhetorical, and thematic structures to bring together epistemologically different worlds—it also takes each specific case as the basis for generating, from these structures, a new perspective on the world as a whole. Hence it is no coincidence that one of the most important recent debates in cultural theory has been about "world literature." At its core, this is a debate about validity and legitimacy—a debate on the question of which modes of narration can lay claim to what forms of worldliness, or in short, which narratives can claim a human horizon.

To put it succinctly, the debate has revealed two major approaches. One approach insists on holding fast to a concept of world literature—although it turns to

---

55 See Dipesh Chakrabarty, "The Climate of History: Four Theses," *Critical Inquiry* 35, no. 2 (2009): 197–222.
56 See Étienne Balibar, *Des Universels: Essais et conferences* (Paris: Editions Galilée, 2016).
57 See again Diagne, "On the Postcolonial and the Universal?".

generic evolution[58] or cultural field theory[59] to explains world literature's emergence from European modernity, while also arguing that this canon has been opened up through new processes of reception.[60] More recently, scholars have traced the idea of world literature to a material basis, showing that concrete mechanisms of the publishing market have played a part in the use of the term as a label since World War II.[61] Nevertheless: because the term originates in the European philosophy of history of the nineteenth century, which mostly assumed that the world could be grasped conceptually from a European point of view, a second approach has concluded that the notion reflects imperial structures. In response, this second approach has attempted to pluralize the concept as "world literatures"[62] and decenter it through a notion of the "vernacular,"[63] developing a counterconcept of "literatures of the world."[64] Precisely this most recent formulation, proposed by Ottmar Ette, points to the need to open up the normative question about the universal legitimacy of literature through questions that recontextualize literatures. And here we find a connection to discussions taking place in the francophone world.

Apart from the fact that this debate has been influenced from the beginning by this French-speaking context,[65] its very terminology has shaped it in a way that is important here, and which has been given too little weight compared to the debate in English. An example is the concept of *littérature-monde*, which a collective of

---

58 Franco Moretti, "Conjectures on World Literature," *New Left Review* 1 (2000): 54–68.

59 Pascale Casanova, *The World Republic of Letters*, trans. M. B. DeBevoise (Cambridge, MA: Harvard University Press, 2004).

60 David Damrosch, *What Is World Literature?* (Princeton: Princeton University Press, 2003); Joachim Küpper, ed., *Approaches to World Literature* (Berlin: De Gruyter, 2013).

61 Gisèle Sapiro, ed., *Translatio: Le marché de la traduction en France à l'heure de la mondialisation* (Paris: CNRS Éditions, 2008); Gesine Müller and Dunia Gras, eds., *América latina y la literatura mundial: Mercado editorial, redes globales y la invención de un continente* (Madrid: Iberoamericana, 2015); Stefan Helgesson and Pieter Vermeulen, eds., *Institutions of World Literature: Writing, Translation, Markets* (London: Routledge, 2016); Venkat B. Mani, *Recoding World Literature: Libraries, Print Culture, and Germany's Pact with Books* (New York: Fordham University Press, 2017).

62 Steven Tötösy de Zepetnek and Tutun Mukherjee, eds., *Companion to Comparative Literature, World Literatures, and Comparative Cultural Studies* (New Delhi: Foundation Books, 2013); Alexander Beercroft, *An Ecology of World Literature: From Antiquity to the Present Day* (New York: Verso, 2015).

63 Francesca Orsini, "The Multilingual Local in World Literature," *Comparative Literature* 4, no. 67 (2015): 345–374.

64 Ottmar Ette, "Wege des Wissens: Fünf Thesen zum Weltbewusstsein und den Literaturen der Welt," in *Lateinamerika: Orte und Ordnungen des Wissens* ed. Sabine Hofmann and Monika Wehrheim (Tübingen: Narr, 2004), 169–184; Ottmar Ette, *WeltFraktale: Wege durch die Literaturen der Welt* (Stuttgart: J.B. Metzler, 2017).

65 Especially by Pascale Casanova in *The World Republic of Letters.*

authors polemically emphasized in a manifesto published in *Le Monde* in order to oppose the separation of "francophone" literature from "French" literature.[66] This notion underscores in particular the problem of worldliness: world literature, this collective argues, is literature that refers to the world and invokes the question of reality. The aim of undoing the world's hierarchies is to be achieved here not through a debate about historical-cultural models or their legitimacy, but rather by referring to the power that literature has to describe reality.[67] This demand has found strong allies in contemporary French literature, which sees its program as renewing the tradition of realism since Rabelais that has been defined by its critique of power. The movement for a *littérature-monde* has, however, also drawn sharp critique focused on moments where it has reproduced hackneyed distinctions—at times, it must be said, following the politics of publishers —in playing off the wider world against the center; or in playing off a notion of *Francophonie* that supposedly possesses worldliness, that would still take pleasure in the "taste of the dust of the streets," against a decadent literature of the center that it deems to have become estranged from the world. "We need not defend the 'periphery' against, but rather *with*, the 'center'—by making it implode, by starting again from the excessiveness, the intermixing, the creoleness of Rabelais, from the call to invention found in Du Bellay, from the original bastardization of the French language, to oppose its fixation, its classical beauty, its whiteness, its purity," writes Camille de Toledo in *Visiter le Flurkistan, ou les Illusions de la littérature-monde*—an essay composed in response to this manifesto that is polemical, albeit marked by solidarity.[68]

The issue is therefore not a simple demand for worldliness, but rather the need to question a centralist attitude toward the world. Yet we see this necessity emerging in France's metropolitan center nearly simultaneously with the publication of this manifesto. For instance, the group of "incultes"—that is, the writers

---

66 The "Manifeste pour une littérature-monde" was published in *Le Monde* on March 16, 2007, and signed by forty-four French-speaking writers. It was also been published in a book with statements by these authors: Michel Le Bris and Jean Rouaud, eds., *Pour une littérature-monde* (Paris: Gallimard, 2007).

67 For the anglophone context, see the substantial contributions proposed by Debjani Ganguly, *This Thing Called the World: The Contemporary Novel as Global Form* (Durham: Duke University Press, 2016); Stefan Helgesson, Helena Bodin, and Annika Mörte Alling, eds., *Literature and the Making of the World: Cosmopolitan Texts, Vernacular Practices* (New York, London: Bloomsbury, 2022); and Pheng Cheah, *What Is a World? On Postcolonial Literature as World Literature* (Durham: Duke University Press, 2016), which inquires about the world-creating power of literature through four philosophical modes: idealism, Marxism, phenomenology, and deconstruction.

68 Camille de Toledo, *Visiter le Flurkistan, ou les Illusions de la littérature-monde* (Paris: Presses universitaires de France, 2008), 83.

grouped around the journal (founded in 2004) and the publishing house of the same name, *Inculte*, whose most famous representative today is the Goncourt prize-winning novelist Mathias Énard—aims not only to dismantle hierarchies among cultural forms of expression. It also opposes the introspective tendencies of postmodernism with their renewed insistence on the problem of reality as the crucial question for the *futures of the novel*:

> Even more important than the question of "why" is the question of "how": "how to build the pyramid," as Flaubert would have said; in other words: how to make it all fit together? If the aim is to evoke and question the contemporary novel (and perhaps the novel itself), one of the most frequent ways is to question its relationship to reality. To the contemporary world.[69]

Here, it is a stance toward the world as a whole that has become a problem. And in this francophone context, the result is a particular emphasis that questions traditional conditions of legitimacy and that contextualizes, in its own way, the connection to the world as a whole.

We see this, for instance, in a study written recently by the Congolese writer and literary scholar Alain Mabanckou, in which it is no longer the premises of French universalism or a supposedly shared community of values of the French-speaking world that are being sought out, but rather the engendering of world itself, through individual articulation, as the central criterion for a movement that crosses over toward universality. For his book *Le monde est mon langage*, Mabanckou carried out interviews with writers and intellectuals in the French-speaking world in order to lend "more ear to the rumors of the world."[70] He is not interested here in sociocultural difference per se, but in how sociocultural difference produces respectively different forms of consciousness of a shared humanity: "The challenge is to recoup, from our different 'belongings,' something that could positively build a destiny that is shared and affirmed by all."[71] This project sets itself apart not only from the essentializing tendencies that characterize singular epistemic regimes, just as its intention goes beyond "globality," as the idea of a potentially increasing delimitation of consciousness toward the diversity of the world. It rather emphasizes, in an awareness of living on one earth, transcending the global world toward a new universality—an intentionality able to ground its own form of critique, that would encompass a critique of the very

---

69 Inculte collective, *Devenirs du roman* (Paris: Inculte/Naïve, 2007), 13.

70 Alain Mabanckou, *Le monde est mon langage* (Paris 2016: Bernard Grasset), 11.

71 Mabanckou, *Le monde est mon langage*, 12–13.

processes of globalization.[72] "Can there be anything that links us to others with whom we can declare that we are together?" asks Achille Mbembe.[73]

It is in this sense that I am interested in the problem of the "world" and its narrative creation. My understanding of narrative, however, differs from notions of *méta-récits*—be they of national societies or a global community. I understand narrative to be a process of bringing experience to language that emerges from a local context under specific material, cultural, social, and conceptual conditions. The concept of consciousness derived from literature thus no longer aims to artic- ulate idealistic creations of world, situated in the realm of a philosophy of spirit. Rather, it generates worlds that are embodied and yet also reflective, in which the form and validity of the world as a whole first comes to light.[74]

Such a notion of universality found defenders beginning with the proponents of *microstoria* in the debates about the "narrative turn" that unfolded in the 1980s. In his examination of Clifford Geertz's cultural relativism, for example, Giovanni Levi held fast to the idea of human rationality, defending it against the accusation that it necessarily leads to models of cultural hierarchy.[75] The projects pursued by *microstoria* are of interest in this context because this decided turn to the local or the regional does not mean bidding farewell to generality; rather, the intention is for microhistorical studies to find a new shape for generality. It is thus no coinci- dence that the school of *microstoria* has emphasized precisely the functions and techniques of narration itself, in how they come to bear in the "jeux d'échelles," the play of different levels of meaning.[76] Especially the procedural form of the inquiry, the *enquête*, which turns to evidence and events to provide plausibility for an over- all context, has made it possible to build relations between historical situations and narrative structures and thus to construct a field of tension between local contexts and a universal horizon. *Microstoria* has in this way generated a comparison of the

---

72 This kind of awareness was thematized by the historical avant-gardes in the context of World War I as "planetary"; see Robert Stockhammer, "Welt oder Erde? Zwei Figuren des Globalen," in *Figuren des Globalen: Weltbezug und Welterzeugug in Literatur, Kunst und Medien*, ed. Christian Moser and Linda Simonis (Bonn: Bonn University Press, 2014), 47–72. The term "planetary" has re- cently been taken up once again in its critical function, under different cultural premises; see Gaya- tri Chakravorty Spivak, *Death of a Discipline* (New York: Columbia University Press, 2003), 72.

73 See Mbembe, *Necropolitics*, 40.

74 See Christian Moser and Linda Simonis, "Einleitung: das globale Imaginäre," in Moser and Simonis, *Figuren des Globalen*, 11–22, on 12–14. On this notion in general, see Marko Pajević, *Poet- isches Denken und die Frage nach dem Menschen: Grundzüge einer poetologischen Anthropologie* (Freiburg: Karl Alber, 2012).

75 Giovanni Levi, "On Microhistory," *New Perspectives on Historical Writing*, ed. Peter Burke (Cambridge: Polity Press, 1991), 93–113.

76 Jacques Revel, ed., *Jeux d'échelles: La micro-analyse à l'expérience* (Paris: Gallimard, 1996).

local with a traditional concept of the universal, or of preformed universal assumptions with the local, that goes beyond facts: it has instead mainly emphasized the narrative processes that can be used to construct this relationship in the first place.

In the sense of a general narrative theory, which considers narrative constructions of the world to be a central component for self-formation and community building,[77] this opens up ways of examining how universality is produced and experienced in our societies. This is certainly not the monumental universality of universalism, which set itself up as a conceptual and historical necessity, and as something that deems itself concluded; one could perhaps call it a "minor universality."[78] Such a perspective would above all take into account that this different consciousness of universality is essentially being articulated beyond globalization's centers and outside its dominant discourses. Literatures written in French outside France make this clear. They raise the intriguing question of the "nature" of this other universality: Does it essentially consist in relocalizing and reembodying central concepts of modernity, such as liberty, equality, and solidarity, in order to give them new legitimacy? Or will it incorporate ideals that we do not yet see clearly today, that cannot be traced back to the realm of European culture—for example, ideas that mark the relationship to nature in a completely different way?[79] The Senegalese writer Felwine Sarr proposes concepts from the Wolof language, such as dignity (*jom*), hospitality or mutuality (*téraanga*), or modesty and humility (*kersa*), as belonging to the "cultural revolution" out of which the "future of humanity" must arise.[80] In any case, as Mbembe writes, "a democracy-to-come will rely on a clear-cut distinction between the 'universal' and the 'in-common.' The universal implies inclusion in some already constituted thing or entity, where the in-common presupposes a relation of co-belonging and sharing."[81] This means taking a new look at the conditions of appropriation and distribution in the world.

Beginning with Montaigne, as Jean Starobinski writes, we can identify a retreat to sensual experience and a rehabilitation of phenomena as strategies for responding to

---

77 See Jean-Marie Schaeffer, *Pourquoi la fiction?* (Paris: Seuil, 1999); Albrecht Koschorke, *Fact and Fiction: Elements of a General Theory of Narrative*, trans. Joel Golb (Berlin: De Gruyter, 2018).
78 This, of course, alludes to the concept of minor literature articulated by Gilles Deleuze and Félix Guattari in *Toward a Minor Literature*, trans. Dana Polan (Minneapolis: University of Minnesota Press, 1986). See also Markus Messling and Jonas Tinius, eds., *Minor University: Rethinking Humanity after Western Universalism* (Berlin: De Gruyter, 2023).
79 See the chapter on Kossi Efoui and the way he develops, in his book, another relationship between humans and nature.
80 Sarr, *Afrotopia*, 118.
81 See Mbembe, *Necropolitics*, 40.

skepticism and the concomitant loss of systems of order.[82] The claim made by the realism that results from this response is precisely not to depict reality. As an "ism," this realism rather reveals reality as a problem; it does not take the world as something given but rather questions its representation as a specific stance *toward* the world.

This can still be seen in a striking way by rereading Erich Auerbach's *Mimesis: The Representation of Reality in Western Literature*. Auerbach writes in his book that the "serious realism of modern times cannot represent man otherwise than as embedded in a total reality, political, social, and economic, which is concrete and constantly evolving."[83] But Auerbach is explicitly guided by the question of how it might be possible to represent the complex history in which the Nazi view of the world took shape, without becoming linked to a propagandistic structure of myth. His foundational work on mimesis is no Western fulfillment of an Aristotelian poetics, but a history of a problem that he derives from the Old Testament.

As is well known, Auerbach locates the origin of the European tradition of representing reality in a tension between the Homeric and the Elohist styles.[84] His aim is to show that the Pentateuch, in contrast to the transparent structure of the *Odyssey*, is characterized by a transcendent reality that makes interpretation necessary, thus creating a historical-philosophical consciousness and endowing the characters with personal depth. Realism for Auerbach is therefore precisely not a depiction of the world. Rather, the term refers to attempts to produce meaning, to determine through a narrative form the place of human beings in the world. For Auerbach, the historical depth of the Pentateuch thus coincides with a social depth. History in this interpretation is the unfolding of this social depth through ordinary people—a principle realized in the New Testament in the son of a "carpenter" from Galilee.[85] The separation between a noble world of action and a prosaic world of the everyday is suspended. This is also what chiefly interests Auerbach in the *Odyssey*, rather than the fulfillment of any royal destiny. One detail draws his attention. According to the poetic rules of Aristotle and his successors, the epic is fulfilled in the restoration of divine order. Yet in the *Odyssey*, it is Odysseus's dog Argos and his

---

82 Jean Starobinski, *Montaigne in Motion* (Chicago: University of Chicago Press, 2009).

83 Erich Auerbach, *Mimesis: The Representation of Reality in Western Literature*, trans. Willard R. Trask (Princeton: Princeton University Press, 2003), 463.

84 See Auerbach, *Mimesis*, 3–23.

85 Jacques Rancière has problematized this claim with reference to Jesus's announcement that he will be denied by Peter. Auerbach cites this moment as an example of how high and low narrative styles can be equalized, but Rancière argues that the announcement of this denial endows Jesus with an inner status of truth that marks him as a tragic hero. See Jacques Rancière, "Auerbach and the Contradiction of Realism," *Critical Inquiry* 44 (Winter 2018): 227– 241, on 232.

nurse Eurycleia who recognize him as who he really is. These figures, and the embedding of recognition in the process of washing Odysseus's feet that reveals his unmistakable scar, have no place in the high genre of the epic. For Auerbach, however, "Odysseus's scar" in the *Odyssey* stands for the European literary tradition of a world poetics because it brings together the sublime material of the hero's homecoming with his recognition by a lowly maid.[86] In this moment, the question of reality and of truth intersect. Auerbach's problematization of reality is a search for the possibilities of developing a free and egalitarian humanity that Jacques Rancière has described as typical of the generation that stood under the immediate impact of World War II and the Shoah.[87]

Building on Auerbach's famous essay "Philology and Weltliteratur," we can say that where literature becomes "realistic" in a strict sense, where its epistemic regime becomes identical with the positivist epistemic regime of materialism (which Auerbach identifies as the great commonality of the bipolar world order during the Cold War), it is reduced to one possible conception: a realism that clings to the things of the world. Not only does this collapse the tension between sensory perception and the question of truth—in the claim to grasp the world in its entirety, this literature instead attempts to universalize itself, as we see in Auerbach's time with the model of the European novel, threatening to subsume the typological difference of the world's various poetics in a totalizing narrative of standardizing processes. "And with this," Auerbach writes in a Hegelian vein, "the thought of world literature would be at once realized and destroyed."[88] For Auerbach, the work of and on world literature has an archival function: of maintaining, in a period of transition, an awareness of what threatens to swallow the present, in order to comprehend achieved conceptions of reality in terms of a critical genealogy. Philology itself thus becomes that "scar of Odysseus" that does not fade, remaining a rift of tension for the European worldview.

Hence if one reads Auerbach's literary history in the sense of the problem launched by Auerbach himself, as an investigation of how a "constantly developing political-social-economic total reality" is narratively shaped, it can also be read as a describing a specific history of social opening. This is what Jacques Rancière did in his reading of *Mimesis*, showing that Auerbach describes a development in which the experience of everyday, unheroic life is increasingly being elevated to the starting point of world experience. As an example, Rancière cites *To the Lighthouse* by Virginia Woolf, which he reads as beginning with the banal history of a family as a

---

86 See Auerbach, *Mimesis*, 22.
87 See Rancière, "Auerbach and the Contradictions of Realism," 238–239.
88 Erich Auerbach, "Philology and Weltliteratur," trans. Maire and Edward W. Said, *The Centennial Review* 13, no. 1 (Winter 1969): 1–17.

"random moment"—as Auerbach is translated, or as Rancière prefers to translate, "any moment whatever"—that is stretched to universality: "Any moment in the everyday life of any character from any class of society appears to have an infinite power of expansion."[89] It is in this potential universalization of space and time into an infinite dimension of humanity that we find Auerbach's egalitarian conclusion. Of course, one can object to Auerbach that the arbitrariness of the moment in the modern novel is by no means developed as a promise of happiness: the great anti-heroes—Julien Sorel, Emma Bovary, not least Septimus in Virginia Woolf's *Mrs. Dalloway*—all fail, and with their deaths the infinite extension of the moment is undeniably revealed to be an illusion. Yet this is precisely where Jacques Rancière begins in his reading of Auerbach—in an attempt to restore access to the political relevance of representing reality.[90]

The invocation of the world in literature, as Rancière shows in *Politics of Literature*, is a republican force that pervades the European nineteenth century. In the same vein as his reading of Auerbach, Rancière emphasizes that realistic literature, the "great novel," no longer follows a poetics defined by rules and norms. Rather, the Aristotelian principle of action of the noble hero, who falls so that the divine order of the world can be restored, has finally been called into question; and this now transforms the world, as well as the phenomena and objects within it, into actors in their own right.[91] But what can these actors—no longer necessarily acting subjects—articulate?

The aesthetics of realism produces a play of intensities that questions traditional patterns of perception—the old way of structuring what is sensual—and subversively undermines the Restoration society of the Bourbons and the Second Empire by enabling a fundamentally different perception of reality. This capability, held by a divergent use that would articulate a different "mode of establishing a certain community," is the politics of literature:[92]

> The sentences of Balzac and Flaubert may well have been mute stones. But those who offered that judgement also knew that, in the age of archeology, paleontology and philology, stones, too, speak. They don't have voices like princes, generals or orators. But they only speak all the better as a result. They bear on their bodies the testimonies of their history. And this testimony is more reliable than any speech offered by human mouth. It is the truth of things as opposed to the chatter and lies of orators.[93]

---

89 See Rancière, "Auerbach and the Contradictions of Realism," 237–238.
90 See Rancière, "Auerbach and the Contradictions of Realism," 239–241.
91 See Jacques Rancière, *The Politics of Aesthetics: The Distribution of the Sensible*, trans. Gabriel Rockhill. (New York: Continuum, 2004), especially 35–41, "Is History a Form of Fiction."
92 Jacques Rancière, *The Politics of Literature*, trans. Julie Rose (Cambridge: Polity Press, 2011), 83.
93 Rancière, *The Politics of Literature*, 14.

In this worldliness, an intensity thus crystallizes with which these authors clearly articulate something about their time that is able to claim validity against official ways of speaking history. The expression this produces is often unsettling. Jacques Rancière describes, for example, how in Tolstoy's *War and Peace* the historiography of great men and their deeds is taken ad absurdum in descriptions of battles: the real actor is now the masses, who, in the turmoil of battle, write the course of this great history less by strategy than by chance. Hence what these realistic depictions of battles describe, Rancière argues, is a tragic, fatalistic feeling of modernity in which the individual becomes lost.[94] In this way, the structure of postrevolutionary conditions tells a different history of modernity than the progressivism proclaimed by the nineteenth century. The world itself speaks more truthfully than the promises of a time that has devoured its own ideals. This is the link between the waves of realism after 1789 and 1989: they stand in a relation to damaged narratives of freedom.

The grand realism of the long nineteenth century is thus bound to the production and universalization of subjectivity and, at the same time, dialectically, to its negation during the nineteenth-century restorations in France and in the structures of modern capitalism. This realism does not seek to present a mirror image of the world, but rather to create an intensity that cannot be fully grasped with traditional concepts of emotion, generating instead an affect in the reader for which a language must yet be found. This is why Fredric Jameson has emphasized the affective function of realism.[95] He argues that the text creates a tension to reality, evoking a strong affect, an "existential present" that interrupts the narrative, the *récit*, and arrests the logic of the triad "past-present-future" on which it is based.[96] He sees these affects as part of a changed embodiment that require a new form of representation in language, describing affect as "the organ of perception of the world itself, the vehicle of my being-in-the-world."[97] Universalist modernity can be said to coincide with a series of structures of feeling and knowledge that were embodied and could be clearly articulated. In the "great novel" of the nineteenth century, Martin von Koppenfels argues, these primarily took a negative cast as feelings of loss, against which the novel tried to immunize itself.[98] By contrast, the affects of our times displaying a tendency toward universality are bound to a form of embodiment that seeks to be brought to language in the first place, in a form that can

---

94 Rancière, *The Politics of Literature*, 72–79.
95 See Fredric Jameson, *The Antinomies of Realism* (New York: Verso, 2015), 27–44.
96 Jameson, *The Antinomies of Realism*, 43.
97 Jameson, *The Antinomies of Realism*, 43.
98 Martin von Koppenfels, *Immune Erzähler: Flaubert und die Affektpolitik des modernen Romans* (Munich: Wilhelm Fink, 2007).

be generalized, as a reality that can be shared. Narratives engender these affects as a stance toward the world, or as its negativity; they create these affects as specific intensities that move us.

Our time is characterized by attitudes and subjectivities that are globally interdependent and interrelated even though they emerge locally. Bundling these particularities into an epistemological or political universalism no longer seems possible. The Parisian cultural theorist Lionel Ruffel has shown that we live in a paradigm in which cultural expressions are diversifying and becoming more independent from institutions—in a time of a great "brouhaha."[99] Its consequences include an increasing complexity of phenomena and a growing awareness of their interconnectedness.[100] In contrast to Hegel's phenomenology, however, this does not necessarily produce a universalizing consciousness developing toward freedom. But then how are truth and justice possible if these opposites cannot be sublated? If we are only able to imagine the sublation in what is (ultimately) valid by way of a relation to an "after"? To this question, Ruffel replies:

> These different *posts* whatever their individual qualities, in one way or another lead us back to the centrality of the modern narrative. Now, it is precisely the deconstruction of the modern narrative, and above all its designation as a narrative, that is decisive for the contemporary period. Must it be marked by tropes indicating an after, a survival, a beyond? And by all those sentiments that go along with them, especially of melancholy?[101]

For years now, Camille de Toledo has described the groundlessness we sense beneath our feet as an *esthétique du vertige*, an aesthetics of vertigo.[102] This perception of vertigo has lost any commonality with the ironic glass bead game that postmodernism has played with the concept of truth and reality. We have long seen the need to give knowing and normativity a form that is globally valid. Otherwise, it will remain impossible to organize knowledge and justice in a diversified, multipolar world. The question of how this might happen continues to provoke despair. The deconstruction of those concepts that have been assumed to be universal is not the evil we must repudiate, but a kind of zero point from which we must rethink how we live together. For it points at once to a subversive

---

99 Lionel Ruffel, *Brouhaha: Worlds of the Contemporary*, trans. Raymond N. MacKenzie (Minneapolis: University of Minnesota Press, 2018).
100 See Doris Bachmann-Medick, *Cultural Turns: New Orientations in the Study of Culture* (Berlin: De Gruyter, 2016), 104–105.
101 Ruffel, *Brouhaha*, 112–113.
102 See his description of himself at toledo-archives.net/biography/, accessed April 1, 2018. The term draws from W. G. Sebald's book *Vertigo*, trans. Michael Hulse (New York: New Directions, 2016).

revolt against Eurocentrism and to those subjectivities that can no longer be subsumed under an abstract universalism, and that we must take into account in reorganizing our coexistence.[103]

Jacques Derrida's brief book *The Monolingualism of the Other* may have been published too late—in 1996 in France, with a translation into English in 1998 and into German in 2003—for it to have had any significant influence on the reception of deconstruction, which is often all too lacking in context. In this book, Derrida writes unequivocally that the painful experience of Vichy policies in Algeria in the 1940s—which denied him, as a Jew, access to the French school and thus to the culture of the French language—led him from then on to deconstruct any claim of interpretational sovereignty over concepts of humanity. At the same time, however, the experience left him long unable to speak about precisely this, since he was capable of speaking only in this one language that did not belong to him, and that was the language of his oppressors.[104]

Derrida describes here an experience that is common to the colonial context, despite its specific characteristics. The inscriptions made in our European languages by such subjugated subjectivities are starting points for rethinking a "we." In the last interview Jacques Derrida gave before his death, he asserted this "we"—as a "we" that assumes responsibility—against his own skepticism about forms of collectivization: "What we call in a certain algebraic shorthand 'Europe' has certain responsibilities to assume, for the future of humanity and the future of international law—that's my faith, my belief. In this case, I do not hesitate to say 'we Europeans.'"[105] Deconstruction—as we find with Derrida, where it is no blind play with signs—gives rise to a responsibility for a "we" that must be more than the sum of our different lifestyles, should we not want to resign ourselves to the cynical position of the spectator in world society.[106] "At the very least, one must understand [one's own time] and assess its significance," writes contemporary philosopher Tristan Garcia,

---

103 Roland Barthes, *How to Live Together: Novelistic Simulations of Some Everyday Spaces; Notes for a Lecture Course and Seminar at the Collège de France (1976–1977)*, trans. Kate Briggs and ed. Claude Coste (New York: Columbia University Press, 2013).

104 See Jacques Derrida, *The Monolingualism of the Other: The Prosthesis of Origin*, trans. Patrick Mensah (Stanford: Stanford University Press, 1998), 59–76.

105 Jacques Derrida, *Learning to Live Finally: The Last Interview*, trans. Pascale-Anne Brault and Michael Naas (New York: Palgrave Macmillan, 2007), 41.

106 See also Albrecht Koschorke's commentary: "The academic left has deconstructed itself. It is time to readjust the terms." *Neue Zürcher Zeitung*, April 18, 2018, 39, https://www.nzz.ch/feuille ton/die-akademische-linke-hat-sich-selbst-dekonstruiert-es-ist-zeit-die-begriffe-neu-zu-justieren-ld.1376724, accessed August 1, 2018.

to seek out what will enable us to strive for a form of peace amid the war between identitarian positions. This peace is not the end of any "we"—it never will be, no more than it will be the end of conflict, fighting, and war. But for those of us who continually hope for something like a provisional peace among ourselves, the time of generalized hostility is the crucial moment for us to work toward resurrecting the desirability of the idea of a "we" that we habitually tend to forget.[107]

At a time when the militant violence that essentially stems from the structures of colonial modernity is coming closer to Europeans, as the presence and testimonies of refugees are massively bearing witness to this violence's existence and effects, refounding this "we" is an urgent task. Freedom from brutal violence and misery cannot only apply to Europe.

Or as Achille Mbembe writes: "the construction of the common is inseparable from the reinvention of community."[108] Mbembe restores to universality its essential, founding impulse: namely, that it only makes sense to speak of universality when each individual has a part in it. He returns here to the historical idea of humanity—no longer deriving it, however, from traditional arguments, whether of religion or the Enlightenment. For him, they stem rather from a planetary horizon of sharing a world:

> There is therefore only one world, at least for now, and that world is all there is. What we all therefore have in common is the feeling or desire that each of us must be a full human being. The desire for the fullness of humanity is something we all share. And, more and more, we also share the proximity of the distant. Whether we want to or not, the fact remains that we all share this world. It is all that there is, and all that we have.[109]

It is only when individuals can preserve their share in the whole that the planetary horizon of reference becomes ethically charged. But colonial power has not only globally undermined this principle of inalienability to an unimagined extent; in its redistribution of goods and resources and its subjugation and annihilation of human beings and animals, it has largely destroyed the possibility of insisting on any balance of relations. In the work of Frantz Fanon, whom Mbembe invokes as a paradigmatic figure of anticolonialism, we clearly see the deep marks this has left on the body, gaping as a wound: "on the one hand, the body of hatred, of appalling burden, the false body of abjection crushed by indignity, and, on the other, the originary body, which, upon being stolen by others, is then disfigured

---

107 Tristan Garcia, *Wir* (Suhrkamp: Berlin, 2018), 285.
108 Achille Mbembe, *Critique of Black Reason*, trans. Laurent Dubois (Durham: Duke University Press, 2017), 183.
109 Mbembe, *Critique of Black Reason*, 182.

and abominated, whereupon the matter is literally one of resuscitating it, in an act of veritable genesis."[110]

Mbembe leaves no doubt that this revival must be a restitution in the sense of a redistribution of goods. Against a politics of enmity, a necropolitics, Mbembe pursues a politics of reparation that would restore the ties that have been destroyed in order to create a new global society. Or more precisely, one should say: to create a new ecology of a global society, because Mbembe understands the planet in the sense of Édouard Glissant as an "all-world," in which everything that exists corresponds with everything else, and in which the idea of the relationality of all living things takes the place of identity. Hence the "cannibal structures of our modernity," Mbembe argues, have entirely consumed our "reservoirs of life."[111] The concept of reparation in Mbembe's work is interesting because it aims not at the restoration of a supposed cultural identity (which is sometimes the case for reparation claims), as though it were possible to return to a pristine state; it refers rather to the abstract notion of the participation of all in the global community. In this sense, reparation certainly means economic compensation. But it is also about the restoration of human relations.

If universal justice is to be achieved, one crucial aspect will be creating psychological balance and symbolic means of access. "In the era of the Earth, we will effectively require a language that constantly bores, perforates, and digs like a gimlet, that knows how to become a projectile, a sort of full absolute, of will that ceaselessly gnaws at the real."[112] The reference here to the voice is central. The voice is directly connected to the body, to the wounded body. It is the articulation of the individual, and at the same time it is communication with the other. It is in the voice that speech finds its liberating and its social dimension—because bringing something to language is community building.[113] One essential habitat of working in and with language, however, is literature—or, to be even more specific, narrative, in which symbolic processes of negotiation are carried out that are not simply empty clattering, as is sometimes claimed by those who scorn literature, but rather determinations of the self and of society. In the space between representation and reality, as Erich Auerbach has shown for Europe in all its depth, what appears is nothing less than an aesthetically formulated understanding of the world. "The challenge of our time," writes Achille Mbembe, "is also to understand which language and which writing will be able to give Africa its strength back, its own power, along with a form for

---

110 See Mbembe, *Necropolitics*, 189.
111 Mbembe, *Critique of Black Reason*, 181.
112 Mbembe, *Necropolitics*, 189.
113 Here, too, see Rancière, *The Politics of Literature*, 83.

representing its place in the world [*figure-monde*]."[114] If one brackets the question of empowerment—all sentimentality aside, the "old continent" is still a center of political and economic power—the formation of a new *figure-monde*, the orientation toward "another heading," applies all the more to a Europe whose claim to explicate the world is melting away, and which must take responsibility for its history by helping to shape the process from which a new universality can emerge.[115]

---

114 Achille Mbembe, "L'Afrique qui vient," in *Penser et écrire l'Afrique aujourd'hui*, ed. Alain Mabanckou (Paris: Éditions du Seuil, 2017), 17–31, on 28.
115 See also Jacques Derrida, *The Other Heading: Reflection on Today's Europe*, trans. Pascale-Anne Brault and Michael Naas (Bloomington: Indiana University Press, 1992).

Égalité—The Melancholy of White Men over Forty

No doubt, the order is wrong—it's *liberté* that actually comes first. *Liberté, égalité, fraternité*: this is how the motto is emblazoned all over France, in every school, civic office, and state palace. But the small, irreverent shift I am making here from this motto's grand history in the French Republic is not accidental. One could say that the modern era began with the demand for equality. It was the materialist foundation for equality of all people under natural law that first radically challenged the genealogical ideal of aristocracy, that is, a society of estates. If all people are equal by nature, differences between them can only be justified socially—and yet social differences are to be fought against and privileges of birth ought not exist. That said, wasn't it the case that equality was sought and established precisely because Enlightenment thinkers—and then an entire social class—wanted to assert claims to freedom? So—it should in fact be liberty before equality?

This question of which of these ideals is primary is as uncompelling as modernity's obsessive search for a beginning, an origin, for authenticity—though hardly less explosive. In his collection of essays *Equaliberty* (*La proposition de l'é-galiberté*), Étienne Balibar has shown that it was only in relation to each other that equality and liberty could be generated as fundamental values of European modernity.[1] His broader aim, however, was to remind us of the condition of equality that has been entirely obscured by the total dogma of liberty we find motivating market-obsessed forms of politics.[2] The idea of the regulative play of markets is misguided in any case, given that the early modern idea of markets was founded precisely on the hope of balancing out destructive individual interests, in the sense of unlimited freedom, in order to produce social equilibrium.[3]

In moving *égalité* to the first position here, I am thus following those who have claimed it as a banner cry against the self-intoxication of liberty's apostles. This is, of course, the very drama of modernity: that liberty's song quickly becomes a victory march—a cry of solidarity demanding that all the nations of the world be led to freedom, even if it is through subjugation. In this *mission civilisatrice*, in the campaigns of the Bonapartist revolutionary armies, the same dialectical drama takes shape that is meant to be evoked by my slight transposition of

---

1 See Étienne Balibar, *Equaliberty*, trans. James Ingram (Durham: Duke University Press, 2014), especially 4–9.
2 See Balibar, *Equaliberty*, 4.
3 Joseph Vogl, *The Specter of Capital*, trans. Joachim Redner and Robert Savage (Stanford: Stanford University Press, 2015).

terms: Napoleon's expedition to Egypt and his campaigns across the European continent ushered in an age of empire heralding the completion of the French Revolution. Liberty, however, not only gave cover to the subjugation of entire societies: it also propagated those "weapons of criticism" that would later be used to crucially undermine imperialism.[4] Those who were conquered came to confront their occupiers with the very idea of equality that now also marked their claims to liberty.[5] To their great amazement, troops sent by Napoleon in 1801 to Haiti to put down its revolution and restore French law arrived to find an army of former slaves singing the revolutionary "Marseillaise."[6] Such appropriations occur in various places.

There is a legend about the carnival held every year along the Rhine, which was banned but then allowed under the Napoleonic occupation. As the story tells it, the festival always begins at 11:11 a.m. on November 11th not only out of silly tradition, but as an abbreviation for *égalité, liberté, fraternité*—ELF, or eleven in German. Initially meant to ironize the high ideals of the French occupiers, the intention was later turned against the Protestant occupation that ensued after the Rhineland was awarded to Prussia at the Congress of Vienna. This is certainly more myth than history, but there is an inner truth in the foolish revolt staged by this string of numbers. It suggests that the order of modernity has been disrupted, that its calculation no longer works out. Strictly speaking, modernity was never a zero-sum game.

Since the French Revolution, the relationship between liberty and equality has been inscribed within the problem of the relationship between materialism and idealism. If Hegel understood history as "the progress of the consciousness of freedom"[7] that passes with the revolution into a state of fulfillment, Marx famously turned the question on its head by considering consciousness as resulting from a history of material relations. The episode of the master and slave in Hegel's *Phenomenology of Spirit* already assigns labor the central function for mediating social relations, in that labor brings forth a subject's consciousness of itself.[8]

---

4 See Dipesh Chakrabarty, *Europa als Provinz: Perspektiven globaler Geschichtsschreibung* (Frankfurt am Main: Campus Verlag, 2010), 12. See also Markus Messling, *Gebeugter Geist: Rassismus und Erkenntnis in der modernen europäischen Philologie* (Göttingen: Wallstein Verlag, 2016), 437–455.

5 See also Balibar, *Equaliberty*, 4–5.

6 See Susan Buck-Morss, "Hegel and Haiti," *Critical Inquiry* 26, no. 4 (2000): 821–865, especially 865.

7 Georg Friedrich Hegel, *Lectures on the Philosophy of World History*, trans. H. B. Nisbet (Cambridge: Cambridge University Press, 1975), 54.

8 On this interpretation of labor as engendering human freedom, see Alexandre Kojève, *Introduction to the Reading of Hegel; Lectures on the Phenomenology of Spirit*, assembled by Raymond Queneau, trans. James H. Nichols (Ithaca: Cornell University Press, 1980), 9–56.

But this consciousness gives rise to demands: the republic must in any case make materialist arguments, because it can only fulfill the ideal of universal liberty if all are furnished with the necessary means, if social impoverishment does not prevent political participation. Here we see that "there are no such things as 'absolutely universal' emancipatory universalities."[9]

The nineteenth century, for instance, is marked by battles over representation and the distribution of wealth, and the great works of European literature tell this history again and again as a story of unkept promises and bitter disappointments. The "realist novel"—meaning the works of Balzac and Stendhal, Tolstoy and Flaubert—develops a politics of literature that counters political language with an archeology of things handed down by tradition and a skepticism toward sensual knowledge, and this opens a rift between literature and the rhetoric of bourgeois ideologies of progress.[10] Walter Benjamin's interpretation of Baudelaire, which constellates Baudelaire's poetry of evil with Blanqui's anarchism, shows how the final destruction of ideals in the French Revolution of 1848 was followed by a leaden powerlessness that no longer permitted any idealism—precisely because its goals had long been sullied, or at least those that would have been worth fighting for.[11] Baudelaire's poems are assertions of the self beneath a transcendence that has collapsed.

In the period after World War II, the question of representation and the distribution of wealth in France and Europe more generally increasingly faded into the background. The principle of social democracy seemed to have been largely achieved, and entire strata of the population had been saved from immiseration.

---

9 Balibar, *Equaliberty*, 12. In Hegel's writings, this disappointment led to a retreat from a heroic to an epistemological concept of freedom. Hans Peter Krüger has demonstrated as much in an analysis of the concept of labor, which in Hegel's writings underlies a political thought process that runs "from 'the labor of the republican for the general' (1795) to the [concept] of 'the general labor of war' (1802) to the 'labor of the concept' (1807)"; see Hans Peter Krüger, *Heroismus und Arbeit in der Entstehung der Hegelschen Philosophie (1793–1806)* (Berlin: Akademie Verlag, 2014), 13. In this respect the anthropological concept experiences a historical shift of meaning, which correlates in the young Hegel with a political republicanism of action; then later with the concept of a "higher enlightenment" as a program of propagating Enlightenment through the revolutionary wars, and of legal and educational reform; and finally in the "systematic Hegel" with the significance of the concept of labor for absolute knowing (see Krüger, *Heroismus und Arbeit*, 293). The republican promise of liberty thus loses its overt political dimension and becomes internalized as a program of *Bildung*, of self-formation or cultivation.
10 See Jacques Rancière, *The Politics of Literature*, trans. Julie Rose (Cambridge: Polity Press, 2011), especially 3–30. Rancière first mentions the "so-called realist novel" on page 15.
11 Walter Benjamin, "The Paris of the Second Empire in Baudelaire," in *Selected Writings*, vol. 4, 1938–1940, ed. Howard Eiland and Michael W. Jennings (Cambridge, MA: Belknap Press, 2003), 3–92.

The central question appeared to concern the fulfillment of individual notions of freedom. In France, beginning in the late 70s, even the Parti Socialiste distanced itself from class struggle and reoriented itself toward the individuals of a liberal majority society. The enormous success of Didier Éribon's autofiction *Returning to Reims* can be explained by the fact that he again directs attention toward the material conditions of political representation and social participation. Why, he asks, have I, as a left-wing intellectual, spent my life dealing with my homosexual identity and not with my social background? His answer: "Let me put it this way: it turned out to be much easier for me to write about shame linked to sexuality than about shame linked to class."[12] If Éribon's path to Paris meant liberation from a homophobic working-class milieu and access to an intellectual world, his journey to the suburbs of Reims is a return to the world of the disadvantaged milieu of his origins. What Éribon understands upon returning to Reims is the abandonment of the lower strata of society, whose affiliation with the Communist left had afforded them an anchor, had given them the feeling of having a voice in society. According to Éribon, the left abandoned the question of class consciousness by embracing individualized consumer society, in order to be electable to the social center. This caused the ideal of equality to fade in left-wing consciousness, Éribon argues, and the lower classes to fall silent. Today, he suggests, their last opportunity to protest, to raise their voice, is to vote for the radical right-wing Front National (since 2018, the Rassemblement National). And as we know, these formerly communist milieus in France have increasingly done just that. Éribon observes that the lower-class milieu has always been latently homophobic, misogynous, and xenophobic. His recognition that the right is the "new left" has shaken old certainties. Yet if we look at fascist movements historically, this is not entirely astonishing.[13] What Éribon finds actually shocking in retrospect, and in particular with an eye toward his own personal and intellectual path, is his own blindness.

Didier Éribon's autofictional social study is insightful—not only in analyzing the embodiedness and habitus of the working-class world (a project inspired by his academic father, Pierre Bourdieu), but in portraying, with such sensitivity, the history of a disappointment. How could the values of modernity—the very ideals that had developed such a liberating force even for Éribon himself—how could the republican ideals lose their political power and turn against themselves? Despite Éribon's pugnacious tone, his book reflects a basic mood that has afflicted

---

12 Didier Éribon, *Returning to Reims*, trans. Michael Lucey (Los Angeles: Semiotext(e), 2013), 25.
13 One thinks here, for instance, of Benito Mussolini's political origin in the Italian Socialist Party (PSI).

France for years: there seems to be a universally shared observation that republican ideals are in decline, to be replaced by slogans in the service of the security state, by insecurity, a sense of decadence, and a fear that power has been lost in a globalized world. It remains to be seen whether Emmanuel Macron's once hopeful presidency might still change this state of affairs. "La France va mal"—"Things are not going well for France"—is a phrase heard regularly. "France is still a rich country, but since my childhood I have felt a sense of loss," says the philosopher Tristan Garcia. "France feels wounded, and one of these wounds has to do with its colonial history."[14] France is not alone in Europe with these feelings of loss and woundedness. But France is where a "tristesse européenne" that has befallen us as Europeans, and that has shaped our epoch, appears with particular clarity.[15]

With his 2011 book *Le Dépaysement* (perhaps best translated as "the estrangeness"),[16] Jean-Christophe Bailly sets out on a voyage through France in that grand tradition of journeys across the country that ranges from Germaine de Staël's *De l'Allemagne*[17] to the *Tour de France par deux enfants*,[18] the nineteenth-century school classic whose intention was to create unity in the minds of the French, or the world-famous race, the Tour de France. Bailly's book, however, is no patriotic celebration of France l'Hexagon, no attempt to educate a nation into being, by depicting a richness of the country that has never been in doubt. Rather, it reflects the loneliness and rapture of Rousseau's *Rêveries du promeneur solitaire*, of an alienation from his own time. Bailly's view of the landscapes between the Rhine and the Atlantic begins with the question of what France actually is—and thus with a loss, an inner emptiness characterizing the country, that becomes increasingly hollow the more it echoes within the constantly repeated slogans of the Front National, and of the supposedly moderate right wing proclaiming the greatness of France. France has lost its way; the certainties of republican universalism are no longer self-evidently valid. Bailly wants to avoid being paralyzed by melancholy, and instead he concretely engages with France: he turns to the country to

---

14 Tristan Garcia, "Frankreich wird gewaltsamer, aber auch ehrlicher," interview with Stephanie von Hayek, *Kulturaustausch: Zeitschrift für internationale Perspektiven* 4 (2017): 19–21.

15 Camille de Toledo, *Le Hêtre et le bouleau: Essai sur la tristesse européenne, suivi de L'utopie linguistique ou la pédagogie du vertige* (Paris: Seuil, 2009).

16 Jean-Christophe Bailly, *Le Dépaysement: Voyages en France* (Paris: Seuil, 2011).

17 Madame de Staël, *De l'Allemagne*, 2 vols. (Paris: Garnier-Flammarion, 1968); Madame de Stael, *Germany* (London: C. Baldwin, 1813).

18 [G. Bruno] Augustine Fouillée, *Le Tour de la France par deux enfants: Devoir et Patrie, Livre de lecture courante, Avec 212 gravures instructives pour les leçons de choses et 19 cartes géographiques, Entièrement revue et augmentée d'un epilogue*, 338th ed. (Paris: Belin, 1907).

gain a new reality, or more specifically, to gain an awareness of landscapes and life realities that elicit astonishment, to once again pose questions about the linguistic surface of political discourse without abetting blind patriotism or a fear of disappearing.

Recent literature has not escaped the crisis caused by the shift into new media and the loss of representation this has entailed.[19] It has responded with tried and tested possibilities, but these have always existed in a complicated relationship to the avant-garde's claim to have left these very methods behind.[20] In order to examine and counteract this perceived "loss," it has focused on narration as an anthropological technique of appropriating and shaping the world. Hence if literature is (also) something like a seismograph for intensities of the present, then the melancholy of the past few years cannot be overlooked; it is the material out of which novels are made. Looking only at the list of France's most important literary prize, the Prix Goncourt, we find more than a few dark books about destroyed relationships and sadistic derangements, about violence and war, decadence, modernity's crisis of meaning, and taking leave of humanity: *The Kindly Ones* by Jonathan Littell (French 2006, English 2009), Gilles Leroy's *Alabama Song* (French 2007), Michel Houellebecq's *The Map and the Territory* (French 2010, English 2012), *The French Art of War* (French 2011, English 2017) by Alexis Jenni, Jérôme Ferrari's *The Sermon on the Fall of Rome* (French 2012, English 2014), and Mathias Énard's *Compass* (French 2015, English 2017). Looking at the same period, one might also think of essays from the genre of cultural criticism: Camille de Toledo's *Essai sur la tristesse européenne* from 2009; Michel Onfray's Spenglerian *Décadence* (2017), certainly Boualem Sansal's *roman à thèse* lauded by the Académie française, *2084: The End of the World* (French 2015, English 2017); and, in a sense, Fabrice Gabriel's unique text *Une nuit en Tunisie* (2017), a melancholy exploration of his estrangement from the world of his youth after 1989. Finally, there is also the sad book *Entre les deux il n'y a rien* (2015) by Mathieu Riboulet, a hybrid of essay and novel, about the lost hope of European youth from the 1970s. Of course, these works are not representative of all literature written in French. But as the list of the Prix Goncourt shows, this thematic convergence is not plucked out of thin air. In it, we glimpse a crisis taking shape as a consequence of world-loss. Is it a coincidence that all these works were written by men? And in almost every case, by White men who long ago left their youth behind?

---

19 See William Marx, *L'Adieu à la littérature: Histoire d'une dévalorisation, XVIIIe-XXe siècle* (Paris: Les Éditions de Minuit, 2005).
20 See the chapter "L'Épuisement de la littérature et son éternel recommencement," in Antoine Compagnon, "XXe siècle," in *La littérature française: dynamique & histoire*, ed. Jean-Yves Tadié, vol. 2 (Paris: Gallimard, 2007), 783–787.

Nearly all these books revolve in one way or another around the position of European modernity in the world. There is pain in all of them—of taking leave, of demise, of the destruction of an idea. Can this appear as anything but the discursive symptom of a narcissistic grievance? If it was the thinking White man, the philosopher, who recognized in history a "progress in the consciousness of freedom," thus embodying a European freedom that had supposedly come to a consciousness of itself, then it is also the achievement of precisely this self-aware European modernity that is now being fundamentally called into question. Like no other country, however, the French nation saw itself as the realization of the ideal of liberty and proclaimed its own universalization as a *mission civilisatrice* that was expected to take place in the medium of French language and culture.[21] In the postimperial age, which often enough still fails to cultivate an awareness for the abysses of the past, even as they conspicuously gape before us, this self-image lies in ruins. Pensive, melancholic, furious—the books noted above revolve obsessively around the possibility of exiting a world that appears hopeless, and whose destruction Europe helped to bring about, by trampling on the universalism it proclaims and elevating its own, mostly male, freedom over equality.

Over the same period of the last ten years, Marie NDiaye's *Three Strong Women* (French 2009, English 2012) and Lydie Salvayre's *Cry, Mother Spain* (French 2014, English 2016) received the Goncourt, and Maylis de Kérangal wrote *The Heart* (French 2014, English 2017; also translated as *Mend the Living*). These books are neither belletristic nor spiritual in nature, nor do they spring from any motherly affection. Such clichés no longer resonate. Healing effects have always been attributed to all those impacted by the modern conquest of the world: to so-called primitive peoples, or to Black Africa, to women. Jules Michelet's *La Femme* from 1860, for instance, dreams of marriages with these specific groups as possessing a healing power, and of an energetic, exemplary Haiti as a "Black France."[22] Yet the site of these books written by women is different. The novels are turned toward the future; they tell of a utopian power and the possibility of survival.[23]

---

21 See Jürgen Trabant, *Der Gallische Herkules: Über Sprache und Politik in Frankreich und Deutschland* (Tübingen/Basel: Francke, 2002).

22 See here Markus Messling, "Ernüchtert ans Meer: Moderne Kritik und (anti)urbane Utopien bei Stendhal, Gobineau und Michelet," in *Literarische Stadtutopien zwischen totalitärer Gewalt und Ästhetisierung*, ed. Barbara Ventarola (Munich: M. Meidenbauer, 2011), 297–320.

23 See also Nastassja Martin, *Croire aux Fauves* (Paris: verticales/Gallimard, 2019), who battles her way through a near-fatal encounter with a bear and then struggles with the conflict she encounters between the shamanic interpretation of the world found in the Eastern Siberian populations of her fieldwork and the hyperrationality of a Paris plastic surgery clinic. From the reparative processes these experiences entail, she draws a hope for a different, nondichotomous consciousness of the world.

I don't want to overemphasize this comparison; one could easily find numerous counterexamples—and the chapter in this book on Shumona Sinha's trilogy of novels about the fate of women in our present day certainly offers a convincing one. In putting things so starkly I hope to make visible a problem, but my intention is not to resubstantialize the sexes. Literature is not an expression of something natural, but of reflection and imagination. It is in and through literature that an embodied consciousness is articulated in language—a language that seeks to give form to the world, that creates a world. It is no coincidence that the overwhelming number of the titles I have mentioned here fall within the scope of the movement within contemporary French literature that can be described as neorealism, which emerged in the early 1980s and has become increasingly established since 1989.[24] The stance toward the world itself is the problem.

The intensity generated by this realistic literature is a melancholy of loss. What has been lost is the possibility of creating individuality in the world, and of creating sense out of the world. Where in capitalist modernity do the ideals of 1789, or ideals at all, still shine forth? Can human beings still shape the world, and themselves, in transcending their individual points of view?

This experience of loss is, however, not the same everywhere. It can arise from grievance and give birth to anger; it can be born of shame and seek solidarity. And we find this illustrated in present-day literary voices who share a deep anthropological pessimism: Michel Houellebecq, Mathias Énard, and Camille de Toledo. All three of these authors interweave the anthropological question of the human condition under materialist preconditions of modernity with the aesthetic question of how the world is sensually appropriated. Their works are a kind of literature that seeks to compensate for this loss under the sign of European melancholy. But their depictions of the present in the novels *The Map and the Territory* on the one hand, and *Compass* and *Le livre de la faim et de la soif,* on the other, bring forth two distinct politics of literature, and two distinct answers to our present, that could hardly be more different.

Michel Houellebecq or The Vehemence of Political Romanticism

There is no other French writer enveloped in Germany by such an aura. Since his novel *Whatever,* Michel Houellebecq has been hailed as a scandalous author for exposing the spiritual impoverishment of White men in late capitalism, for

---

24 Wolfgang Asholt, "Un renouveau du 'réalisme' dans la littérature contemporaine?," *Lendemains* 38, no. 150/151 (2013): 22–35.

putting misogynist and homophobic attitudes on display and writing about nudist camps and anal sex.[25] Just recently, in January 2019, he was celebrated by some for having supposedly foreseen, in *Serotonin*, the violent protests of the "yellow vests."[26] Others have asked whether he did not also predict, in *Platform*,[27] Islamist acts of terror carried out against international capitalism, and in *Submission*,[28] the growing influence of Islamism in France. Does Houellebecq have prophetic abilities, as some in the media have suggested?[29]

Such characterizations, of course, follow the marketing strategies of Flammarion, Michel Houellebecq's French publisher, who by now spares no effort in planning the publication of his books and keeping press interest high. More aura means better business. Contrary to Houellebecq's doomsday scenarios, his novels have been highly successful in one respect, regardless of the millions he has received in royalties: they have earned his publisher enormous sums of money.

But Houellebecq is no prophet. It was a gruesome coincidence that the long-planned publication of *Submission* on January 7, 2015, coincided with the attack on the editorial offices of the satirical magazine Charlie Hebdo. This attack shockingly displayed the polarization of French society. It may have initially suggested more. But anyone who has carefully read *Submission* will likely understand that, even if the book is tremendously Islamophobic, it is not primarily a reckoning with Islam, but rather with European modernity. The fact that we find dairy farmers setting up roadblocks in *Serotonin* is hardly astonishing, considering the decades-long tradition of protest among French farmers. Nevertheless: the spread of this fury to the lower middle class, as it finds itself threatened with falling behind, is nothing new since the electoral successes of the Front National (now Rassemblement National);

---

25 Michel Houellebecq, *Whatever*, trans. Paul Hammond (Burnaby, B.C.: University of Simon Fraser Library, 2014 [1994]).

26 Michel Houellebecq, *Serotonin: A Novel*, trans. Shaun Whiteside (New York: Farrar, Straus and Giroux, 2019 [2019].

27 Michel Houellebecq, *Platform*, trans. Frank Wynne (London: Vintage Books, 2003 [2001]).

28 Michel Houellebecq, *Submission*, trans. Lorin Stein (London: W. Heinemann, 2015 [2015]).

29 For instance, the *Frankfurter Rundschau* from January 1, 2019, headlined its review, by Stefan Brändle, by noting: "The prophet of the 'yellow vests': In his new novel *Serotonin*, Michel Houellebecq describes the impoverishment of the French rural population." See www.fr.de/kultur/literatur/michel-houellebecq-der-prophet-der-gelbwesten-a-1646182, accessed February 7, 2019; similarly, on January 3, 2019, *Deutschlandfunk Kultur* broadcast a discussion among critics under the title "Warten auf den neuen Houellebecq: Prophet der 'Gelbwesten'-Proteste" (Waiting for the new Houellebecq: Prophet of the "yellow-vest" protests); www.deutschlandfunkkultur.de/warten-auf-den-neuen-houellebecq-prophet-der-gelbwesten.1013.de.html?dram:article_id=437421, accessed February 7, 2019; or the German television program *ZDFheute* announced on January 4, 2019: "Provokateur und Prophet: Houellebecqs neuer Roman" (Provocateur and prophet: Houellebecq's new novel); see www.zdf.de/nachrichten/heute/houellebecqs-neuer-roman-ist-da-serotonin-100.html, accessed February 7, 2019.

it has already become a focus of sociological research. The *gilets jaunes* themselves do not appear in *Serotonin*—nor could they, because the manuscript had been completed long before they entered onto the stage of history. Hence if Michel Houellebecq is a prophet, then only, in the apt, polemical words of Alex Rühle, as a "prophet of decline,"[30] an Oswald Spengler of our time.

There is no doubt that Michel Houellebecq is a clever analyst who for years now has been describing the destructive effects of neoliberalism on the cohesion of society. Yet what he uncovers is less any new political or economic insight and more an affective stance toward the world, a deeply felt lack. In this regard, he is schooled in the great tradition of the French social novel, which does not depict reality but rather makes it possible to experience how reality is shaped by the inner tension that an observer brings in encountering it. Like few other writers, Houellebecq has thus captured the fear of falling behind and the outrage, the isolation and the melancholy, of the anxious middle classes. He admitted that he has long since ceased to be counted among them when he noted critically of himself, in a television interview during the 2017 French presidential election, that he belonged to the globalized elite and no longer understood the French people.[31] His intention in *Serotonin*, however, is to hear what the people have to say, to give them a voice. In literary terms, he only succeeds to a limited extent, because for page after page the book simply reworks typical Houellebecq topoi and slang.[32] At any rate, it is mainly for Michel Houellebecq himself that Houellebecq's way of writing is a form of serotonin—the happiness hormone whose release in the brain is induced by antidepressants, and without which the narrator Florent-Claude Labrouste cannot bear reality. Houellebecq's narrator—as always, a game with Houellebecq's alter ego, even if this time his name isn't Michel—skillfully trots out for his readers what they already know from countless novels: sexual obsessions, the merits of the orifices belonging to this or that woman, contempt for his Japanese partner (even before he finds a video of her having sex with dogs), the malice with which he gloats over his environmentally conscious fellow citizens, and the inner joy he takes in the damning environmental impact of his diesel SUV. Labrouste works as an expert for the Ministry of Agriculture, writing reports to further its interests in Brussels—until he quits his job and sets off into

30 Alex Rühle, "Der Prophet des Untergangs," *Süddeutsche Zeitung*, January 4, 2019, https://sz.de/ 1.4274668, accessed March 29, 2023.

31 See www.lesinrocks.com/inrocks.tv/michel-houellebecq-je-fais-partie-de-lelite-mondialisee-jai-perdu-le-contact/, accessed February 2, 2019.

32 See the brilliant critique by Jürgen Ritte, "Schlechtes Kabarett," https://www.deutschlandfunk. de/michel-houellebecq-serotonin-schlechtes-kabarett.700.de.html?dram:article_id=439318, accessed February 7, 2019.

the misery of the provinces to join the dairy farmers who cannot prevail amid global competition, and whose protest is brutally shot down.

Houellebecq is by no means the first to point to the downward spiral of milk prices as a symbol for the decline of the agricultural sector. In his illuminating film *On the Road in France* (*La Traversée*), for instance, Daniel Cohn-Bendit had already traveled to visit various farmers—some farming conventionally, others following ecological or organic methods—shortly after Macron's election, in order to comprehend a society in fear fifty years after 1968.[33] In Houellebecq's novel, the dairy farmer episode is drawn more pointedly, as the basis for a critique that is not only economic but also spiritual and moral. When Michel Houellebecq once claimed that he didn't think much of parliamentary elections and only voted in referendums,[34] he exemplified the recourse to "the people" taken by both right-wing and left-wing sovereigntists in France in their campaigns against its democratic representatives. As far as the writer's prophetic powers are concerned, then, deep down the relation between cause and effect is reversed: Michel Houellebecq has long contributed to the production of this voice of the people; his texts are its intellectual expression, the educated side of the rage against the system of *La France en colère*. He did not foresee the yellow vests, but his literature is ideologically aligned with the parts of their revolt that the antidemocratic forces within the movement have exploited. Yet as he himself has not failed to see, he is free from the threats to his existence that affect and rightly outrage parts of our societies. Houellebecq's thinking instead belongs to the ideological superstructure that has formed in educated right-wing circles. But he does not offer imagined political scenarios within the democratic spectrum; he is not concerned with reform. There is a reason that the tragic character in *Serotonin*, Aymeric d'Harcourt, who leads the farmers' roadblock, is the scion of an old French family from the landed gentry. His downfall stands for the downfall of all "real values" that France supposedly once represented. Houellebecq stands in the tradition of the antimodernism that emerged from the aristocratic rancor after 1789.[35]

---

33 Daniel Cohn-Bendit and Romain Goupil, *La Traversée/On the Road in France,* documentary, March 16, 2018, Paris.

34 See the interview by Alex Rühle with Michel Houellebecq: "Das Leben ist ohne Religion über alle Maßen traurig," *Süddeutsche Zeitung*, January 22, 2015, www.sueddeutsche.de/kultur/interview-mit-michel-houellebecq-das-leben-ist-ohne-religion-ueber-alle-massen-traurig-1.2316339.

35 See Dominique Rabaté, "Extension ou liquidation de la lutte? Remarques sur le roman selon Houellebecq," in *Le Discours "néo-reactionnaire": Transgressions conservatrices*, ed. Pascal Durand and Sarah Sindaco (Paris: CNRS Éditions, 2015), 265–279, on 276.

Like historical realism before it, Houellebecq's literature is also an anti-politics of perception: it exposes the empty promises of politically liberal democracy, which Houellebecq portrays as corrupt and in decline. He presents a world in which all ideals are being crushed by unlimited materialism, and from which there is no escape. Unlike historical realism, however, Houellebecq's literature no longer seeks to capture moments of freedom, but rather to document the supposed hopelessness of this situation, with its spiritual disintegration. In doing so, it tracks a politics of feelings. Michel Houellebecq has in this way made himself the protagonist of a movement that hurls its fury—which reaches across all classes, as has long been clear—against modernity, exposing modernity's destructive forces without asserting its emancipatory achievements. There is nothing left to defend; the only solution is a radical scission. To check the ingredients of this stance, one need only read Michel Houellebecq's arguments in "Donald Trump Is a Good President," published in *Harper's Magazine* on January 5, 2019.[36] The text is polemical, certainly ironic in places, but it does reveal basic assumptions: a concept of Christian, Western culture, sovereignism, nationalism, political antiliberalism, and contempt for the EU and parliamentarianism. This is what Trump and the Brexiteers stand for, whom Michel Houellebecq openly admires. More and more clearly, his literature reveals itself as a call for a sharp turn.[37]

For Michel Houellebecq, the modern world is a place where human beings have no future. In this vision, the model of the human as a thinking and acting subject is being culled in our present day by the machinery of evolution—which is regarded as having implanted into humans the very drives to devour the world that are now themselves, at the end of a development governed by natural law, tearing human beings apart. *The Map and the Territory* offers a potent poetic image for this in the video montage that the main character of the novel, the artist Jed Martin, creates in his refuge in the countryside. Here, a camera films little Playmobil figures as they are overgrown and overrun by nature—at an almost grotesquely slow pace, but inexorably: "Le triomphe de la végétation est total." The novel ends with these bitter lines:

> The work that occupied the last years of Jed Martin's life can thus be seen—and this is the first interpretation that springs to mind—as a nostalgic meditation on the end of the Industrial Age in Europe, and, more generally, on the perishable and transitory nature of any

---

36 See www.harpers.org/archive/2019/01/donald-trump-is-a-good-president/, accessed February 7, 2019.

37 In that sense Houellebecq at once incorporates the two neoreactionary "ideal types" that Gisèle Sapiro has described for the intellectual field: the aesthete and the polemicist. See Gisèle Sapiro, "Notables, esthètes et polémistes: manière d'être un écrivain 'réactionnaire' des années 1930 à nos jours," in Durand and Sindaco, *Le Discours "néo-reactionnaire,"* 23–46.

human industry. This interpretation is, however, inadequate when one tries to make sense of the unease that grips us on seeing those pathetic Playmobil-type little figurines, lost in the middle of an abstract and immense futurist city, a city which itself crumbles and falls apart, and then seems gradually to be scattered across the immense vegetation extending to infinity. The feeling of desolation, too, that takes hold of us as the portraits of the human beings who had accompanied Jed Martin through his earthly life fall apart under the impact of bad weather, then decompose and disappear, seeming in the last videos to make themselves as the symbols of the generalized annihilation of the human species. They sink and seem for an instant to put up a struggle, before being suffocated by the superimposed layer of plants. Then everything becomes calm. There remains only the grass swaying in the wind. The triumph of vegetation is total.[38]

The position of observer remains empty behind a camera that films without interruption. The highly elaborate depiction of the laws of nature, as if discovered under laboratory conditions, and the disappearance of human beings in the triumph of evolution go hand in hand. It is in this sense of fusing anthropology and aesthetics that *The Map and the Territory* is an art novel, and its protagonist Jed Martin is the artist who makes it possible to rehearse, in every step, the supposed unleashing of a materialistic modernity that consumes itself.

Realistic aesthetics and social description are also directly linked in Houellebecq's contribution to the novelistic tradition. "Houellebecq is to globalized society what Balzac was to France of the Bourbon Restoration and the July Monarchy," writes Bruno Viard. "He pursues the project of portraying society as a whole, as well as the currents that cut across it."[39] The comparison with Balzac is apt not only in terms of realistic aesthetics, but also of the authors' skepticism toward a republican modernity that is becoming entangled in struggles over distribution of wealth and representation without being able to deliver real profit and salvation. Viard continues: "This author is a typical representative of the romanticism of the twenty-first century—a writer who bases his work on the Manichaean dualism of political economy, on the one hand, and a paradise of ideals such as love and literature, on the other."[40]

Houellebecq's world view is based on a pessimistic anthropology with forerunners in Schopenhauer and Baudelaire. For him, the collapse of Christian transcendence in European culture means it is no longer possible to transcend life.

---

38 Michel Houellebecq, *The Map and the Territory*, trans. Gavin Bowd (New York: Alfred A. Knopf, 2012 [2010]), 269.

39 Bruno Viard, *"La Carte et le Territoire*, roman de la représentation: entre trash et tradition," in *Michel Houellebecq: questions du réalisme d'aujourd'hui*, ed. Jörn Steigerwald and Agnieszka Komorowska (Tübingen: Narr, 2011), 87–95, on 94.

40 Bruno Viard, *Littérature et déchirure de Montaigne à Houellebecq: Étude anthropologique* (Paris: Classiques Garnier, 2013), 94.

Existence finds itself trapped in the suffering of total immanence that no longer bestows meaning upon life, while also remaining impervious to spiritual experience or faith, and thereby becoming a permanent source of lack. In an interview with Jean-Yves Jouannais and Christophe Duchatelet in 1995, Houellebecq responds to a question about the inner coherence of his work: "There is above all, I believe, the intuition that the universe is based on separation, suffering, and evil; and the decision to describe this state and perhaps overcome it. . . . The starting point is the radical rejection of the world as such—and also an assent to the concepts of good and evil."[41]

This pain of constant privation is thus the catalyst for attempts to create things that are ideal, such as art, love, and truth—in order to silence, if only for a moment, the torment of meaninglessness. This had historically been the power of literature in the modern age: as a platonic symbolism that emphasized moments of experiencing truth, moments of realism aimed at the experience of distancing oneself from "reality" in order to assert freedom and individuality. In *The Map and The Territory*, Houellebecq demonstrates how in Western materialism this function of art, as the last refuge for the transcending of life, is in danger of dissolving. Capitalist consumerism—which for Houellebecq is the ultimate social form of human beings striving for more, striving to transgress a limit in appropriation—can assimilate any and all ideals. Houellebecq retraces this with painful meticulousness.

At first, Jed Martin's true feelings for Olga, the woman he adores, have no chance at all, because she is a modern businesswoman who is constantly traveling, which leaves his love riddled with her absences. The conditions of flexibilization mean that women can no longer be worshiped as ideal, and in this constellation Jed is increasingly unable to maintain and admit his feelings. One can read this as Houellebecq's critique of equality, inasmuch as traditional gender difference assigns women an idealized function that melts away under the force of egalitarian materialism. In Houellebecq's book, this fails to engender any joyful, emancipatory power, while love falls by the wayside.

Jed's painterly realism, which stands for both the artistic idealism of the character's beginnings and the author himself, is dragged to ruin by his commercial success. Here, we find all the classic motifs of critiques of capitalism. Demand drives production; individuality and uniqueness give way to reproducibility; motifs and design are arbitrary. The Platonic question of the good, the true, and the

---

41 Interview in *Art Press* 199 (1995): 37–48, reprinted in Michel Houellebecq, *Interventions* (Paris: Flammarion, 1998), on 94.

beautiful degenerates to the question of a sales price. Jed becomes rich and unhappy.

Finally—and this is the narrative strand that gives the novel its name—the subjective appropriation of the world, as carried out by Jed in the form of photography and the editing of regional Michelin maps, is itself called into question. The experiment set up here by the author Houellebecq could hardly be more splendid: cartography is the practice of putting the world into perspective according to criteria that are as intelligible and "objectifiable" as possible; its dream is to master the world itself. By employing aesthetic criteria to edit these maps, Jed creates his own world, creates an individual perspective, and achieves a victory of freedom over any prefabricated idea. But this delivers only a brief satisfaction, because the regional maps from the tire company Michelin are iconic. Jed's images become the expression of a turning to the *terroir*, the native soil, to the region with its products. They thus also become objects of desire to a conservative movement that seeks to preserve "traditional values" and thereby reconciles commercialized ecoproducts, monastic retreats, and SUVs. In this way, Jed Martin's images become the lubricant of capitalism: they create values in the struggle for values, but they lose their emancipatory power. Nothing could be more comical than Houellebecq's description of a Michelin reception—a scene with all the ingredients for a conservative role-playing game that Houellebecq mercilessly ridicules by portraying the reception of Jed's art alongside wine and sausages and in the limelight of TV starlets. The attempt to preserve ideals within a system that devours them—conservatism itself—is presented by Houellebecq as an undertaking doomed to failure. Houellebecq makes the same point even more viciously in the novel *Submission*, which followed in 2015. Here, Houellebecq's protagonist is a literary scholar in a desperate search for spirituality who is led to the particular abbey, the Abbaye Saint-Martin de Ligugé near Poitiers, that the Benedictines were forced to temporarily abandon under the anticlerical laws of 1901, and where the actual writer Joris-Karl Huysmans completed his turn from naturalism to piety. François, however, finds no enlightenment in the abbey, as banality catches up with him: he can't avoid spending the whole time thinking of smoking, and he leaves his "journey in the light," as the monk calls it, by saying he "had a terrific time."[42]

Houellebecq is not interested in conservatism. As he sees it, conservatives fail to recognize the dramatic consequences of the hollowing out that comes from materialism. They fail to understand that modernity tears everything down, including language. It is in keeping with these premises that Houellebecq does not cultivate the literary form of French that stretches from *bon usage* to Marcel Proust, turning

---

42 Houellebecq, *Submission*, 182.

instead to a language that is simple, meager, almost colloquial. This is a recognition that the art of language, like all forms of art, can no longer have a transcendent effect; clinging to this would be a desperate gesture. Houellebecq thereby unmasks a language of contemporary society that no longer demands conceptual effort and has flattened out to become pure communication. For him, art and language no longer give rise to any freedom. Herein lies the vehemence of his attack on modernity. But can pessimism itself still develop a power to liberate, or at least to delay?

The question arises as to whether and how writing might remain possible at all when an aesthetic that relies on idealistic surpluses founders, because these surpluses can always be transformed into capital. Houellebecq's anthropological reply is clear: when the grinding machine of capitalism has finally assimilated idealism, life itself will remain as the only area where transgression might be possible, the only area, in short, that holds any opening. Only life itself would remain as something capable of being modeled, extended, worked into a new form—but this also makes it available to be possessed or used, it becomes a commodity, in the way presumed over several strikingly grave pages in Houellebecq's *The Map and the Territory* devoted to policies of dying in the Dignitas euthanasia clinic. In the end, human beings consume themselves.

Just as Jed Martin represents, in the first part of the novel, an alter ego for a young, idealistic Houellebecq, "Houellebecq" makes an entrance in the second part as the alter ego of the experienced author. And this Houellebecq is brutally murdered after a brief friendship with Jed Martin, the very figure he had so generously supported. The body of this Houellebecq is cut into a thousand pieces and arranged by the murderer so that the ensemble of limbs and pieces of flesh splayed on the carpet is reminiscent of the abstract expressionism of a Jackson Pollock. A fusion of art and life is announced here, in the form propagated by the historical avant-gardes, and from which Italian fascism in particular drew its lessons. And with this, the final horizon of biopolitics has now been drawn: life itself has become a mass to be shaped. The farewell to the idealistic figure of the human artist evoked one last time in Jed Martin, as an artist who desired to create subjectivity and freedom, entails saying farewell to the human *tout court*. The late capitalist society that the author Houellebecq repeatedly brings to our attention in his work thus becomes the natural habitat for a transformation of the human being, carried out through medicine and genetic engineering, as a creature who follows its needs and life instincts. It is in this sense that the capitalist game for Houellebecq is the structure of evolution itself.[43]

---

43 This is interesting insofar as Joseph Vogl has shown that the idea of the market was originally invented out of a pessimistic anthropology, which arose in the shadow of Europe's religious wars

The murder of the novel character Houellebecq marks a break in Houelle-becq's narrative program. Here, Houellebecq introduces a detective method that Carlo Ginzburg demonstrated, in his essay on microhistory, as a fundamental pro-cedure of modernity: the examination of small pieces of evidence—of threads, traces, or clues—serves as the starting point for a pathological interpretation of the big picture.[44] A kind of crime thriller thereby unfolds that ostensibly serves to solve the murder but more profoundly reflects a change in anthropological presup-positions: Houellebecq no longer allows us as readers to remain in the realistic age that the first parts of the novel describe, to remain in its idealistic attempts at trans-gression; instead, we find ourselves caught in a social pathology whose indications are evoked by the novel's content and aesthetics. The investigation of the case leads into the dark room of the plastic surgeon Adolphe Petissaud—a name that bespeaks a short hop or jump, and here connotes a character whose intellectual leaps fall short. Quite the opposite, though, he is one who "took himself for God,"[45] who plays like the creator with various insects by allowing them to attack each other in large terrariums and fight to the death. His concept of evolution is stamped with brutal-ity; questions about adapting to the environment play no role; nature is a great eat-or-be-eaten. This once again clearly shows the pessimistic anthropology of Houelle-becq with which we began—yet in a form that now regards the suffering that comes from immanence as no longer being ameliorated by ideals, but by the co-opting and reshaping of this immanence itself. Nothing remains capable of tran-scending nature except the technical processing of life itself into a supposedly higher stage in the evolutionary process. In his caricature of conventional bour-geois desires, Houellebecq sketches dark shadows of the future: the physician as the god of human beings, and his creatures as members of the master race. The choice of "Adolf" as a first name is hardly a coincidence.

Dr. Petissaud's basement is also where the painting of Houellebecq with Jed Martin's dedication is to be found—the same image that had been stolen from the fictitious writer's living room, just above the scene of the gruesome murder. Not only does this prove Petissaud to be the murderer; the image, together with paint-ings by Francis Bacon and two plastinations by Gunther von Hagens, forms a

---

and out of a deep mistrust of human passions. The hope was that the market, in the free play of its forces, could create a balance that the political structure had not been able to achieve. See Vogl, *The Specter of Capital.*

44 Carlo Ginzburg and Anna Davin, "Morelli, Freud and Sherlock Holmes: Clues and Scientific Method," *History Workshop* 9 (Spring 1980): 5–36; see also Carlo Ginzburg, *Clues, Myths, and the Historical Method,* trans. John and Anne C. Tedeschi (Berkeley: University of California Press, 2012).
45 Houellebecq, *The Map and the Territory,* 265.

kind of art-historical panorama rendering visible a development to naturalism, both aesthetically and in terms of the philosophy of history. The gaze shifts from Bacon's depiction of creatureliness and Martin's late realistic painting to one of von Hagens's plastinations. The walls are decorated with sculptures made by Petissaud from parts of human bodies. Here, evolution has symbolically realized its final stage in a cabinet of Frankensteinian horrors.

The gap between historical naturalism and the naturalism depicted here by Houellebecq lies in the disappearance of any capacity for hope—the kind of hope that in Émile Zola, for example, always remains recognizable thanks to a moral standpoint outside literature's experimental laboratory of evolution, which in Zola drew its strength from a reformist and republican-socialist worldview.[46] This worldview expected the representation of the laws of social development to serve scientific knowledge and social change. But Houellebecq's account is governed by the determinism of his anthropological assumptions, which no longer release any transformative energy, not even a dystopian force.[47] This explains the calm, serene narrative stance in *The Map and the Territory*; the work no longer elicits that angry and provocative cynicism that pervaded every line of Houellebecq's earlier works—in *Whatever* or *Atomised*[48]—and suddenly made him a "phenomenon."[49] *The Map and The Territory* marks a departure from any liberating force of realistic aesthetics; neither immanent transcendence nor subversive features of articulation persist in the novel. The last function that still belongs to literature, as to art in general, is to document the evolutionary processes in the habitat of late capitalism. The creation of perspective via maps becomes a documentation of the territory of late capitalism and the forces at work within it. It is in this sense that Houellebecq employs the art form that Jed Martin calls "videograms" to create, in his poetological epilogue, an amalgam of anthropological disposition and aesthetic correspondence. So back to the beginning: little Playmobil figures are being filmed by a fixed camera as they are bleached by the elements and overgrown by a gigantic miniature jungle. This is the decline of subjectivity, the victory of vegetation.

---

46 Rita Schober, *Auf dem Prüfstand: Zola – Houellebecq – Klemperer* (Berlin: Edition Tranvía, 2003), 198–199.

47 See Markus Messling, "Anthropologie du Mal et politique de la littérature: Michel Houellebecq et Roberto Bolaño," *Revue des Sciences Humaines* 321 (2016): 51–66.

48 Houellebecq, *Whatever*; Michel Houellebecq, *Atomised*, trans. Frank Wynne (London: Vintage House, 2007 [1998]).

49 See the contributions in Thomas Steinfeld, ed., *Das Phänomen Houellebecq* (Cologne: DuMont, 2001).

But if nothing remains, if even the romantic belief in the function of art is left destroyed, and the only role that writing still has is not to transgress but to document an unstoppable pathology, then any moralistic position is out of the question. A powerful image for this hopelessness is Houellebecq's depiction of an anal sex scene in *Submission*: François pays a call girl yet feels no satisfaction because sex on demand has the potential to be continued ad infinitum, rendering it aimless; the call girl, by contrast, suddenly feels pleasure, which is something forbidden by her professionalism and why she stops the penetration. In opposition to modernity's image of sexuality as liberated from morality and reproduction, Houellebecq articulates in his image a coitus interruptus that captures the impossibility of transgression and transcendence through orgasm. When sex is bought, orgasm brings no liberation.

Against this hopelessness of total materialism, the French characters of *Submission* choose a conservative alternative represented in Houellebecq's vision—in which Catholicism is nothing more than a sclerotic, sterile tradition—by moderate Islamists. Here, Islam can still claim to be a "hot" religion that would revolutionize society. The moderate Islamists, however, commercialize the values they proclaim and buy their power through materialistic slights of hand, such as dynastic politics or cronyism; in this regard, they differ in no way from the political calculations of Christian conservative parties. They are subject to the same criticism that Houellebecq hurls against bourgeois rationalism: "We all know that. We may prefer Baudelaire. Or even Karl Marx, who, at least, is not mistaken when he writes that 'the triumph of the bourgeoisie has drowned the sacred shivers of religious ecstasy, chivalrous enthusiasm, and sentimentality in the icy waters of selfish calculation (*The Class Struggles in France*).'"[50] Nonetheless, the assertion of ideals that are derived in Marx from the material transformation of social relations seems, to Houellebecq, to be an impossible undertaking. We are stuck here in the horror of a destructive materialism from which there is no escape, that lacks any dialectic, even a negative one. The end of utopia. Houellebecq's novel plays with fear—a fear in which the emancipatory possibilities that narratives might reveal die away.[51] His most recent novels are part of the long history of

---

50 Houellebecq, *Interventions*, 94.

51 Analyzing Houellebecq's early works of fiction, Niklas Bender comes to a similar conclusion in his chapter "Die Lehre des Scheitern III: Das Ende der Möglichkeiten." See also Bender, *Verpasste und erfasste Möglichkeiten: Lesen als Lebenskunst* (Basel: Schwabe, 2018), 63–75. Bender has also written an enlightening essay that highlights the significance of H. P. Lovecraft for Houellebecq's poetics of fear, titled "Angst als literarisches Lebenselixier" (Fear as a literary elixir of life): "Few authors are as polarizing as Michel Houellebecq. His new novel has just been published. To understand what has made it so successful, you have to know how he got started as a writer—and know his literary idol." Published in the *Frankfurter Allgemeine Zeitung*, January 12, 2019, 18.

European narratives of decline aiming to provoke an abrupt, sudden revolt. In truth, the destroyers of democratic modernity are always at the ready in the background of *Submission* and *Serotonin*. The political explosion of the neo-right-wing anger generated out of the feeling of an aggrieved humanity and its ideals, which has been catapulted into the forefront of politics in Western democracies by a considerable number of voters, crystallizes here as the intensity of the present. In *The Map and The Territory*, Jed Martin, Michel Houellebecq's idealistic alter ego, tries to visit his terminally ill father in Switzerland before his father can commit to the process of assisted dying. But he arrives too late. Jed is gripped by an immeasurable sadness and blind rage, in which he almost kills the staff member at the Dignitas center with his own hands, as she stands surrounded by the center's administrative records. The bloody deed has a liberating effect on him: "On arriving at the hotel, he realized that this bout of violence had put him in a good mood."[52]

Mathias Énard or Nostalgia as a Resource for the Future

Mathias Énard shares the deep skepticism toward a modernity that has betrayed its ideals, and that loses sight of what it means to be human. What he does not share is the notion that the situation cannot be changed, that there is no longer any hope for humanity. Énard's somber little book *L'alcool et la nostalgie* is based on a radio play he wrote for the broadcaster France Culture about a journey on the Trans-Siberian Railway.[53] Its German title, *Der Alkohol und die Wehmut*—a word that is often translated as "melancholy" but has no true equivalent in English— seems almost more fitting than the original:[54] "Wehmut" means "restrained grief, silent pain at the memory of something past, irretrievable," and Énard's book is

---

52 Houellebecq, *The Map and the Territory*, 255. Despite the aesthetic impact of Houellebecq's novels, which culminates above all in a sense of hopelessness and paralysis afflicting modern life, it remains possible to insist on a distinction between the feelings of the novel's protagonist and author. Nevertheless, it must be noted that in a revealing interview with Michel Onfray, Houellebecq appeared to offer pretexts for possible massacres against immigrants or people with a migratory background by making racists statements. See Michel Onfray, "'Dieu vous entende, Michel': L'entretien entre Michel Houellebecq et Michel Onfray," in "La fin de l'Occident," special issue, *Front Populaire: La revue des souverainistes* (November 29, 2022): 2–45. In *Serotonin*, Houellebecq fictionally played out the transformation of right-wing anger into action; since then, the real-world implications of this transformation has become abundantly clear in Western societies.
53 Mathias Énard, *L'alcool et la nostalgie* (Paris: Inculte, 2011).
54 Mathias Énard, *Der Alkohol und die Wehmut*, trans. Claudia Hamm (Berlin: Matthes and Seitz, 2016).

less about the memory of days gone by than about world-weariness itself.[55] Yet the book ends with an evocation of love and hope. Jeanne is standing at the sickbed of Mathias, who has tried to kill himself with pills after suffering an insurmountable loss, the loss of his kindred soul and friend Vladimir. Mathias's life hangs in the balance. Jeanne, who had lived with the two men in an unspoken *ménage à trois* during the wild Russian years of the postreunification period, unfurls a tapestry of words aimed against death:

> I could have left, too. / Not on a train to Siberia, that's for sure, but I could have decided to leave you to your story, both of you, I didn't do it, for you, among other reasons, for him, too, because all of this is complicated. / Very quickly, I understood. / I understood that Russia was eating us like an ogre. / All these stories, all these tales, all these songs. / We move forward. / We always move forward. / . . . Your heart beats in my hand, our hearts beat in our hands, all hearts beat in all hands. / The sun will eventually rise.[56]

Mathias Énard's work is like this song of love: an attempt to wring life from world-loss, to counter in some way the fear of loss. It is the counterproject to Houellebecq's swan song.

Like Houellebecq, Énard also writes from the standpoint of an ailing imperial center that has brutally absorbed the world and yet cannot satisfy its own hunger. Unlike Houellebecq, though, Énard does not write from Paris, Walter Benjamin's "capital of the nineteenth century." Énard lives in Barcelona, the republican Mediterranean metropolis, where neither the Spanish bridge to the Arab world nor the Reconquista are to be forgotten, and which defiantly nurtures a utopian spirit in its own cruise-ship hypercapitalism. Even in its nationalist tensions, Barcelona is a countercity. This biographical decentering finds its literary counterpart in the novel's relocation to Vienna: *Compass* is conceived from this metropolis on the Danube, the capital of the Habsburg Empire, where it was no more possible to ignore the diversity of peoples and languages than the land bridge to the Ottoman Empire. Paris is the center of universalistic modernity. But for Énard, Vienna is the center of another modernity that has always been aware of its enmeshment with the Other—a center that has been able to find, in this enmeshment, a saving grace, or at least a reorientation, while the self-universalizing French Republic was busy burying its ideals in Jacobin terror and France's subsequent imperial mission.

For Énard, Vienna is the romantic city par excellence and the city of Romanticism, the gateway to the East, a place of erudition and of a turning toward the Orient, a place from which music and poetry, ideality and spirituality, have been

---

55 "Wehmut," in Duden Onlinewörterbuch, https://www.duden.de/rechtschreibung/Wehmut, accessed January 14, 2021.
56 Énard, *L'alcool et la nostalgie*, 87–88.

able to flow back to Europe. This, though, is the past; the Habsburg Empire has long since lost itself and its "inner Otherness." And yet something has remained, covered with the rust of time, because this history is sedimented in Énard himself: in his knowledge of Oriental languages and love of Persian poetry, in countless changes of place and experiences of traveling, in the knowledge of the scholars of Orientalism and in the shared longing of Romanticism to transcend a leaden immanence.[57] Vienna's empty grandeur, in which we, with Franz Ritter, can present to a psychoanalyst our discontentment with the world, is the perfect starting point for Mathias Énard's tour of our present day. Beginning from this nostalgia he slowly, at first almost imperceptibly, draws hairline cracks through our melancholy.

He draws these cracks out of a nostalgic knowledge that the loss is irreversible, even as it leaves behind in us a residue, as a kind of fault line engendering a distance to reality. This is an attitude that confronts what is here now, even as it is always located at a different psychological place, in a sunken world of history, of childhood, of language. Within us, a life brightly appears that is unreachable, lost, sometimes imagined, liberating us from the power of what is immediate. What thus emerges here—out of such experiences of a leap in time, of linguistic difference and psychological rupture—is a complex world that can be described as "cosmopolitan," in contrast to a mere spatial change that need not continue to offer any promise of freedom in times of flexibilization and ubiquity.[58] With its poetic power, the attitude to which this gives rise subverts the tendencies of our present to negate the countless stratifications of our existence. And in this sense, nostalgia carries within itself a force directed toward the future. Énard conjures this force against the "European sadness" he sees afflicting us—an assumption that he shares with Houellebecq. For Énard, however, this assumption is a beginning, not a conclusion.

Franz Ritter, the protagonist of *Compass*, is a musicologist shocked by an alarming medical diagnosis that fearfully keeps him awake at night. During his

---

57 These are the terms that Leyla Dakhli employed in the poetic eulogy she delivered at the Leipzig Book Prize for European Understanding in 2017; see Leyla Dakhli, "Accolade for Mathias Énard," trans. Holger Fock and Sabine Müller, in *Leipziger Buchpreis zur Europäischen Verständigung 2017: An Mathias Enard = Leipzig Book Award for European Understanding*, ed. City of Leipzig (Leipzig: Leipzig Book Award, 2017), 69–74.

58 For a discussion of this non-elitist interpretation of cosmopolitanism, see the astute text by Olivier Remaud, *Un monde étrange: Pour une autre approche du cosmopolitisme* (Paris: Puf, 2015), as well as Markus Messling, "Réalisme esthétique et cosmopolitisme littéraire: Poétiques de la perte chez Giorgos Seferis et Kossi Efoui," in *Décentrer le cosmopolitisme: Enjeux politiques et sociaux dans la littérature*, ed. Guillaume Bridet et al. (Dijon: Éditions Universitaires de Dijon, 2018), 71–84.

vigils, he unfolds a fragmented and stratified ego stretched between narrative modes of philosophical thoughts, memories, perceptions, and interpretations. The resulting stream of consciousness is what in fact constitutes the novel and, ultimately, an introspection on our Europe. As with the novel, we can no longer find our place in the world:

> We are two opium smokers each in his own cloud, seeing nothing outside, alone, never understanding each other we smoke, faces agonizing in a mirror, we are a frozen image to which time gives the illusion of movement, a snow crystal gliding over a ball of frost, the complexity of whose intertwinings no one can see, I am that drop of water condensed on the window of my living room, a rolling liquid pearl that knows nothing of the vapour that engendered it, nor of the atoms that still compose it but that, soon, will serve other molecules, other bodies, the clouds weighing heavy over Vienna tonight: over whose nape will this water stream, against what skin, on what pavement, towards what river, and this indistinct face on the glass is mine only for an instant, one of the millions of possible configurations of illusion.[59]

Énard places the ending, the diagnosis of Franz's illness and his fear of death, at the beginning. This is where we stand. But from here we can now also set out, seek hope in the past, recognize in history that alternatives are available. Énard invokes one of these alternatives with historical Romanticism. *Compass* is pervaded by references to the works of the Romantics, and Romantic motifs fill its pages:[60] music and poetry, scenes of nature and ruins, wanderlust and the Orient, dreaming and the intoxication of opium, epistolary novels and spiritual kinship, madness, an enraptured self, and loneliness. Franz Ritter cautiously writes a few lines full of longing to Sarah, whom he adores, across the pages of a scholarly article. Unable to sleep, he searches for a reply that would truly be able express his feelings. He ultimately finds what he is looking for in the four lines of Schubert's *Winterreise*, which also conclude the novel, in their uncertainty and mild hope: *"I close my eyes / My heart still beats fervently. / When will the leaves at the window turn green again? / When will I hold my love in my arms?"*[61]

The romantic motif of an unfulfilled yet longed-for union is the novel's central theme, because Énard's book explains the rift through our time as an irretrievable loss of the Other. The problem is not the worldliness, the transcendental homelessness of modernity itself. To this, the Romantics had reacted with a

---

59 Mathias Énard, *Compass*, trans. Charlotte Mandell (New York: New Directions Publishing, 2017 [2015]), 9.
60 For a discussion of Romantic problems and motifs and their social and historical conditions, see the chapter "Der romantische Durchbruch" in the standard work by Wolfgang Asholt, *Französische Literatur des 19. Jahrhunderts* (Stuttgart: J.B. Metzler, 2006), 88–108.
61 Énard, *Compass*, 445.

transcending of the self that led to an opening toward the Other, to an encounter with other cultures and people, an enthusiasm for the "Oriental world," even to the idea of a universal poetics of the world in which everything corresponds to everything and all people are connected. The diversity of the world, its linguistic points of view and forms of poetic fashioning, its narratives and lifestyles—this is the material that represents the possibility of experiencing otherness, or even more, of immanent transcendence. *Compass* therefore operates simultaneously on two levels that are developed in different narrative strands. One is the level of historical Romanticism, whose works are cited, discussed, and debated. The other is the level of our present day, in which Franz Ritter, Sarah, and their friends set out along the paths of the same experiences mapped out by the Romantics and their heirs—by figures like Hammer-Purgstall and Nerval, Félicien David, Liszt, and Debussy, or Delacroix and Max Ernst—in Istanbul and Aleppo, Palmyra and Jerusalem, Tunis and Budapest, Vienna and elsewhere.

The levels are intertwined via a book within a book. With its fictional title *On the Various Forms of Madness in the Orient*, this work has a structuring and, especially in its motifs, historicizing effect. The novel's literary conceit also integrates the thematic complexes it evokes into Franz's and Sarah's life, interweaving these characters' experiences with the book and fusing their reality with tradition, and it is the relationship between these two levels that in fact first drives the pain of modernity to the surface. The richness of historical Romanticism functions here as a structure of knowledge stretching, at times, across multiple pages of musical-historical excursus, where it comes to resemble a Parisian parlor game played for social distinction; and from the very beginning of novel, the permanent threat Romanticism faces of becoming stiff and stilted is exposed in Franz Ritter's reaction to Sarah's disputation at the Sorbonne—as an "exercise," as he says, "that filled me with bitterness and melancholy."[62] But the novel focuses in on a site where this knowledge becomes fluid, becomes embodied and true-to-life, as Sarah and Franz set out into a world of discovery, of self-estrangement. These two levels in the novel open up a terrible, gaping wound of our present day: Iraq, the land of the Tigris and the Euphrates; Syria, the fertile crescent; in short, the cradle of the Orient, bombed to pieces, buried under rubble and ashes, with conflict smoldering and burning all around, in Palestine, on the Gulf of Aden, in Libya, in the Balkans. Nothing remains of the romantic landscapes; death fixes its gaze at the protagonists and at us as readers.

---

62 Énard, *Compass*, 14. See also the author's discussion of his own experiences in the academic world; Fabien Ribéry, "Tramways de porcelaine, pour clochettes, zarb, et bols tibétains," interview with Mathias Énard, in *le poulailler*, November 5, 2015, www.le-poulailler.fr/2015/11/tramways-de-porcelaine-pour-clochettes-zarb-et-bols-tibetains/, accessed August 25, 2018.

Romanticism is a feeling and a remembrance that has lost any surface for its projection. With the loss of this relation and the depth of its history, Europeans have become monolingual. They have lost the opportunity of "this life that was not [their] own."[63] This does make it possible to once again experience the historical feeling the Romantics had—the feeling of suffering from a rift through time that cannot be healed. But Europe has been destroyed by this possibility of fleeing from the horror it feels at itself; its egalitarian materialism has not produced equality in the world. Like Zeus abducting Europa, the daughter of the Phoenician king, it has rather robbed the Orient, expropriated its treasures, and implanted in it a logic that equalizes everything and contributes to those longings and struggles that are tearing it apart today. In his novel *Street of Thieves,* Énard narrates the story from the other side of the Mediterranean, from where Europe obsessively appears as a horizon that finally dissolves—painfully and mercilessly—into a promise that cannot be kept.[64] The experience of culture—or in other words, the experience of difference and interweaving giving rise to an opening toward something new, toward ideals—has melted away. Where should ideals come from now?

Herein lies the profound gulf separating Énard from Houellebecq's critique of materialism, inasmuch as what Énard is criticizing in modernity is not secularization itself but rather the force with which it has simultaneously torn down and brutally realized its ideal of equality. *Compass* is a literary archeology that would once again make it possible feel, hear, and see the Orient, its longing and curiosity. The book is intended to resemble the delirium of opium to which Franz Ritter first surrenders in Istanbul, which brings him "closer to Novalis, Berlioz, Nietzsche, Trakl"—an intoxication that makes "you feel as if you are touching eternity," that "draws us out of ourselves . . . and projects us into the great calm of the universal."[65]

As a reminder that there is an inner "East" whose Europe must reflect on its own melancholy in order to forget itself and thus overcome its loneliness in the world, Énard gives his novel the title of *Compass.* In the novel, this appears concretely as a replica of a compass owned by Beethoven: a small device made of brass or copper that Sarah gives to Franz as a present, with a manipulated needle that stubbornly points to the east, against the laws of nature. It is a sign of the marriage of egalitarian materialism and mystical self-transcendence that "reconciled Hegel with Ibn Arabi," and which Franz Ritter finds enthusiastically in Ernst

---

63 Énard, *Compass*, 214.
64 Mathias Énard, *Street of Thieves*, trans. Charlotte Mandell (Rochester, NY: Open Letter, 2014 [2012]).
65 Énard, *Compass*, 74.

Bloch's interpretation of Avicenna—a text he continually reads aloud to his former lover Sigrid, to her annoyance.[66]

Compass is a novel as deviation, as wondrous transposition—a transposition to the place, in Damascus, in Tehran, where a small group of scholars of the Orient, of many different origins and religions, study together and celebrate humanity under the immeasurable starry sky of Palmyra. It is a brief epoch of community. An equality appears in this in-between place, a new universality that leaves behind the possessive character of European universalism. But the events in Iran of 1979/1980 had already foreshadowed separation.

The reading of Romanticism that Énard gives us in his novel is, of course, selective. One could even call it quintessentially French. Only one who has lived and breathed French centralism and its monocultural vehemence could celebrate German Romanticism as a cosmopolitan and culturally tolerant antidote. Peter Hacks's sharp tongue functions here as an unsparing contrastive agent: "A Romantic author is an author," he writes in *Zur Romantik*, "who has read English literature, whose works are published by Georg Reimer, who consumes opium, is sexually served by patriotic groupies, and has Karl Justus Gruner as his commanding officer."[67] Yet we need not agree with all of Peter Hacks's vicious jabs in order to concede the entanglement of many Romantics in "Germanomaniac patriotism."[68] It was Viktor Klemperer who outlined the dark features of the Romantic legacy in *LTI*, his great work on the language of the Third Reich: "Both linguistically and in its literature, German Romanticism had established a connection with the Indian prehistory of Germanic civilization and an Aryan common ground between the different European peoples. . . . The construction of the Aryan has its roots in philology rather than science."[69]

In *Compass*, however, the Romantics appear largely in the pure light of a countermovement against a simplistic analytical materialism, and a universalism derived from this materialism that exposed its destructive, even totalitarian power in the revolution of 1789. This is indeed opposed by Jena, by early Romanticism, which clings to the ideals of humanity, to the idea of the freedom and equality of the human race, of a great universal poetry, which nonetheless insists that it can only be woven from multiplicity and translation. This is the origin for the discovery of the Orient and of other sources of human spirituality, such as

---

66 Énard, *Compass*, 183.
67 Peter Hacks, *Zur Romantik* (Hamburg: Konkret Literatur, 2008), 54.
68 Hacks, *Zur Romantik*, 81.
69 Victor Klemperer, *LTI: The Language of the Third Reich* (London: Bloomsbury Academic, 2013), 142.

Persian poetry, the Bhagavad Gita, or Buddhism, that come to fundamentally occupy Europe in the nineteenth century.[70]

The Napoleonic Wars, however, dashed the belief in universality. "France" was radically rejected by many intellectuals in the German-speaking countries, who questioned the modern ideals of freedom and equality in also asserting what they claimed as their own. In 1808, Friedrich Schlegel published his extremely influential book *On the Language and Wisdom of the Indians*—an anti-French, antimaterialist, anti-Enlightenment manifesto that laid the foundation for a respiritualization of Europe in Oriental philology.[71] Schlegel admired Brahmanism and regarded it as a model for a feudal aristocracy that would be capable of representing spirit and ideality. He says yes to European unity, and to a multiethnic empire, but under the banner of a renewed Catholic monarchy. After converting to Catholicism, he finally moved to Vienna, where in 1828 he delivered his lectures on the *Philosophy of History*.[72] Influenced by the French aristocratic reaction, and especially by Louis-Gabriel-Ambroise de Bonald and Joseph de Maistre, these lectures sketch out a Christian history of salvation as a luminous stream emanating from the Indo-Europeans, as a people supposedly inclined toward higher spirituality. Schlegel argues that the peoples who have supposedly fallen into materialism, above all the peoples of Africa, share with the Republic the fate of stultification and decline. Europe, though, should be able to save itself, he continues, by reflecting on its spiritual roots, by returning to these roots in a philological search for its origins. The "primitive" peoples of Schlegel's history, those who have yet to discover writing, are by contrast practically lost in his account. His division of the world into spheres of "clear intelligence" and "animal instinct" proved to be as equally inspiring to the Romantics as it did to imperial strands of Enlightenment.[73] "Higher forms" of

---

70 On this point, see the still centrally relevant book by Raymond Schwab, *The Oriental Renaissance: Europe's Rediscovery of India and the East, 1680—1880*, trans. Gene Patterson-King and Victor Reinking (New York, Columbia University Press, 1984).

71 The original text was published as Friedrich von Schlegel, *Ueber die Sprache und Weisheit der Indier: Ein Beitrag zur Begründung der Alterthumskunde, Nebst metrischen Uebersetzungen indischer Gedichte* (Heidelberg: Mohr und Zimmer, 1808). Two English translations have been published: the first by E. J. Millington in *The Aesthetic and Miscellaneous Works of Frederick von Schlegel* (London: Henry G. Bohn, 1849, reissued Cambridge: Cambridge University Press, 2014); and more recently by H. H. Wilson, *On the Language and Wisdom of the Indians* (London: Ganesha Pub., 2001).

72 Friedrich Schlegel, *Philosophie der Geschichte: In achtzehn Vorlesungen gehalten zu Wien im Jahre 1828*, in *Kritische Friedrich-Schlegel-Ausgabe*, ed. Ernst Behler et al., vol. 9 (Munich: Thomas, 1971). An early translation into English was published by James Burton Robertson as *The Philosophy of History in a Course of Lectures* (London: Saunders and Otley, 1835).

73 On this distinction, see Schlegel, *On the Language and Wisdom of the Indians*, 454.

spirituality, it seems, frequently follow a path that runs over the crest of Indo-European ideology—and it was not least because of this "Indomania of the Romantics" that the Islamic Orient soon came to be seen as separate from this splendid spiritual history.[74] The same city where Schlegel held his lectures was, after all, also the site of the Vienna Congress and the Restoration.

Has Mathias Énard never read Edward W. Said?[75] Does he not know that the desire for the Orient was a European longing that reached out to take hold of Egypt in 1798, Algeria in 1830, and Syria and the Levant in 1918? Is Franz Ritter's search for alterity, for intoxication and poetic immersion, for love in times of war, and for the Orient perhaps little more than kitsch oblivious to the political dimension of its own thirst?

On the contrary: Énard knows all too well the dangerous game of alterity. He knows that one who is different can become entirely, wholly Other, and that fascination can quickly turn into self-assertion. The figure who stands for this danger in *Compass* is Richard Wagner, especially the late Wagner of *Parsifal*, whom Énard uses to launch his alter ego Franz Ritter into lengthy discussions of music history and critiques of ideology. Wagner appears as the composer who drove Oriental melodies and themes out of European music to construct, in their place, a monumental Gesamtkunstwerk whose political significance lies in the cementing of a Christian-Western consciousness. Wagner is the bulwark. Musically, artistically, and politically. He is the rock blocking all bridges over the Bosporus. Wagner thus represents the European obsession of exaggerating what it claims as its own because it feels threatened by cultural contamination. This obsession believes that Europe's "own culture" must be cured in the same way as are sufferers of tuberculosis who need not be ashamed of their illness—indeed, for whom sanatoriums were erected as nothing less than a display of the "body of the people," the "Volk," in its purity from decadent foreign infestation. This contrasts to syphilis, which was taken to originate from proximity, from intimacy, from contamination by the Other, and whose signs are shamefully shrouded in loneliness and silence. Such an intertwining of discourse on music theory, poetry, and the history of hygiene characterizes the particular stream of Ritter's consciousness titled "3:45 A.M.," which begins with "Sometimes I wonder" but then shifts, almost imperceptibly in its narrative modes, to become a veritable treatise on European obsessions with purity.[76]

---

74 Rudolf Haym, *Wilhelm von Humboldt: Lebensbild und Charakteristik* (Berlin: R. Gaertner, 1856), 582.
75 Edward W. Said, *Orientalism: Western Conceptions of the Orient*, 4th ed. (London: Penguin Books, 1995).
76 Énard, *Compass*, 317.

Franz Ritter alias Mathias Énard knows about Edward W. Said; he knows about the theory of Orientalism, about the enmeshment of knowledge, art, and imperial power. He knows that Said himself has written about Wagner,[77] as have so many others, and that one can continue Ritter's line of thought about Romanticism to ask about its consummation or possible betrayal in Wagner—musically, ideologically, and politically. *Compass* does not disseminate any kind of historical kitsch; the book does not propagate a simple romanticism. It takes recourse to a belief that inspired at least some to find a way out of the transcendental homelessness of modernity by immersing themselves in reading and knowledge, in interpreting, translating, and adapting Oriental poetry and music—"in art" *tout court*, as that fundamental "experience of otherness."[78] Here, the religion of art is an opening to the Other. Wherever the emphasis on diversity that emerged from Romanticism was linked to the idea of the universality and equality of human beings, it has historically been able to develop an epistemology opposed to the logics of empire.[79] In those places, it has also been an opening to freedom in diversity—not least of all in Wilhelm Müller and Franz Schubert's *Winterreise*, which has been interpreted as a work of political resistance to the repressions of the Restoration period.[80]

In any case, the unconditional transcending of the self is the smoldering core that interests Énard. But the fact that this ember has failed to spark any enduring fire is not, for him, the flaw of this attitude; the problem stems rather from those who put an end to this opening. Herein lies the reason for the immensity of the division that modern European nationalism has torn open, and whose seeds it eventually sows in the Oriental world, too.

From this ambivalent Romantic history, what might be reactivated is the longing for a transcending of the self and for connection. But in the meantime, Europe has long since squandered this chance, which is why there something else in this core that Énard touches upon in his appeal to historical Romanticism: the

---

77 See for example Edward W. Said, "Wagner and the *Ring* at the Met," *The Nation*, June 18, 1990, and "On the Importance of Being Unfaithful to Wagner," *London Review of Books*, February 11, 1993. Republished in Edward W. Said, *Music at the Limits*, with a foreword by Daniel Barenboim (New York: Columbia University Press, 2009), "Wagner and the Met's Ring," 105–114, and "The Importance of Being Unfaithful to Wagner," 166–174.

78 Énard, *Compass*, 357.

79 See Andrea Polaschegg, *Der andere Orientalismus: Regeln deutsch-morgenländischer Imagination im 19. Jahrhundert* (Berlin: De Gruyter, 2005); Messling, *Gebeugter Geist*, especially 182–317; Marcel Lepper, *Goethes Euphrat: Philologie und Politik im "Westöstlichen Divan"* (Göttingen: Wallstein Verlag, 2016).

80 Reinhold Brinkmann, "Musikalische Lyrik, politische Allegorie und die 'heil'ge Kunst,'" *Archiv für Musikwissenschaft* 62 (2005): 75–97.

feeling that everything is sinking. An immeasurable melancholy: "Dear Franz," Sarah writes in a letter she sends to Vienna,

> thank you for this diplomatic note, which managed to make me smile—not an easy thing for me to do right now. I miss you a lot. Or rather I miss everything a lot. I feel as if I'm outside the world, floating in mourning. I just have to meet my mother's gaze for us both to start crying. Crying for the other's sadness, that void we each see on our exhausted faces. Paris is a tomb, tatters of memories. I continue my incursions into the literary territories of opium. I don't really know where I am any more. With sad kisses, till soon, Sarah.[81]

In the speech Énard gave upon receiving the Leipzig Book Prize for European Understanding in 2017, he reminded his listeners that "Europa" was a Lebanese princess whom Zeus kidnapped on a beach near Sidon—a "spoil of war" whom he brought to Crete, and who was never to set foot on today's European mainland. "In *Compass*, I made a renewed attempt to cast some light on the eastern part of Europe's cultural history, particularly in literature and music."[82] This is Énard's mode for interweaving everything with everything else: Europe and the Orient; Arabic, Persian, and Ottoman sources with European culture, literature, and music; our fragmented modern self with the fear-filled vigils of our time and with the exploratory journeys taken by young idealists out into the world; European materialism and the Iranian revolution; historical erudition and contemporary skepticism. One could go on like this forever. Énard creates all of it, as a whole, by blending genres, narrative perspectives, and linguistic styles. Repeatedly, in the form of fictitious letters, events, and memories, an outside world breaks in on Franz Ritter's contemplations. Our idea of Europe's separateness from the Islamic world—a world that seems all the more dangerous because it is marked by permanent repression[83]—is to be undermined and deconstructed as "chimerical purity."[84] Whether the novel succeeds in shaping Franz Ritter's stream of consciousness into that of our own may ultimately depend on whether we, along with the author, believe in the redeeming power of knowledge.

The political structure of Énard's poetics lies in this shaping of perception. Its aim is not to discover alterity and raise it to an absolute that would, in the sense of a Romantic poetics, open up a spiritual experience, a moment of transcendence. Rather, it rather wants to obtain, in its interlacing of identities, a

---

81 Énard, *Compass*, 410.
82 Mathias Énard, "Prize Winner's Acceptance Speech," trans. Holger Fock and Sabine Müller, in *Leipziger Buchpreis zur Europäischen Verständigung 2017*, 77–81, on 78.
83 See the study by Monika Walter, *Der verschwundene Islam? Für eine andere Kulturgeschichte Westeuropas* (Munich: Wilhelm Fink, 2016).
84 Énard, "Prize Winner's Acceptance Speech," 79.

consciousness of the world that contains a dimension of humanity: the game of difference must not lead to an absolutization of the Other, as has happened since the 1990s, when the thinking of alterity took a cynical turn and became a cultural clash. We are fundamentally and always intermeshed with the world in which we live. Difference, which exists in and around us as a transcending of the self, does not mean invalidating equality. Here, *Compass* goes beyond the political dimensions of postcolonialism as a form of representation. Énard is aiming toward a new universality that appears as a planetary horizon:

> The construction of a European identity as a friendly puzzle of nationalisms erased anything that didn't fit into his ideological boxes. Goodbye difference, goodbye diversity. A humanism based on what? What is universal? God, who makes Himself very discreet in the silence of the night? Between the throatslitters, the starvers, the polluters—can the unity of the human condition still be based on anything? I have no idea. Knowledge, perhaps. Knowledge and the planet as a new horizon.[85]

But how can the alter ego that we find here pondering these things still believe in the power of knowledge, as it endures in fear, paralyzed through the night? Does Franz Ritter not embody the narcissistic grievance of Europe that suffers from the loss of its extension into universality. *Compass*, the title of the novel, always indicates the loss of all the points of reference that the novel affirmatively evokes. In *Zone*, Énard led us through the night of a Mediterranean world born from the violence of the twentieth century—a world that must invariably sink, time and again, into violence.[86] Now, however, with this compass in his hand, Énard conjures love and knowledge. And is it not so that these two possibilities merge in the concept of *philology*, in the love of the word that *Compass* is able to evoke for line after line without falling prey to its great passions of origin and nation? Sarah is a strong figure embodying this belief.

Michel Houellebecq's female characters are always caught in tension between two poles: between the inability to attain the ideal of true love, on the one hand, and the unfulfilling fact of prostitution, on the other. Franz's love for Sarah, by contrast, has a modern, passionate character that is rooted in Romanticism and buttressed by its motifs of longing, distance, and epistolary exchange. Sarah is no "sweetheart"—neither a virgin nor committed to any man, she is independent and active, a "savage detective"[87] who refuses to let herself be restricted in continuing to explore the world. She shares with Franz depression and grief over the loss of the world, but this kinship has its limits in the searching restlessness that drives

85 Énard, *Compass*, 368.
86 Matthias Énard, *Zone*, trans. Charlotte Mandell (London: Fitzcarraldo Editions, 2014 [2008]).
87 Énard, *Compass*, 46.

her, that moves her to set out for new shores.[88] Sarah is at once a lover, friend, and vigilant fellow traveler. Above all, however, she is the one who slips into the classically male role of the modern explorer, the anthropologist, during her ethnographic journey to the Malaysian archipelago, where she corresponds with Franz. But, and this is the decisive point, the postcolonial context of knowledge also prevents her from completely merging with this role.[89] Sarah harbors a deep interest in the difference that she sees disappearing from the world, an interest that propels her to a nearly inaccessible region of Borneo. It is difficult here not to think of Claude Lévi-Strauss's *Tristes Tropiques*, of its tragic dialectic of strangeness and sublation. Acting with an awareness of this dilemma, Sarah is a figure who may be tragic, but she is certainly not cynical. Immersion into the unknown does not serve her as a means of exotic edification or as a healing intuition of an ossified other. For her, inhabiting the world means carrying difference within herself, because this is the fundamental criterion of a human being: having curiosity, transcending oneself toward something else. In an article she writes about Ignaz Goldziher, Gershom Scholem, and Jewish Orientalism, Sarah notes that "Orientalism should be a humanism."[90] This is reminiscent of the late Edward W. Said, of his work *Humanism and Democratic Criticism,* and the return to Auerbach's philology that he formulated there.[91] For Auerbach, the task of philology is to preserve, in a time of standardization, a knowledge of the diverse ways in which humans appropriate the world.[92] Sarah certainly represents empathy and solidarity. Above all, however, she represents an ideal of the human being as a poetic creature, as one who creates worlds.

Franz Ritter, by contrast, remains frozen in despair. The night is long. The shock of his diagnosis detaches him from the world; his melancholy entails turning inward. His condition is symbolized by a drop of water in which he sees a reflection of himself—the very drop that is entirely determined by its external world. Against this existential stance in the world, which silences, as it were, the novel's prelude, *Compass* seeks to develop a skeptical turn to reality that transcends the

---

88 This is particularly evident at that moment, during an excursion to the Austrian battlefield of Saint Gotthard, where a Christian alliance defeated the Ottomans in 1664. Here, Franz experiences Sarah as wild and free.

89 On the structural connection between travel experiences, literary comparatism, and the construction of postcolonial theory, see Pascale Rabault-Feuerhahn, ed., *Théories intercontinentales: Voyages du comparatisme postcolonial* (Paris: Demopolis, 2014).

90 Énard, *Compass*, 393.

91 Edward W. Said, *Humanism and Democratic Criticism* (New York: Columbia University Press, 2004), 57–118.

92 Erich Auerbach, "Philology and Weltliteratur," trans. Maire and Edward Said, *The Centennial Review* 13, no. 1 (Winter 1969): 1–17.

monad of despair in the form of memories, poetic recollection, and the essay that Sarah sends to Franz. The last hope lies in salvation through the seriousness of knowledge and the power of art; it lies in the union with Sarah. Franz sends her the verses quoted above from Schubert's *Winterreise*. The song cycle leads into the cold night of political trepidation and existential homelessness: "I arrived a stranger, a stranger I depart," begins its first line. To which Franz responds with the "warm sunlight of hope" from the song "Dream of Spring": "My heart still beats fervently."[93]

Camille de Toledo or The Book Read from Its End

Camille de Toledo is no less skeptical of modernity than the other authors discussed in this chapter. His writing draws from the inherited pain of the Shoah that makes all writing a writing of what comes after, that finds itself exposed to the "holes that have crept into language."[94] For Toledo, the crimes of the twentieth century have destroyed any idea of an authentic originality and a reality that is immediately accessible. "Reality settles as sediment,"[95] Toledo writes. It settles as sediment in language, creating layers whose diversity displaces us into a "vertigo of meaning."[96] We find ourselves in a Benjaminian time in which we are trying to wrest truthfulness from the world through an archaeological uncovering of its manifold "strata of fiction."[97] For Toledo, this is the "Jewish moment of the novel"—the realization that "the deciphered earth is a book."[98] The notion that *littérature-monde*—world literature as it emerged from the end of the Cold War— might possibly be a postideological form of literature capturing the reality of the world against the introspection of a decadent modernity is something he regards as an ideological and geopolitical game. Its merit for him is nevertheless to make visible once again the political dimensions within the narrative appropriation of the world.[99] What the advocates of a gap between the narrative modes of the periphery and those of the center "took to be 'a return of the world' was just one

---

93 Énard, *Compass*, 445.
94 Camille de Toledo, *Visiter le Flurkistan, ou les Illusions de la littérature-monde* (Paris: Presses universitaires de France, 2008), 85.
95 De Toledo, *Visiter le Flurkistan*, 96.
96 De Toledo, *Visiter le Flurkistan*, 80.
97 De Toledo, *Visiter le Flurkistan*, 31.
98 De Toledo, *Visiter le Flurkistan*, 96.
99 De Toledo, *Visiter le Flurkistan*, 37, 39, 95.

more step in its fictionalization."[100] Camille de Toledo concludes from historical experience that there is no gap between reality and its expression in language, between theory and the world itself.[101] It is precisely for this reason that he accords legitimacy to the claims made by *littérature-monde* about the power of non-European narratives to break up and decenter European ones—especially in the politics of memory and history.[102] In this political sense, he does in fact admit a "return of the world." For Camille de Toledo, however, there is no unspoiled, paradisaical reality beyond community and thus beyond language: "They [the postcolonial proponents of *littérature-monde*] are right to believe in literature. / But the reasons they give are unreasonable. For it is not the 'return of the world' that offers an opportunity. / But rather its loss. The world is lost, and only the words remain."[103] Camille de Toledo considers work on narratives that build community to be the great task of our time, and it is this task to which he has dedicated his work. He has not only revived the literary essay as a form of diagnosing the times but also invented his own way of writing, which fuses the characteristics of narrative and analytical forms of text. This corresponds to his theoretical expansion of a deconstructivist approach to include aspects from another epistemic mode—a thinking of disorder, creolization, and bastardization—that Camille de Toledo gleans from Aimé Césaire, Édouard Glissant, and the dimensions of historical depth found in *littérature-monde,* not to mention a subversive European tradition stemming from Rabelais.[104] All too often, this idiosyncratic way of writing is concealed by the marketable label of novel printed on the covers of his books.

"De Toledo," or the one from the Spanish city of Toledo—this nom de plume is not only a conscious reference to the Jewish part of his family history, which serves to transform a rebellious literary youth[105] into a lifetime of seriousness.[106] The name furthermore alludes to a historical epoch in Europe that for Camille de Toledo symbolizes both the disaster of separation and the hope of reinvention.

---

100 De Toledo, *Visiter le Flurkistan,* 71.

101 De Toledo, *Visiter le Flurkistan,* 39.

102 See Camille de Toledo, *Le Hêtre et le bouleau: Essai sur la tristesse européenne* (Paris: Seuil, 2009); see also the opening arguments in the following chapter of this book.

103 De Toledo, *Visiter le Flurkistan,* 97.

104 De Toledo, *Visiter le Flurkistan,* 73–109.

105 Camille de Toledo, *Coming of Age at the End of History,* trans. Blake Ferris (Brooklyn: Soft Skull Press, 2008 [2002]).

106 It is clear from Camille de Toledo's graphic novel about Theodor Herzl that this is not only about a commitment to his Jewish family history, but also a Jewish tradition of the diaspora and the thinking bound up with it. The graphic novel about Herzl in fact turns out to be a story about the invented boy Ilia Brodsky and the hopes of the diaspora of Eastern European Jewry. See Camille de Toledo, *Herzl: une histoire européenne* (Paris: Denoël, 2018).

This is the Toledo School of Translators, which flourished after the Spanish kings pushed the Caliphate of Cordoba out of the center of the Iberian Peninsula. Here, we find foreshadowed the violent separation of the Muslim and Christian worlds that was completed with the fall of Granada in Spain in 1492. At the same time, the scenario emphasizes a significant intellectual debate: a knowledge of the Arabic language, which had served as the *lingua franca* of a flourishing philosophy and science in Moorish Spain, led Christian and Jewish scholars of the twelfth and thirteenth centuries in Toledo to translate numerous works into Latin that had been handed down in Arabic. This may never have produced a "school" in the sense of a theory of translation, and certainly not in any institutional form. In practice, however, treatises of Greek philosophy and science, by authors such as Euclid, Hippocrates, or Aristotle, that were preserved in Arabic in Toledo were translated alongside important texts of the scientific culture of the Islamic world itself, including writings by famous scholars such as Ibn Rushd (Averroes), Ibn Sina (Avicenna) or the *Algebra* of al-Khwârizmî, as well as foundational works of Islam such as the Koran.

As a symbolic site of translation, Toledo thus represents a historical turning point and a new beginning. This does not emerge here, as is so often the case, from a reference to what is claimed as own's own, from any "original" culture, but from a search for connections, from translation as a practice carried out through intermediate steps. It was Arabic-speaking Christian ("Mozarabic") and Jewish translators who stood between the Arabic of Islam and the Latin of Christianity. The translators often worked in teams of two, some of whom are vouched for by name, such as Dominicus Gundisalvus and Avendaut (Ibn Dawûd), or Gerardus Cremonensis and Ghâlib (Galippus): a Mozarab or a Jew translated the texts from Arabic into intermediate versions in Hebrew or a Romance language, which the Christian clerics then translated into Latin.[107] Only later, as the monarchy grew stronger, were texts increasingly translated directly into Castilian. Since many terms originated from scientific knowledge and forms of thought that had been developed in Arabic, and for which no equivalent existed in the target languages, the translators invented numerous loanwords from Arabic, a fact that contributed considerably to Spanish's development as an all-encompassing language of science and culture.[108] For Camille de Toledo, the medieval city of Toledo thus represents the paradigmatic site of the in-between, a bridge, a beginning that lacks any obsession with origins. Here, Europe's separation from the Oriental

---

107 For the history of the Toledo School of Translators, see the overview in George Bossong, *Das maurische Spanien: Geschichte und Kultur*, 3rd ed. (Munich: C.H. Beck), 73–79.
108 See Bossong, *Das maurische Spanien*, 78.

world, its obsessions with the purity of blood and the nation that already announced themselves in the Reconquista, are once again pacified by a belief in the knowledge of humanity.

His name says it all: translation is the crux, the pivot of Camille de Toledo's thinking, a key to his work. His aim is to transfer the memory of the murder of the Jews and of the total war into a twenty-first-century way of life that does not remain frozen in terror, but rather transforms this paralysis into a reflection that liberates Europe from itself—and that integrates colonialism as a worldwide experience of the twentieth century to allow a new idea of humanity to emerge.[109] In the years since 1989, the certain belief that the victory of capitalism would per se bring freedom has begun to teeter among Europeans, too. Everything has begun to teeter. We find ourselves in an *inquiétude d'être au monde*, in a state of unrest in and toward the world that combines fear and hope. This is the title Camille de Toledo gave to a speech he delivered in August 2011 at the Maison du Banquet et des générations in Lagrasse, in the south of France, and which he later published under the same title.[110]

L'inquiétitude d'être au monde is a kind of long poem—introduced by a speech; interrupted by comments, questions, sometimes even by chants resembling a chorus; sometimes rhymed, but mostly not; structured in verses of different length and without any formal scheme. Its lyrical character resides not only in its metaphorical language and the individuality to which this gives voice, but rather—formally less perfect, but structurally comparable to Baudelaire's sonnets—in a referential context of the sublime that European poetry traditionally evokes through form. Such reference to the ideal by means of formal quotations—and that is the most one can say about this here—stands in stark contrast to the poem's content, which thematizes the abysses of the twentieth century and their material, physically destructive power. As in the poetry of classical modernism, an effort to assert subjectivity can be discerned in the creation of this tension. Faced with the collapse of order, the lyrical I seeks a new language. What has collapsed here is the idea of something that is absolute, whole, actual, which can now be quoted only by means of form. If this representation previously ordered the world, the experience of its loss has played a part in begetting the obsessions of purity that separated out and ultimately annihilated "[t]he mixed, the bastards, the imperfect products of Europe's nations."[111] De Toledo argues that after 1945, for example, attempts were

---

109 "I am aiming here for a connection between [Claudio] Magris and [Édouard] Glissant"; Camille de Toledo, *L'inquiétude d'être au monde* (Lagrasse: Éditions Verdier, 2010), 29.
110 The speech has been translated into German as Camille de Toledo, "Die Unruhe über das In-der-Welt-Sein," *Lettre International* 107 (Winter 2014): 61–71.
111 De Toledo, *L'inquiétitude d'être au monde*, 26.

made to fill the "holes" left by this annihilation by clinging to memory, rather than fundamentally acknowledging the hybridity of culture:

> Here, poetry, philosophy of the hole / and of shoveling full, using / and abusing the great words of *hollowness, nothingness*. / We now learn them at school: / they form a rosary. / The upside-down anthem of a Europe / that has killed all the *peoples of the in-between*. / Its two souls, Jewish and Gypsy. / Its two stateless songs. / And in passing, / without any medal, the soldiers of its islands, / of its old colonies.[112]

For Camille de Toledo, the experience of the twentieth century is one of separation and murder, arising from the rejection of transculturality, translation, mutual intelligibility and exchange, and hence even culture as such. But he sees this rejection as resulting from an attempt to make absolute what is claimed as one's own—to strip it of particularity in asserting it as a norm, to elevate it into a conceptual framework for grasping the world, whether it be that of universalism or its dialectical opposite, "the sick Romanticism obsessed with (re)foundings."[113] This is also the reason, he continues, for the rejection of the idea of universality, of the "trick of thinking without a body" that seeks to transcend "skin," "forms," and "languages"—in short, anything that is concrete.[114] It is in this regard, he suggests, that European, Western universalism is solipsistic, a monolingualism full of "bitterness,"[115] a uniform, unified, yet singular tongue, a "langue *uni.*"[116] And from the suffering of this all-encompassing claim, what he sees left in the world is nothing but its aggressive rejection: "The only thing universal is rage."[117]

Europe, however, unsettled after the catastrophe, trapped in the fearful paralysis of an uncertain future, would exclude the world right down to the memory of this guilt, would still teach the following generations "mots-morts"—"deadwords."[118] Camille de Toledo plays here with this doubling of death, which refers to "the dead" in the sense of "words devoid of meaning," but also to the "deadly" character of these words: "I alone am the language and the meaning of the world. I discover, under the crust of words, pure ideas."[119] Yet since it is at least intuitively clear to everyone that "this time has passed,"[120] a discontent is spreading in the Western world. He sees the tribunes from the right playing with this fact to their own ends,

---

112 De Toledo, *L'inquiétude d'être au monde*, 27.
113 De Toledo, *L'inquiétude d'être au monde*, 47.
114 De Toledo, *L'inquiétude d'être au monde*, 48.
115 De Toledo, *L'inquiétude d'être au monde*, 48.
116 De Toledo, *L'inquiétude d'être au monde*, 48.
117 De Toledo, *L'inquiétude d'être au monde*, 36.
118 De Toledo, *L'inquiétude d'être au monde*, 46.
119 De Toledo, *L'inquiétude d'être au monde*, 36.
120 De Toledo, *L'inquiétude d'être au monde*, 36.

offering identity, nation, and civilization—or even "earth" and "root"—as supposed alternatives. But their words are "wrongly named words, *acccursed ones*, indebted-words, poorly spoken and damned" ("Mots-mal-nommés, *maledetti*, / mots-endettés, mal dits et maudits")[121] representing nothing but the fearful flip side of European hubris. Who, then, should prepare the children for this uncertainty when we "grow up within / frames that implode every single day"?[122]

This is where the pedagogy of the speech de Toledo gave in the Maison du Banquet now unfolds. He proposes an "école de l'entre,"[123] a school of the in-between, that would performatively prepare Europeans for this insight: "In the space between languages, *il n'y a kein universal*," is how one might translate—or transpose—his original line: "Dans l'entre des langues, *there is kein Universel*."[124] What is central here is thus the diversity of languages. For Camille de Toledo, this comprises, on the one hand, the discovery of the diversity of thought as proposed by a European tradition since Leibniz, and especially since Wilhelm von Humboldt.[125] But it also entails, on the other hand, the discovery of the opacity of the world, which is the prerequisite for its acceptance. In this linguistic quality—which stands, as the materiality of thought, for the material, corporeal dimension of culture itself (it is worth remembering here de Toledo's triad of skin-form-language)—the world once again becomes recognizable in its reality as the very discrepancy between life realities. It is here, in this "in-between," this "hole," this "*gap*," that the horizon of the twenty-first century looms.[126] In the place of a language that "selects, classifies, and exterminates,"[127] Europe must think of itself as translation and learn to "live between languages."[128] In 2008, Camille de Toledo came together for this purpose with the writer, journalist, and publisher Maren Sell to found the European Society of Authors, which dedicated itself over the ten years of its existence to translation as the true language of Europe. With its yearly "Finnegan's List," it recommended for translation forgotten or rarely translated works in various languages.[129]

---

121 De Toledo, *L'inquiétitude d'être au monde*, 35.
122 De Toledo, *L'inquiétitude d'être au monde*, 58.
123 De Toledo, *L'inquiétitude d'être au monde*, 44.
124 De Toledo, *L'inquiétitude d'être au monde*, 42.
125 On this point, see the essential study by Jürgen Trabant, *Traditionen Humboldts* (Frankfurt am Main: Suhrkamp, 1990).
126 See de Toledo, *L'inquiétitude d'être au monde*, 43–44.
127 De Toledo, *L'inquiétitude d'être au monde*, 50.
128 De Toledo, *L'inquiétitude d'être au monde*, 58.
129 The Société Européenne des Auteurs was dissolved in 2018, after ten years of activity. For an account of its aims, see Camille de Toledo, "La traduction ou comment émouvoir l'Europa," https://web.archive.org/web/20120312122309/http://www.seau.org/fr/about, accessed August 2, 2018.

But these lessons were not easy. In a round table discussion on "World Translations: Europe and Its Languages" in November 2018, Camille de Toledo spoke of what felt to him like a failure in the German language, which he so intently pursued in Berlin after the death of his brother, but which left him in fear of being disempowered.[130] His move to Berlin had been bound up with the hope of leaving his own biography behind and entering a new, fluctuating life. Post-reunification Berlin is evoked here as a site of fusion and in-between, as a utopian place whose language, unlike English and French, was not linked to the claim of universalist centers. But over the years, Berlin has increasingly emerged as a locus of national power. What remained for him was a feeling of failure, in which Germany had pointed him back to his Jewish family history in an overpowering gesture, leaving him in fear. This loss of faith then became the focus of his most recent book, *Thésée, sa vie nouvelle* (Theseus, his new life), where he reworks this loss into an unconditional new beginning as he enters into the labyrinth of a family history that entangles him in a long chain of suicides.[131]

One can gently object to this way of telling the story. We could point to the Catholic family heritage of Camille de Toledo—of Alexis de Mital—and to his incorporation of a specific, normative concept of language. We could point out that this utopian view of postreunification Berlin was quite Parisian, in that its hope lay in being delivered from centralism. Yet regardless of how we might assess these various individual aspects, what is still revealing in any case is his reference to the power of language to enable or take away belonging.

Language is essential for the production of community. All politics, de Toledo claims, draws its life from direct address, from the power that political speech can develop only in a national language. And the field of politics cannot tolerate any in-between, the argument continues, because this would mean disempowering any capability to speak performatively; it would undermine the language of community-building from which politics lives. For this reason, according to de Toledo, small communities such as those of the "République des lettres" are unusual in the political game. They refer all the more insistently to the incredible importance of translators whom he regards as capable of creating a transnational community beyond language differences. And having a European politics would require enlarging this community, as the community that could be addressed in political terms. He thus concludes that Europe must exist as a genuine politics of translation; it must incur the massive costs required to enable the formation of a

---

130 One example was during an evening of the international writers conference "Europe and Its Borders/L'Europe et ses frontières," in a discussion panel with Priya Basil, Camille de Toledo, and Jürgen Trabant, moderated by Maike Albath, November 15, 2018.
131 Camille de Toledo, *Thésée, sa vie nouvelle* (Lagrasse: Verdier, 2020).

political community that it cannot afford to lose to simplistic dreams of exchange, fluctuation, and hybridization. Europe is translation or it is an elite project that must fail.

Is Camille de Toledo himself not proposing a radical relativism that gives such weight to the individual internal coherence of cultures—in thinking and living—that nothing can penetrate them, that there is nothing they might share in a human horizon? Doesn't de Toledo's idea of the "impermanence of knowledge"[132] conceptually belong—despite its emancipatory thrust—to the same essentialization of life forms and cultures that are deployed with such skill by proponents of neo-identitarianism and their Kulturkampf obsessions?

Faced with the bombing in Oslo's government district and with the mass murder committed by the right-wing extremist terrorist Anders Behring Breivik in July 2011 on the island of Utøya, at the campground run by the youth organization of the Norwegian Social Democratic Party, de Toledo directed the pedagogy of *L'inquiétude d'être au monde* against that "phantasm of refounding" that would still distinguish "between what is *propre*"—meaning both "one's own" and "clean"—"and what is dirty."[133] Utøya is the name for a catastrophe of our present, brought about by the obsession with fixed concepts of identity. Seventy-seven souls murdered, seventy-seven individuals who were working to bring about an open society. Suffocated hopes whose despair can be opened up only in narrating toward potential futures. What might have become of them?

Vies pøtentielles—"Pøtential lives"—is the title of Camille de Toledo's volume of narratives countering the despair of life demolished, the catastrophe of endings closing in, with new possibilities.[134] Narration appears in this work as an anthropological force of survival that is wrested from death.[135] And Utøya is the political starting point inscribed into this force. This is then supplemented by autobiographical events—a chain of suicides in the family on the father's side—and by

---

132 De Toledo, *L'inquiétitude d'être au monde*, 55.

133 See de Toledo, *L'inquiétitude d'être au monde*, 56.

134 Camille de Toledo, *Vies pøtentielles* (Paris: Seuil, 2011). The stories and "exege§es" 20–24 from the book have been translated into German as "Pøtentielle Leben," in Jerôme Ferrari and Cornelia Ruhe, eds., "Den gegenwärtigen Zustand der Dinge festhalten: Zeitgenössische Literatur aus Frankreich," special issue, *die horen: Zeitschrift für Literatur, Kunst und Kritik* 267 (2017): 138–152.

135 On the cultural and historical significance of narration after the catastrophe, see Ottmar Ette, *Konvivenz: Literatur und Leben nach dem Paradies* (Berlin: Kulturverlag Kadmos, 2012). For a discussion of (post)catastrophic narratives, see Ette's book *ÜberLebenswissen: Die Aufgabe der Philologie* (Berlin: Kulturverlag Kadmos, 2004), as well as Ottmar Ette and Judith Kasper, *Unfälle der Sprache: Literarische und philologische Erkundungen der Katastrophe* (Vienna: Turia + Kant, 2014).

fictitious or real incidents, told as flash fictions indicating life constellations as quickly and succinctly as possible. An example is the story of Inge Denktrup in the GDR. Denktrup pretended to be the daughter of a woman named Sarah Weltman who was murdered by the Nazis. Her aim was to achieve a "restitution" of Sarah Weltman's property, which she did in fact accomplish, only to then be exposed as a tragic impostor. The texts always deal with the question of how the narratives that people weave from their lives enable them to continue living. This is symptomatic of Camille de Toledo's entire oeuvre.[136] His writing composes a counterpoint of reality and its appropriation in order to reveal the vital function played by our interpretations, our narratives of ourselves. What is more "real" here? Reality or its narration?

Following the traces of his own parents' honeymoon through South America, the first-person narrator, only barely concealed as the voice of the author, encounters a man in Buenos Aires who has failed as a director and must now leave his little son at home every day to collect leftover food for them to eat. The man is ashamed that his settled life has come to an end, and especially at having to lie to his son day in day out to give him false hopes amid their struggle to survive: "He fought for his son and told me, aware of his guilt: 'Ahora, nos contamos historias falsas, historias para vivir.'"—"Today we tell false stories, stories to live."[137] This little story moves us because we are gripped by empathy. The tale expands to become something general that we are able to sense because we feel, when faced with such a limit, such an end, the need for the hope that narration gives. This hope tears open a possibility that transcends this limit, even if only for a few moments. "His son, snuggled up against him, patted him back. They could have stayed like this forever, in a tight embrace."[138] In the fragile finitude of life, the narrative thus reveals a general "as if," which is thrust between our different world views. Camille de Toledo does not simply let this "as if" stand on its own. Perhaps he doesn't trust its power to resonate? Perhaps he wants to grasp it himself? In any case, he inserts "exege§es" between the narratives, graphically marked with the typographical symbol § as another discursive level based on reason and argumentation.

As always in his texts, the in-between is characterized by a blending of genres, of narration and reflection, in which he and we are to become aware of what makes it possible for the narrative to be accessible to experience. In this story, it is the narrator's own interpretation that interferes. In the letters his father wrote

---

136 See also Johan Faerber, "Camille de Toledo: à livre ouvert (Le Livre de la Faim et de la Soif)," *diacritik,* August 2, 2017, www.diacritik.com/2017/02/08/camille-de-toledo-a-livre-ouvert-le-livre-de-la-faim-et-de-la-soif/, accessed August 10, 2018.
137 De Toledo, *Vies pøtentielles,* 140.
138 De Toledo, *Vies pøtentielles,* 136.

while in South America, in their description of its great rivers, the narrator had mistakenly read the term "ramification" as "ramifiction." The world appears as the ramification of his *histoires, historias*—his (hi)stories—and thus the narrating self declares:

> But there are no *historias falsas*, Jorge, only, *nur, seulement, una ramifiction infinita, entiendes!* infinite, *donde estamos*, we, you understand, *donde estamos*, are condemned to live, *vincere, ou mourir*, to live or die. Then I would have added: Look again, Jorge, at how I got lost in this book, between your life, mine, and all those I think I remember.[139]

Vies pøtentielles is a polyphonic construction that evokes life worlds and narratives in order to extract something of humanity in the face of catastrophe. Its actual core plays out between the (hi)stories of its human characters. Camille de Toledo's aim is not to set the languages and materialities of cultures against each other, but rather to emphasize the in-between, that space which can be frightening because it unsettles firmly believed certainties, because it fails to offer the solid ground for which we long and because it constantly demands a plethora of references. Yet this space also holds the possibility of establishing culture in a way that frees itself from such opposition by opening up a human perspective.

Different languages are, to quote Wilhelm von Humboldt, "world views"— not simply vessels of sounds into which one might always and everywhere pour the same thinking, as European rationalism believed.[140] Rather, they shape our thinking, color our view of the world, such that they are the forms available to us to appropriate our life world. That is why they hold something opaque, obscure, that we understand when we learn other languages. One philosophical position close to Camille de Toledo, which Barbara Cassin has expressed concisely, emphasizes that philosophizing, that is, understanding the world, is only ever possible multilingually, inasmuch as different historical and cultural aspects are sedimented in the words of different languages for the same objects. Languages are in this sense untranslatable, *intraduisibles*.[141] This applies above all to concepts that do not pertain strictly to objects but rather belong to human beings and their apprehension of the world. Recognizing this untranslatability, however, means taking a standpoint "beyond" that is only generated after the complex process of translation has been completed. This point of view arises in recognizing the efforts of both languages to grasp the object to which they refer; it recognizes, in

---

139 De Toledo, *Vies pøtentielles*, 140–141.
140 See Jürgen Trabant, *Mithridates im Paradies: Kleine Geschichte des Sprachdenkens* (Munich: C.H. Beck, 2003).
141 See Barbara Cassin et al., ed., *Dictionary of Untranslatables: A Philosophical Lexicon* (Princeton University Press, 2014).

these efforts, a common ground. Even Wilhelm von Humboldt's linguistic anthropology, which has often been co-opted as the prelude to a modern cultural relativism, aimed at a point of view that already incorporated linguistic diversity, since it epistemologically manifests both difference *and* universality.[142]

In everyday life, the process of relating to another linguistic world is of course not rational per se. Rather, as the Parisian philosopher Olivier Remaud has pointed out in relation to narrated experiences of exile, it is a process of making oneself familiar, a slow incorporation of speech into the complex social and cultural facets of this process.[143] Against this background, the ability to translate proves to be an art of dealing with difficulties that allows us to think through and beyond differences to arrive at a new "monde commun," a common world.[144] In *L'inquiétude d'être au monde* we read: *"The word 'World' is like the swan; it floats. / Welt, Terre, Mundo, Salt of the Earth."*[145] The verse's concluding turn opens up this notion toward the dimension of humanity; it locates the world in the "childhood remembrance of an age before language, / in the in-between in which we are connected."[146] That which lies between the worlds points to a space of separate, yet shared and sharable, experience—in the same way that the narratives in *Vies Pøtentielles* are intertwined on various levels. This is precisely the strength of Camille de Toledo's composition, which opens up something general to experience without negating or suspending its individual narratives.

It is in reference to this generality, yet to be discovered in the spaces between narratives, that the contemporary significance of literature develops in the work of Camille de Toledo. The search for this in-between is what allows him to turn the "tristesse européenne" toward hope. If the universalistic validity of European narratives is waning at the same time that a diversity of narratives is claiming validity, this reflects first of all a situation of confusion and chaos that Europe finds frightening. It raises the question of how to preserve a general perspective,

---

142 Markus Messling, "W. von Humboldt's Critique of a Hegelian Understanding of Modernity: A Contribution to the Debate on Postcolonialism," *Forum for Modern Language Studies* 53, no. 1 (2017): 35–46.

143 For example, in the lecture "Le choc des cosmopolitismes?" that Olivier Remaud delivered on May 17, 2017, at the Chair of European Philosophy at the University of Nantes. I have the speech as a manuscript; I refer here especially to pages 14 and 15. An extract of the text has been published in advance under the title "Les frontières sont des portes" in *Le Monde des Idées*, May 6, 2017, page 7 ("Débat").

144 Barbara Cassin, ed., *Après Babel, traduire*, catalogue of the exhibition of the same name at the *Musée des civilisations de l'Europe et de la Méditerranée* (MuCEM Marseille) (Arles: Actes Sud, 2016), 16.

145 De Toledo, *L'inquiétitude d'être au monde*, 42.

146 De Toledo, *L'inquiétitude d'être au monde*, 35.

a perspective of humanity, that can be claimed as a reference point for emancipatory principles. The melancholy also gripping Camille de Toledo, which he shares with Mathias Énard, springs from a concern for erudition and a culture shaped by books: if the standing of text culture is dwindling, where can a space be found to negotiate this very question of narratives and their validity? In the same way that Michel Houellebecq's thought proceeds from the end of art and its emancipating power, Camille de Toledo grasps narrative from the end of the book: "What can the book still do? What will become of the book?"[147] While Houellebecq remains fixated on the implosion of the center and ascribes only a documentary function to literature, Camille de Toledo takes the end of the book as a starting point, as an opening to the world:

> For me, it was a way not to give in to melancholy, to fight against the intimate, pleasant pitch of regret. The contemplation of the past, of what disappears in the stifling, savage process of modernity, is, in many ways, a tread worn of habit, and there will be plenty of time for me to fall into this groove as I grow old. But for now, I wanted to see if I could recognize the vitality of our metamorphoses, the alliance of energy and brazenness, of anger and joy, that accompanies the amalgamations in the new world—in short, all the energy of our furious confusion. I stood up against our collective inclination to grief, to the sadness and regret of lost hierarchies.[148]

But how might this happen—concretely, specifically? How might literature make it possible to (en)counter the chaos of narratives? How might the loss of a single narrative structuring the world be overcome?

Camille de Toledo's answer is radical: we must turn insecurity into curiosity, we *ourselves* must turn toward the world, as it manifests itself in all its narratives; we must have a hunger and a thirst for diversity, must take up all of this worldliness in(to) ourselves, in chaos and disorder, in the hope that we will find, in it, the reality of the world, that we will find life. *Le livre de la faim et de la soif,* "The Book of Hunger and Thirst," is the name of the grand text that sets out on this quest. It wants to drink in the narratives of the world with utter excess, to absorb them all, to live through them by telling them, to *be* their view of things— until it becomes lost among them, amid this telling; until it demands too much of itself, drives its own personality to falter, unswervingly, to the point of madness. As a book within a book, the book itself is the novel's protagonist. In its unlimited taking up of the world, "dans son délire,"[149] threatened by its own delirium, it must finally submit to medical interventions, which one of Alexander Pavlenko's

---

147 Camille de Toledo, *Le livre de la faim et de la soif* (Paris: Gallimard, 2017), 88.
148 De Toledo, *Le livre de la faim et de la soif,* 12–13.
149 De Toledo, *Le livre de la faim et de la soif,* 230.

illustrations shows us with a disconcerting realism.[150] The leap from narration in the book to the book as an actor is the answer that Camille de Toledo gives to our present disorder, to our "charnel-house age."[151] His novel is a book about the book as living subject. By elevating the book to the status of protagonist of his novel, he contradicts the departures from literature so cleverly proffered by others;[152] he tests "the resilience of this form that is called the novel" by capturing the metamorphoses of our narrating without classifying or judging them.[153] In averting the hopeless death of the book, he finds a chance to escape melancholy:

> A book, yes, as a character. For the book, too, is morphing. It is becoming embodied, disembodied, reaching immateriality, trembling at the thought of dying or falling into oblivion, and some say: "This is it, this is the end. The end of literature and the end of the book." In my opinion, this is one of the most incontrovertible explanations for our inclination to melancholia: we feel that a disappearance is imminent, and from this point on, the entire filter of our glances and expressions appears contaminated by the shadow of this end. The dead, the faces, and finally the books.[154]

Camille de Toledo certainly can't be accused of underestimating the importance of narration for building community. For him, "world" does not mean reality in any objectifiable sense, but rather always a construction of reality. Realism in this context thus means taking seriously the narrating of the world. But this makes realism no less powerful. As an appropriation of the world, it is a potent principle with immense historical and political force. On this point, *Le livre de la faim et de la soif* leaves no doubt. It begins its tour through various mythological prehistories with the tale of a giant who first consumes his own mother from within, then brutally murders her, only to become a world-eater who shamelessly gorges on planets and celestial bodies.[155] In the archaic beginning is greed; the world, its course of time, *Chronos*, is born in crime. As the giant prepares, like Goya's *Saturn*, to devour the earth, he is suddenly seized by a satisfied fatigue, a calm before feasting on this colorful planet so different from the others. He falls asleep, time passes, the earth and its people live—for now. The facticity of life and the world is beyond our reach, the story tells us; we live in an unlikely deferral. In this way, it testifies to this elemental force while also banishing it. In bringing this world-eater to a halt with cunning, the story creates the world, even if

---

150 De Toledo, *Le livre de la faim et de la soif*, 237.
151 De Toledo, *Le livre de la faim et de la soif*, 138.
152 See the recent history of "intrinsic" reasons for the decline of "literature" as a social institution written by William Marx, *L'Adieu à la littérature* (2005).
153 De Toledo, *Le livre de la faim et de la soif*, 13.
154 De Toledo, *Le livre de la faim et de la soif*, 13.
155 De Toledo, *Le livre de la faim et de la soif*, 26–30, 53–55.

the world's outcome remains uncertain. This is essentially reminiscent of *Thousand and One Nights*. The mythological story of the world-eating giant is a story about the necessity of narrating.

The biblical *Genesis* by contrast—which the novel then calls upon as the ur-narrative of salvation by the one God, of a return home, of a political identity between people and empire—creates historical depth and a philosophy of history that have grounded Europe's notions about the course of humanity into the present day. The book, "this reactionary,"[156] remains tied to this narrative, perpetuating it by repeatedly returning to ideas of genesis, lineage, and teleology through language.[157]

The parts of these (hi)stories that might appear archaic are in truth powerful and current. Camille de Toledo immediately reminds modern readers of this in order to prepare them for the journey through his world of narratives. At first glance, this path may remind us of the postmodern play with meaning and truth that Italo Calvino works through with his readers in his novel *If on a Winter's Night a Traveler*,[158] where he leads them through beginnings to the book that start over and break off again and again, in order to make his readers aware of the role they themselves play in constituting meaning.[159] In Calvino's novel, readers are protagonists in a double sense: as figures of the novel and as real readers addressed with the familiar form of "you," whose reading is linked to the events as though it were decisive for the progress of the narrative. But Camille de Toledo is not interested in a game of representations. The question of which telling might circle more closely around the truth, might be better able to grasp it, appears unanswerable here not simply because of the book's processes of subjectification. Rather, each story claims a right to its own validity. The distanced external standpoint that might be able to playfully demonstrate to the reader, through the composition of the text, the relativity of each narrative, that standpoint of a postmodern attitude, has long since been drowned in the blood of narratives of an identitarian stripe. As in archaic history, narration is always a twin of violence. The recognition of all (his)stories, the search for something new in their simultaneity, for the opportunities of a common ground opening up between them, is a question of life and death. Herein lies the seriousness with which the book within the book speaks: "We will not go out, my friend. We will not escape. There is apparently no longer any outside. We are in language, possessed, enclosed. And we have to accept that yesterday's (hi)stories are

---

156 De Toledo, *Le livre de la faim et de la soif*, 83.

157 De Toledo, *Le livre de la faim et de la soif*, 22–24.

158 Italo Calvino, *If on a Winter's Night a Traveler* (London: Picador, 1982).

159 See Renaud Pasquier, "Camille de Toledo, Le livre de la faim et de la soif," *La Nouvelle Revue Française* 624 (May 2017): 153–154.

resurfacing, like old stones."[160] In the spirit of the French tradition since Derrida, the deconstructivist gesture does not appear here as a kind of ironic relativism. Rather, it points to the fact that the act of positing meaning is *about* something. What is at stake is existential.

Le livre de la faim et de la soif is a furious book. The narratives on which its journey takes its readers draw their universes from old and new myths, from the Old Testament and the Koran, from Rabelais, Cervantes and Borges, Dostoyevsky and Melville. They spring from the legends of Westerns and of Japanese modernity; they lead from the biblical Orient via Russia to India, to Saudi hypermodernity on the Gulf and to Japan. Dreams and reflections, poetry and criticism blur together. In a great stream of events, the book drifts around the world, telling and retelling, reshaping, its narratives. In the end, the polyphonic noise and rumbling of the world is stronger here than individuation. The content can hardly be summarized any other way than to say it is about this experience, about living through this diversity of (hi)stories. This is where their inner coherence comes from. The book wants to discover just what it can tell. And it dictates all of it to a dactylographer, an assistant who writes down everything the book experiences, thus bringing together, on a formal level, the points of view from which it narrates—the experiences of a protagonist characterized by many kinds of belonging. What is at stake here is the possibilities of the book. But the very point of view that is supposed to be suspended, neutralized, in the book's nonhuman figures is marked as a site in its literary constellation. The blatantly obvious model of the journey taken by the novel's two heroes, the book and its typing companion, are Don Quixote and Sancho Panza. As in Cervantes's parody of the picaresque novel, here too the ghosts of the past appear; the distorted images of reality are reflected everywhere. Restlessly, breathlessly—breath, breeze, and wind all play a large part as metaphors of the spirit and of spiritualization—the book throws itself into the old and new narratives collapsing upon it, which it then seeks to appropriate in acts of retelling in new form. If Cervantes's novel is taken to be the expression of a European modernity that is losing its transcendental certainties, and which must therefore find a new way to articulate itself in language,[161] then the book's furious ride across time and space, with its dactylographer Camille de Toledo by its side, must be read precisely in the sense named in the novel itself: "Letting go, leaving this ancient age of beginning and end, of controlling meaning, of mastered language."[162]

---

160 De Toledo, *Le livre de la faim et de la soif*, 206.

161 In the sense classically formulated by Georg Lukács, *The Theory of the Novel: A Historico-philosophical Essay on the Forms of Great Epic Literature*, trans. Anna Bostock (Cambridge, MA: MIT Press, 1989), 97–107.

162 De Toledo, *Le livre de la faim et de la soif*, 147.

The book, the blurb on its cover tells us, is the author's alter ego. But if Cervantes's Don Quixote comes to repeat Sancho Panza's experiences,[163] the same is true of the relationship between this book and its dactylographer. The book's "hunger" and "thirst" for (hi)stories and their worlds may be those of the author. But it contains moments that reveal the function of the writer who already sees what that book is yet to experience—an experience that has already been had, a view that has already been shaped. One such moment occurs during the Arab episode of the book's world tour, when the snow in an artificial ski slope in Dubai melts, exposing "all the successive strata laid down by modernity's profanations" and, with them, all the violence and sacrifices that "progress" or "modernity" demand.[164] Do we not find here, shining through, a historical view grown wise with age that cautiously orders things in the world?

This points to the philosophical problem of the novel: today's narratives are not equally valid. This is not because the author has a different knowledge of the world's various narratives. To achieve the novel's aim, it would be best for these to be representative, but they need not be. The potential of a diversity that would encompass the globe clearly emerges in reading de Toledo's book. But sometimes ghosts of the past, such as the book's censorship in a Saudi fatwa,[165] also appear, weaving threads of value judgments into the narrative. These are not trivial—for example, when we read that "censorship endows books with spirit," that it spurs them to invent "deeper forms of intelligence" in the form of "indirectly told (hi)stories."[166] The book is not making any superficial comparison of civilizations. Rather, it has a critical function that emerges as an organizing principle in the novel. This is already invoked in the preface, entitled "Pardon." If we might say, with Ernst Bloch, that the novel's motto is "joy is greater than the law," then the author excuses himself in this preface for wanting to indulge, against all the "laws" he embodies, in the joy of plumbing the openness and futurity of the book amid the chaos of world narratives: against the catechism, against the Talmud commentaries of Rabbi Rachi, against modern science's notions of truth. The gathering together of all the narratives the novel invokes, of all their many universes, is thus subject in the novel's events to a certain opacity, but this is by no means the real aim of bringing all these things together. This aim lies rather in the hope that the critical power of the book might shape these narratives toward a new world in giving them form. Such a hope is symbolized in the

---

163 I take this beautiful observation, which makes recourse to Giorgio Agamben, from Johan Faerber, "Camille de Toledo: à livre ouvert," https://diacritik.com/2017/02/08/camille-de-toledo-a-livre-ouvert-le-livre-de-la-faim-et-de-la-soif/, accessed February 7, 2019.
164 De Toledo, *Le livre de la faim et de la soif*, 310.
165 De Toledo, *Le livre de la faim et de la soif*, 275–297.
166 De Toledo, *Le livre de la faim et de la soif*, 290.

novel's final image, in which the book and its writer join an oceanic stream of dead children and bodies of destroyed humanity, of all its vanished hopes and dreams, its memories and gestures. "'Are you there?' I ask again / And the book, far away, responds: / 'I am right here.'"[167]

We might say that the book's protagonist descends into madness, the madness of a bondage to the world and its voices, almost to the point of unconsciousness; that he drifts through this world for long stretches without really being able to appropriate it and shape it. At the end of the book, however, we are left with his desire to find an image for the experience of horror that would exhort us to live on in peace. The novel's conclusion is a wild reshaping of Melville's tale of Captain Ahab, in which the whale and the characters of other great (hi)stories, and with them the great traditions of world narratives themselves, decompose in the ocean current of memory into mud. Here, the vivid action breaks off and transforms into a kind of scenic dialogue, a cosmic echo enveloped in darkness that returns the book to its immateriality. But it remains present: "Je suis là," "I am right here," it affirms repeatedly. If we identify the task of the book's protagonist as listening to the (hi)stories of the world, then Camille de Toledo's novel is itself the principle of taking this up by giving it a form. The most powerful force the medium of the book can mobilize is fictionalization—the transformation of, the giving of form to, the overwhelming noise of world (hi)stories.

One of the universal (hi)stories taken up in the novel, in the sense noted above, is the biblical telling of the Israelites' exodus from Egypt. Every child knows this story, in which Moses leads the Israelites, caught in mortal danger, across the Red Sea with the help of God, who causes the waters to miraculously part while they pass through. And this is why a child is the character in Camille de Toledo's novel who overturns the meaning of the narrative. While the Israelites are fleeing through the cordon of the sea, the children stop to look at the walls of water, which have become a kind of aquarium displaying hundreds of sea creatures. The children are enthralled. Fearing for their children's lives and following Moses's command, the parents drag the little ones along the path toward the Promised Land. But one child, the son of Ishmael, runs in the opposite direction to prolong his zoological delight. The Israelites are at odds over the question of what to do—leave the child behind or face the danger of the approaching Egyptian army? The narrator, for one, remains with the boy. And what became of the child? That depends on which tradition is told, the narrative voice says. Some say that Nile fish helped him, that they saved his life. Other say that the boy turned into a fish, and that he then traveled the world, reappearing again and again to its fishermen in the form of an

---

167 De Toledo, *Le livre de la faim et de la soif,* 377.

air bubble carrying a muffled sound: "I told you so." Yet the father, Ishmael, cannot make peace with the loss of the son. Day after day, year in year out, for centuries, he walks along the beach, only to one day finally receive certainty:

> After many years, one day the father took a dead hand, the body of a drowned child covered with seaweed, on the shore, his arms covered by small shells, to be the fulfillment of his wish. That day, Ishmael believed to have found his son again. This is why another tradition tells that the child was actually carried away by the water and that he traveled around the earth until finally he once again reached the shores of the Mediterranean, where he washed up, in front of the trembling legs of his father, who took the boy in his arms and shook him beneath the sun. A small anchor of feet, head, and arms, brandished toward the sky, until Ishmael finally kneels down and lays his son's body on the sand and says, "But how! How can God want *this*?"[168]

Here, the genealogical story that tells of the salvation of the Israelites and their arrival in the Holy Land becomes a story of distraction by the world and its diversions. In this version, the narrative takes a much more suggestive form, as an eternal story of flight and exile. The literary image of the child's corpse immediately evokes a photo burned into our visual memory—of the body of the drowned Syrian boy, the refugee who washed up near Bodrum in September of 2015. Whereas the biblical story is the narrative of a rescue that is structurally linked with the *Odyssey* and other narratives of homecoming, Camille de Toledo insists on the necessity of its retelling in new forms. A future is only possible in a different understanding of our genealogical narratives.

Camille de Toledo's theater-of-world-narratives is ultimately based on an anthropological theory of narration, which extends the concept of narrative beyond the literary framework to become a basic structure of human community. "What can it do, after all, if from now the weaving of its connections is outside its control, if the writing finally takes place without the book, beyond it?"[169] Sounding this out is the task of his novel's protagonist. On a performative level, however, the pain plays out beyond the end of the book, while the search for a new way to narrate humanity still takes place within the medium of the book itself. In a sense, here the level of the novel's composition constantly runs counter to the level of its plot, with the effect that, in the face of chaos and polyphony, the great

---

168 De Toledo, *Le livre de la faim et de la soif*, 95. Dieter Hornig translated the story for a reading at the Deutsches Theater Berlin, which took place on November 3, 2017, as part of the evening "Fluchtpunkt: Das Mittelmeer und die europäische Krise" (Fluchtpunkt: the Mediterranean and Europe's crisis). The German word "Fluchtpunkt" means "vanishing point," but "Flucht" (flight) can also be read in the sense of fleeing or escaping. I thank Camille de Toledo for providing me with the German translation.

169 De Toledo, *Le livre de la faim et de la soif*, 146.

power of the novel remains subjectification. An order of universal world history and structure, as found in totalizing works such as those of Melville or Dostoyevsky, no longer seems possible. But this means the hope of wresting a new perspective from polyphony is that much greater. The novel thus does not show how life across the globe can be given narrative structure, or to what end its narratives might weave themselves together. But it shows the hope *that* this might happen by relying on their shared telling, their wildness, the fullness of life they hold— and on the ability to thereby narrate community, even under postuniversalist circumstances, in a new, different way. Hope in the works of Mathias Énard can be said to consist of another, living form for the genesis of knowledge—a form that makes it possible to transcend the self in curiosity about the world, embodied in the figure of the "savage detective." In Camille de Toledo, by contrast, this hope is born from the integrative and critical power of the book itself. The premises of both works are clear: they lie in a belief in the power of the word and in a profound knowledge of the history of its tradition and interpretation. But they themselves also call out the crisis they see besetting this history. The only escape from this dilemma is to declare our solidarity with them. This will provide us with something against Houellebecq's documentarianism of decline. To speak with Erich Auerbach, Mathias Énard and Camille de Toledo bring to life in our time, as a time of transition, a knowledge that is often all too easily banished to the dusty shelves of archives: a politically relevant knowledge of the potential of narrating the world.[170]

---

170 Here, too, see the remarks on Auerbach in the introductory chapter to this book, "Universality after Universalism."

Liberté—The Language of the Villa Sésini

We find ourselves walled in, pinned down by the weight of memorial plaques and monuments. Beneath them, we lose our relation to the world around us. This is the thesis of Camille de Toledo's book *Le Hêtre et le bouleau: Essai sur la tristesse européenne*—"The Beech and the Birch: An Essay on European Sadness."[1] But Camille de Toledo's essay does not add his voice to the chorus of others after 1989, some of them problematic and others revisionist, who wish to finally wipe away the weight of history, to forget it entirely. He is not seeking any final liberation from guilt and remembrance. On the contrary: if he is left skeptical by these monumental sites erected in stone to remember the crimes of European totalitarianisms, and especially to remember the crimes of the Holocaust, then this is because it seems to him that the European twentieth century has walled itself off from the world by encasing itself in its own guilt. These monuments are memorials for the European victims of European violence. But where does one find monuments to the immensurable systematic violence that was inflicted on the non-European world?

Frantz Fanon and Hannah Arendt have shown that European totalitarianism is inconceivable without imperialism, without the colonial masters' formative experience of having total control over the labor and life of other human beings.[2] These structural historical connections are almost never invoked by memorials made of stone (one exception is the monument to the victims of the Atlantic slave trade that was opened in 2012 in the French city of Nantes, the Mémorial de l'Abolition de l'Esclavage). Yet they have become increasingly significant in the post-1989 world, as the question of which system would prevail has vanished within a form of global capitalism that is reinvigorating, in new ways, the political significance of imperial borders, laws, and imbalances in wealth and participation. Who could ignore that the destruction of Syria is in fact a fading ember of the imperial order imposed upon the Middle East by the Sykes-Picot Agreement in 1916, in the midst of World War I?

Camille de Toledo's 2009 essay—a piece as visionary as it is relevant to the present—prompts the question of how a Europe that had based its postwar order on the moral foundation of its own victims' culture might take up, and take seriously, the grief of others for which it is in fact largely responsible. How can Europe

---

1 Camille de Toledo, *Le Hêtre et le bouleau: Essai sur la tristesse européenne, suivi de L'utopie linguistique ou la pédagogie du vertige* (Paris: Seuil, 2009).
2 Frantz Fanon, *The Wretched of the Earth*, trans. Richard Philcox (New York: Grove Press, 2004); Hannah Arendt, *The Origins of Totalitarianism* (New York: Schocken, 1951).

respond to the reordering of the world after 1989 if it constructs its internal moral cohesion solely around a relation to itself? How can the people who come to Europe find a suitable place in European societies if Europe conceals essential elements of the prehistory that conditioned their flight and migration? Camille de Toledo bespeaks the hope that the culture of remembrance expressed by the monuments of European cities—epitomized by Berlin, the new center of Europe— might prove to be just one, though certainly central, starting point for a historical consciousness that is increasingly being called to interweave itself with the world.[3] Yet if we follow Camille de Toledo, this interweaving is not to be carried out by monuments but by narration that is capable of interweaving grief and trauma, that can layer these experiences in complex ways and process them together without casting hierarchies in concrete.[4] Europe must find a new way of relating to the world—in books, in public forums, in museums.[5] The colonial world is returning to Europe, and European societies must acknowledge and address its experience of violence. But of course this articulation already has its own history of speaking and writing.

The Kenyan writer and intellectual Ngũgĩ wa Thiong'o rejected the language of English because he found that, when used retrospectively to describe his own colonial fate, it retained a colonizing impact on his own thinking through its way of speaking, through its cultural implications. For him, turning to local languages was thus an act of decolonizing the mind.[6] Like English, all European colonial languages are weighed down by the domination for which they have been instrumentalized. Some things can no longer be said in these languages, or at least they cannot be said as they once were, inasmuch as the way these languages have come to be used repeats hierarchical, racist, demeaning, and aggrandizing patterns of thought.

---

3 See also Michael Rothberg, *Multidirectional Memory: Remembering the Holocaust in the Age of Decolonization* (Stanford: Stanford University Press, 2009).

4 Ottmar Ette has also emphasized this as a criterion for the fact that the changes in the world in which we live cannot be grasped by economic-social-scientific analyses alone, but that validity must rather be given to narratives and their reflection; see Ottmar Ette, *TransArea: Eine literarische Globalisierungsgeschichte* (Berlin: De Gruyter, 2012), and *List, Last und Lust literarischer Konvivenz im globalen Maßstab* (Berlin: Kulturverlag Kadmos, 2010).

5 See Bénédicte Savoy, *Die Provenienz der Kultur: Von der Trauer des Verlusts zum universalen Menschheitserbe*, revised version of the inaugural lecture given upon assuming the international chair Cultural History of Artistic Heritage in Europe, 18th–20th Century, at the Collège de France, March 30, 2017 (Berlin: Matthes & Seitz, 2018). See also Arno Bertina, *Mona Lisa in Bangoulap: Die Fabel vom Weltmuseum* (Berlin: Matthes & Seitz, 2016), as well as the afterword written by Bénédicte Savoy, "Das Erbe der Anderen," 51–76.

6 Ngũgĩ wa Thiong'o, *Decolonizing the Mind: The Politics of Language in African Literature* (London: J. Currey, 1986).

Languages are not simply containers of sound into which meaning can be arbitrarily packed. Rather, they become historically charged; they convey experiences, color our view of the world. In the same way that English has been shaped by an ongoing history of exercising power in contexts defined by unequal power relations, French has a particularly dramatic history of its own. Like no other nation, France has based its cohesion on a unified language, to be asserted from the position of the center as the language of reason and freedom—first against multilingualism and cultural diversity within the multiethnic state of France itself, and then, outwardly, on a global scale as the rational medium of modernity.[7]

Of course, this ideological history of French is long and convoluted. From the beginning, it was accompanied by deep insecurities. The unification of France's culture in and through the language of the royal court and the small Parisian upper class, instigated by Cardinal Richelieu with the founding of the Académie française in 1635, directly stemmed from the fears of disintegration that France had faced since the bloody religious wars of the sixteenth century. Its policies regarding language and culture have long served to level out confessional, cultural, and linguistic differences and to centralize the structure of the state. France exemplifies with great historical depth how the modern nation-state is formed through cultural assimilation. Without the force of this linguistic centralism, it is impossible to understand the energy of the opposition that thinkers such as Roland Barthes, Julia Kristeva, Jacques Derrida, Gérard Genette, Pierre Bourdieu, Gilles Deleuze, and Michel Foucault ultimately unleashed, through their critiques and deconstructions of language, in the context of the *Tel Quel* movement and beyond in the 1960s and 1970s. Since then, it has been quite rare for any emphasis to be placed on those emancipatory aspects that have, historically speaking, *also* come from the standardization of French—here one thinks of liberation from provincial confines, or the enabling of educational advancement that can be found in some biographical accounts penned by the protagonists of the Enlightenment.[8]

The obsession with French as the language of the nation was reinforced by the Revolution of 1789, as the constitutional concept of the "République une et indivisible," the one and indivisible Republic, collided with a political reality that did not correspond to the claims made by the Republic's constitution. Given the

---

7 See Jürgen Trabant, *Der Gallische Herkules: Über Sprache und Politik in Frankreich und Deutschland* (Tübingen/Basel: Francke, 2002); Joseph Jurt, *Sprache, Literatur und nationale Identität: Die Debatten über das Universelle und das Partikuläre in Frankreich und Deutschland* (Berlin: De Gruyter, 2014).

8 One widely discussed affirmation of the tradition of language policies in France can be found in Hélène Merlin-Kajman's *La langue est-elle fasciste? Langue, pouvoir, enseignement* (Paris: Éditions du Seuil, 2003).

extreme military pressure from the forces of restoration that were attacking France from all sides, as well as the internal debilitation caused by *terreur* and *fronde* and by the counterrevolution staged by the nobility in the Vendée, the fact that only about a third of those living within the multiethnic state of France spoke French posed a real existential threat. The Revolution responded by making massive demands that discourse be translated into French.[9] Speaking a "false" language such as Breton, Corsican, or Alsatian ran the risk of being stamped as counterrevolutionary. There has been no other time where France more brutally repressed its own diversity than during the early days of the Republic.

Aiming to assert French against other languages, a discourse has developed since the Renaissance that sees French as possessing special characteristics: a "Discours de la défense et de l'illustration de la langue française."[10] It attributes, for instance, specific grammatical advantages to French—above all, a sentence order of subject-predicate-object that is taken to be especially logical, to form the basis for a clarity of thought that is believed to have carried over into intellectual achievements. The cultural supremacy of France, its literature, its theaters, its rhetoric, its courtly style, its knowledge, its political greatness—all of these supposedly ensue from a French *esprit* generated in French. During the Revolution, however, this layering of culture acquired a new dimension: the spirit of freedom. Since then, French has also claimed to be the language of modernity. Since then, French has not only laid claim to the highest degree of cultural prestige: as the language of enlightened reason, it also presents itself as giving birth and reality to the republican values of *liberté, egalité*, and *fraternité*. For this reason, since the French Revolution it has been even more insistently elevated ideologically as the "langue de la liberté," the messenger of freedom. This means that all republican pedagogy must therefore be oriented toward French, both inside and outside France. How else could republican values be universal if they are not de facto universalized, that is, understood and recognized by all?

This discourse also makes French into the line dividing nature and civilization: on one side, we have the ostensible language of reason and freedom, and on the other, languages that are more familiar—suitable at best for everyday life but not higher, intellectual activities; or we have a single medium of clear thought versus a plurality of languages that limit thinking through the very media of their

---

9 See Michel de Certeau, Dominique Julia, and Jacques Revel, eds., *Une politique de la langue: La Révolution française et les patois; L'Enquête de Grégoire* (Paris: Gallimard, 1975), and Jürgen Trabant, "Die Sprache der Freiheit und ihrer Feinde," *Zeitschrift für Literaturwissenschaft und Linguistik* 41 (1981) (= Sprache und Literatur in der Französischen Revolution): 70–89.
10 This is the title of Joachim Du Bellay's famous treatise, *La Deffence, et Illustration de la langue Francoyse*, ed. Henri Chamard (Paris: Fontemoing, 1904).

articulation. Was French not one of the central reasons for France's rise as a world power? An expression of the universality of its civilization?

This line of thought gave birth to the civilizing mission of modernity, which other powers—Germany, Italy, to some extent England—each adopted in their own way in their imperial endeavors. Throughout Europe during the nineteenth century, the superiority of French was translated into a superiority of the "Indo-European" languages.[11]

Against this background of emphasizing European languages, it is anything but banal that numerous writers formulate the experience of their subjugation in the language of former imperial masters. Given the particularly massive tradition of viewing colonialism as cultural mission, this is especially true of the countries of the French-speaking world, where nonfrancophone literatures—despite their more or less extensive beginnings in Arabic or various creoles—have not been able to establish themselves, or for various reasons have done so only to a limited extent, even after decolonization. Yet how can any articulation be subversive when language itself lies at the center of the problem, and when its use entails structural violence?

Recognizing France's loss of standing within the largely anglophone globalization since the 1970s, French governments have increasingly sought out allies for French, and for cultural and linguistic diversity, through their language and cultural policies. One result is the *Francophonie*, founded in 1970, which essentially began as a cultural alliance with France's former colonies but later grew into a more far-reaching political alliance reflected in the founding of the Organisation Internationale de la Francophonie in 2005.[12]

A distinction between the terms *français* for the center and *francophone* for the periphery has stubbornly persisted in the marketing of literatures in French, with "French" still indicating that a text "stands within the great tradition of French" that was itself once seen as universal, and "francophone" meaning something like "world literature," in a sense similar to that of "world music."[13] This is the context for the polemical reversal demanded by the Congolese writer Alain Mabanckou in the lecture he delivered upon assuming the chair of artistic creation (Chaire de création artistique) at the Collège de France: that the 66 million citizens of France should finally integrate themselves into the large community of 220 million francophone speakers; and not, as is usually imagined within the hexagon of France, that the

---

11 For a discussion of the *longue durée* of all these processes, see Markus Messling, *Gebeugter Geist: Rassismus und Erkenntnis in der modernen europäischen Philologie* (Göttingen: Wallstein Verlag, 2016).

12 See Jürgen Erfurt, *Frankophonie: Sprache – Diskurs – Politik* (Tübingen: Francke, 2005).

13 Pascale Casanova, *The World Republic of Letters*, trans. Malcolm de Bevoise (Cambridge, MA: Harvard University Press, 2007).

Francophonie should continue to be defined by its relation to the center. In any case, one thing is clear: the francophone world today is above all not French.[14]

Alain Mabanckou belongs to a generation of intellectuals who find it possible to write with confidence about the relationship of the *Francophonie* to the former center. He ironizes not only France's cultural self-image but also the lack cultural independence and the inferiority complex of the political classes in its former colonies. In his novel *Broken Glass*, he tells how a coterie of advisors is asked to invent a phrase that will allow the president of an African country to go down in history. The president is jealous of his minister, who had declared "J'accuse!" with the grand gesture of a statesman and thus placed himself in the intellectual tradition of the French Republic. But since, as the narrator says, "there's plenty of petrol in this country, but not many ideas," the president's advisors decide to write a letter to the Académie française in Paris—specifically, to Léopold Sédar Senghor, at the time in which the narrative is set, its only Black member.[15] They proceed to compose a convoluted missive in Alexandrines, showing off with the literary form of past subjunctive that is today almost never used, the "subjonctifs imparfaits bien roulés," with the intention of proving how exceptionally educated they are. But the endeavor runs into a crisis because they cannot agree on a choice of punctuation—should it be a comma or semicolon?—which leads to more and more problems. Finally, they discard the letter. And on the next day, at the cock's first crow, someone comes up with a phrase after all. Henceforth, it shall be said that while "the minister accuses, the president understands."[16]

It is telling that, like Achille Mbembe, Alain Mabanckou does not teach in France, but at the University of California in Los Angeles. Writing from this position outside France and the *Francophonie*, he rejects French centrism as well as the "integristic" attitude of the "nostalgic Senegalese Tirailleurs," who would also have one write from a position of opposition.[17] His view is that doing so would clog the universal "highway of literature." Differentiation here is everything. For Mabanckou, there is no such thing as "French" and "francophone" literature, or, as one could say with Taiye Selasi, "French literature" and "African literature."[18] There are rather many different contexts from which literatures emerge—each in its own French. *Le*

---

14 Alain Mabanckou, "'Lettres noires': Afrikanische Literaturen heute," *Sinn und Form* 1 (January/February 2017): 70–89.

15 Alain Mabanckou, *Broken Glass*, trans. Helen Stevenson (Berkeley: Soft Skull Press, 2009), 10.

16 Mabanckou, *Broken Glass*, 32.

17 See here, for instance, the narrator's passionate tirade in *Broken Glass* about literature, which can clearly be read as the voice of Mabanckou's alter ego (130–131).

18 Taiye Selasi, "African Literature Doesn't Exist," opening speech at the internationales literaturfestival berlin 2013 (Berlin: Berliner Festspiele, 2016).

monde est mon langage, "the world is my language," is accordingly the title of Alain Mabanckou's documentation of conversations he held with writers around the world who write in French,[19] and by this he means that worldliness, in the sense of an awareness of belonging to humanity, is more important than any affirmation of belonging to French culture.

It is certainly not all poets, especially from formerly colonized countries, who are able to so nimbly disregard the deeply ingrained arrogance embedded in language; too strong is their perception of how this violence is perpetuated in today's prejudices and racism. The famous slogan uttered by Kateb Yacine at the end of the Algerian war of liberation—"la langue française est notre butin de guerre," "French is our spoils of war"—still expresses both a triumph and a process marked by pain.[20] Appropriating a language, inscribing oneself into the very language meant to be used as a tool of cultural assimilation, perhaps even without having tasted freedom, remains a challenge in a world in which the balance of power relations has only partially shifted. Language is too closely interwoven with us, with the memory held in our bodies and our appropriation of the world, for us to accept what we hear when it quietly whispers to us that it was never ours, anyway. Jacques Derrida's oft-quoted phrase—"I only have one language; it is not mine"[21]—is often rashly taken as a recognition of the fact that language is something supra-individual, inaccessible. Derrida, however, concretely wrested this insight from the pain he experienced in being denied access as a Jewish-Algerian child to public school, and thus to French language and culture, when the Vichy government revoked the emancipatory Décret Crémieux (1870) in 1940; and from the fact that even within the colonial regime a fine distinction was made between the "proper" speakers of French from *France métropolitaine* and the francophone Algerians.[22] Derrida was aware that a language can very well be "withdrawn" under conditions of domination. His famous dictum is thus no statement of fact. Rather, it signifies an ethical turn founding his deconstruction of the concepts used to define what it means to be human, along with his decision to nonetheless say "we" in specific contexts for political purposes.[23] It was this, his true passion for French, that led him to

---

19 Alain Mabanckou, *Le monde est mon langage* (Paris: Bernard Grasset, 2016).

20 See, for example, Boualem Sansal, *Poste restante; Alger: Lettre de colère et d'espoir à mes compatriotes* (Paris: Gallimard, 2006). For a broader discussion, see Jean-Marc Moura, *Littératures francophones et théorie postcoloniale* (Paris: PUF, 2017); Lise Toft, ed., *Une francophonie plurielle: langues, idées et cultures en mouvement* (Copenhagen: Museum Tusculanum Press, 2009).

21 Jacques Derrida, *Monolingualism of the Other; or, The Prosthesis of Origin*, trans. Patrick Mensah (Stanford: Stanford University Press, 1998), 1.

22 Derrida, *Monolingualism of the Other*, as well as *Learning to Live Finally: The Last Interview*, trans. Pascale-Anne Brault and Michael Naas (Basingstoke: Palgrave Macmillan, 2007), 34–38.

23 See Derrida, *Learning to Live Finally*, 38–45.

emphasize his individual idiom over the French tongue, to unfold his own way of speaking a foreign language, as a constant positing and questioning of meaning, a critique of centralized rationalism.[24] Taking something as a spoils of war also always means bringing home the memory of the conflict.

Alexis Jenni—The Violence of Linguistic Rationalism

It is this very idea of understanding France through the history of its recent conflicts, its colonial wars, that is found at the heart of Alexis Jenni's first novel, *The French Art of War*, which won the Prix Goncourt in 2011.[25] Written in the first person, it tells the story of a factory worker who is laid off because of cost-cutting measures in 1991 during the Second Gulf War. Left adrift, he becomes acquainted at a market in Lyon with a former parachutist named Victorien Salagnon. Fascinated by Salagnon's skills in calligraphy, the narrator promises that he will take down Salignon's life story in exchange for lessons in Chinese painting. This story then unfolds for readers as a history of the "twenty-year war" in which France was embroiled between 1942 and 1962, running from the final German occupation of France in World War II and the *Résistance* to Dien Bien Phu, Indochina, and the Algerian War. The bloody episodes of torture and massacre recounted by Salagnon are interspersed with the narrator's present, which is marked by a general indifference in mainstream society and unrest in the suburbs of Lyon.

The thesis advanced by *The French Art of War*, left largely undiscussed in the French public despite Jenni's Goncourt prize, is simple and can be summarized as follows: since World War II, the idea of universalism has entangled France in an increasingly deadly relationship with the world. After finally losing its own territory to the Nazis, France was left dependent on the help of France's former colonies to fight back. The international *Résistance* embodied in the novel by the Greek-Algerian military doctor Kaloyannis is thus presented as an integrative force of French universalism.[26] When France then loses its colonies, the idea

---

24 Derrida, *Monolingualism of the Other*, 56–57; see also Jürgen Trabant, "Sprach-Passion: Derrida und die Anderssprachigkeit des Einsprachigen," in *Exophonie: Anders-Sprachigkeit (in) der Literatur*, ed. Susan Arndt, Dirk Naguschewski, and Robert Stockhammer (Berlin: Kulturverlag Kadmos, 2007), 48–65; Markus Messling, "Behauptung (in) der Schrift: Zur Problematik von Schrift und Individualität bei Wilhelm von Humboldt und Jacques Derrida," *KODIKAS/CODE: Ars semeiotica, An International Journal of Semiotics* 27, no. 3–4 (2004): 163–179.

25 Alexis Jenni, *The French Art of War*, trans. Franck Wynne (London: Atlantic Books, 2017 [2011]).

26 In this regard, the history of the French state's attitude toward troops from the colonies and toward female soldiers has been consistently ambivalent throughout the twentieth century; see Elsa Dorlin, *Se défendre: Une philosophie de la violence* (Paris: La Découverte, 2017), 36–50.

of universalism *within* France that had already begun to teeter is itself put to the test, transformed into a narrative that Jenni describes as a struggle of identities. In one section of the novel, the narrator indicates bald astonishment at the abstraction from reality expressed in this universalism couched in nationalism:

> Because the Mediterranean is right there! Rumour would confine us to the kingdom of Bourges, but I hear voices speaking in French, with different phrasings and strange accents, but in French I understand everything spontaneously. Identity is pure make-believe.[27]

What this abstraction from reality leaves out is France's diversity. Diversity appears on one level, in the different ways in which French is spoken, only to then be suppressed by an insistence on a linguistic norm as the guarantor of a national identity. To follow Jenni, then, the universalist understanding of the French language has served to construct a glorified nation, a *France* "with the big, emphatic 'F,' the capital 'F' you can hear when De Gaulle pronounces it."[28] And from a historical perspective, what underlies this sense of national grandeur is the idea discussed above that France serves as a cultural model for other nations and has been engaged in a civilizing mission since the Revolution. This "certaine idée de la France" wraps itself like an aura around the Grande Nation, as a nation whose dynamism springs from a unique clarity of thought grounded in the clarity of French. This ideology was summed up by the Italian-born publicist and faux aristocrat Antoine de Rivarol, a staunch monarchist, shortly before the Revolution when he was expelled in 1784: "Ce qui n'est pas clair n'est pas français"—"anything that is not clear is not French."[29]

The tension of this tradition thus lies from the outset in the contradiction between a political rationalism linked to universal validity of natural rights and an attempt to locate this rationalism within a certain territory. On Salagnon's mission to Indochina as a parachutist in the French armed forces, during a calligraphy lesson in Hanoi, the following dialogue unfolds with his Vietnamese drawing teacher: that France is to be found in its purest form in the West Indies

> among the Africans, the Arabs and the Indo-Chinese. The white French born in what is narrowly defined as France are always astonished to find that we embody those values they heard tell of in school, which, to them, represent some unattainable utopia and to us are life itself. We perfectly exemplify a France with no superfluity, no excess. We, the cultivated,

---

27 Jenni, *The French Art of War*, 597.
28 Jenni, *The French Art of War*, 310.
29 Antoine de Rivarol, "Discours sur l'universalité de la langue française," in Pierre Pénisson, ed., *Académie de Berlin: De l'universalité européenne de la langue française* (Paris: Fayard, 1995 [1784]), 127–186, on 162.

indigenous people are the crowning glory and the justification of the Empire. We are its triumph, and that will bring about its downfall.[30]

Salagnon responds by asking: "Why its downfall?" This answer is: "How can one continue to be what is called indigenous, while simultaneously being utterly French? One is forced to choose. It is fire and water contained within a single vessel."[31]

In constantly juxtaposing Salagnon's tales of atrocities with statements made by his contemporaries, the novel develops a narrative strategy with far-reaching political implications: it confronts the self-conception of the French nation with the historical reality of France. The politics of this national myth are no longer tenable. Jenni's point, though, is not simply to invalidate an idea, because the reality is much more painful. The more the contradiction between the history of France with a capital "F" and its own universalist claim comes to a head, the more often the "festin de sang," the bloodbath wreaked in obsessively enforcing this idea, repeats itself. There is thus an increasing urgency to communicate and legitimize the growing brutality in the French colonies—by means of language, by means of a form of French that abandons its claim of clarity, that produces obscurity. The more language degenerates into propaganda, the more it must obfuscate and nullify its relation to reality.

What is even more immense, however, is the effect of direct violence on language—of systematic torture such as that practiced by French troops in places like the Villa Sésini. This nineteenth-century neo-Moorish-style palazzo, which housed the German Consulate General for a time from 1927, became a French prison during the Algerian War of Independence and the headquarters of the infamous 1st Parachute Regiment of the Foreign Legion (1er REP). During the Vietnam War, this regiment had been almost entirely wiped out and reestablished—not just once, but twice; in the Algiers putsch of 1961, it belonged to the hard core of the failed coup d'état staged by French generals wanting to force de Gaulle to keep Algeria. The regiment was disbanded for this reason in April 1961. In the Villa Sésini, French troops systematically carried out torture, in particular during the Battle of Algiers in 1957, with the deliberate aim of terrorizing the population in order to break any resistance and sympathy for the Front de Libération Nationale (FLN). As a member of the 1er REP, the same unit in which he had already been in action in "Indochina," Jean-Marie Le Pen, the founder of the radical-right Front National, was also stationed at Villa Sésini during this period as an information officer. Le Pen justified torture in various statements he made in the 1950s and 1960s, for instance, in the magazine *Combat*; in his later political career, he tried without success to have the courts prohibit accusations of torture from being made against him.

---

30 Jenni, *The French Art of War*, 420.
31 Jenni, *The French Art of War*, 420.

Jenni's decision to have his protagonist Salagnon transferred from Vietnam to Algeria, and to the Villa Sésini, is thus quite realistic. Salagnon carries in himself the language of military interrogation and torture, as do many others who come to France after the war. The narrator notes about France in one of the "commentaries" that reflexively structure the novel's chapters that it will from then on be a community of people "who can speak to one another because they share the same language, but who fail to speak to each other because they stumble over dead words."[32] The dead words are the words of the dead.[33] They are drenched in the blood of colonial crimes. They are words charged with a reality that official discourse strives to conceal. For Salagnon, it is utterly impossible to use them: "we speak with gobbets of blood in our mouths that hinder the movement of our tongues; we feel we might choke and, in the end, we say nothing."[34]

For the narrator, however, these wars not only change the community defined by French and how this language is used: they change the language itself.

> Language, like an apple, rots where it has been bruised. It dates back to the time when French, the language of empire, the language of the Mediterranean, the language of teeming cities, of deserts and jungles, the time when French, from one end of the world to the other, was the international language of interrogation.[35]

The historical charge with which language has been burdened seems so fundamental to Jenni's understanding of social tensions in contemporary France that, for him, the latent continuation of the colonial period in this language seems like the prolongation of war itself. The sore throat that plagues the narrator during the riots in Lyon is a symbolic affliction. It requires him to literally leave language behind. And this explains the interest the narrator takes in the painting done by the war veteran Victorien Salagnon: "ink-wash painting does not represent," the narrator says, "it is."[36] This art thus stands opposed to the representational logic of language: its structure does not delineate "them" and "us"; for the narrator, its brush moves in the rhythm of breathing, of life itself. In this way, ink-wash painting brings to the page everything that animates life, free of any presuppositions. The strokes of its brush pulsate; the ink appears to the narrator like blood. He begins to surrender to a simple, elemental realism that is finally able to endow life with an undistorted form. Only the gesture counts. It is this movement that brings forth the act of love the narrator experiences

---

32 Jenni, *The French Art of War*, 563.
33 On this point, see again the reflections in the previous chapter on Camille de Toledo's use of the "mots morts" in *L'inquiétude d'être au monde*.
34 Jenni, *The French Art of War*, 563.
35 Jenni, *The French Art of War*, 564.
36 Jenni, *The French Art of War*, 590.

with a French woman of Algerian origin whose story he does not know. This woman enters his life like a miracle who needs no words. And the act of penetration is no longer a lethal act of violence, but an act of reception without precondition.

To reach this moment of inner peace, the narrator-author must fill more than 600 pages with text. Contrary to his impassioned pleas for ink-wash painting, it is language in which he has worked himself to the core—as though writing were not only a means of numbing his sore throat, but the only method of uncovering its causes. Indeed, Jenni counters any illusory escape from language or a longing for a pure presence with this painful telling of history. Could it generate a language for new narratives of freedom?

Kossi Efoui—The Infinite Revolution of Language

For the Togolese-born, France-based writer Kossi Efoui, modern human beings are anxious creatures, persevering in the expectation of a future that looms at best as shadowy signs in the cavern comprising our life world. The title of Efoui's magnificent 2011 novel *The Shadow of Things to Come* is illuminating on an epistemological level: he reveals, with this allusion to Plato's Allegory of the Cave, his distrust of rationalist modernity.[37] His view is that even if modernity has subjugated the entire world, it has not managed to make it more legible or habitable. As in his 2008 novel *Solo d'un revenant*,[38] which won the Grand Prix Littéraire de L'Afrique Noire and the Prix des Cinq Continents de la Francophonie, Efoui narrates our present as an era of dubious progress reduced to nothing but naked survival; he consequently prefaces his narrative with a somber yet rebellious quotation from Imre Kertész, a survivor of Birkenau: "The sole method of suicide that is worthy of respect is to live."

The Shadow of Things to Come appears to be set in West Africa, in an autocratic system that bears numerous structural similarities to the country where its author comes from. The childhood of its narrator-protagonist is overshadowed by the violence of colonization. His distraught mother falls ill after his father is deported to "the Plantation," a place that is emblematic of the horrors of the colonial system in which thousands of individuals were used up as raw human material through forced labor. "The Plantation," this nonplace, is disfigured in the present of the narrative by a gigantomaniacal and absurd memorial erected by the postcolonial dictatorship as a memorial to the time of enslavement. Its shadow is a foreboding premonition that the postcolonial era will by no means be an unqualified era of

---

37 Kossi Efoui, *The Shadow of Things to Come*, trans. Chris Turner (London: Seagull Books, 2013 [2011]).
38 Kossi Efoui, *Solo d'un revenant* (Paris: Editions du Seuil, 2008).

freedom. The opening of the story epitomizes the novel's title: the protagonist is sitting in a narrow dark room, its walls black as night, pierced solely by the light of the moon that shines through a slender opening in the ceiling. Power has gone out everywhere, across the entire country. Dodging military service is dangerous. He must hold out until the smugglers come, the ones who know the way in the dark.

Setting out into a vague future means almost completely leaving his past behind. The only item the narrator has kept on this journey has sentimental value: a photograph showing him with his adopted brother, Ikko, and their father, who is holding a saxophone. His father's skills as a musician had allowed him to preserve a minimum of individuality under the cruel conditions of forced labor: the father took it upon himself to play "right," "juste"—a French word that also rings with the dual sense of correctness and justice. The narrator's father will never return from this retreat into music as a medium of existential self-assertion. After being liberated from the camp as a hero of liberation, he sinks into a deep silence:

> And he, my father, uttered not a word, not a sound. He had come back silent, as silent as those severely disfigured children who issue from their mother's bellies with the same stigmata on their bodies as the war-wounded; those children doomed to a hard life, their heads drooping to one side, leaning permanently towards the same shoulder under the weight of some unknown heavy thought; those children who one already knows at their birth will not speak, who will say nothing of what they have seen in the world, having arrived in it wounded before they are big enough to fight.[39]

The image of this vulnerable creature encapsulates the historical psychology of the loss of language in systems of total domination. Efoui gives us the means to understand how from the very beginning this speechlessness suffocates all social bonds within a postcolonial order. Efoui's book is in this sense a book about language—or more precisely, about its loss.

Louis-Jean Calvet has shown that the abuse of referentiality is *the* principle of colonial language, in that it appropriates and subordinates the world by designating things according to the logic of one particular rationality.[40] This creates a tension between the life world of the colonized and its description in language. Kossi Efoui makes it possible to feel the effects of this alienation by permanently reproducing, in his narrative, the preconditions of speaking under the semiotic weight of imperialism. These preconditions revolve around three central aspects.

First: the conception of Africa as pure nature. This precondition reflects and cements Europe's longstanding prejudice about Africa, which Hegel systematically incorporated into the European idea of progress: Africans do not act, they do not

---

39 Efoui, *The Shadow of Things to Come*, 29.
40 Louis-Jean Calvet, *Linguistique et colonialisme: Petit traité de glottophagie* (Paris: Payot, 1974).

make history, they simply *are*; their happiness and their suffering are the result of evolutionary drives aside from civilization. Africa just is nature.

Second: the conception of Africa as a world that does not need to be explained. When things just are the way they are, they are clear and unambiguous, "aren't they?"— "n'est-ce pas?" Kossi Efoui constantly repeats such rhetorical forms of re-assurance by peppering his text with expressions of colloquial speech such as *n'est-ce pas, après tout* ("after all"), or *tout de même* ("all the same"). These insidiously in-troduce narrative perspectives into the text that cannot be attributed to the narrator himself but are aspects of a textual fabric into which a new discourse is incessantly and subtly inscribed beneath the surface—a discourse that Efoui has called "les grandes rumeurs."[41] These rumors are ultimately nothing other than the ahistorical prejudices underlying the European *grands récits* about the African continent.

And third: the disappearance of colonial subjects in the language of colonial ad-ministration. The world of those who are colonized is first (re)named beyond recog-nition and linguistically expropriated, even before the brutal impact of this violence on any human beings. In the language of power, this means, to quote the words of Efoui: "On account of the circumstances, prepare yourself to be temporarily removed from your nearest and dearest."[42] Or to put it more plainly, it means deportation, forced labor on the plantations, and often death. The cynical intention, the violence, of this forced disappearing is the formulation "the black diet": "the isolation blocks where people were put on the so-called black diet when the final punishment was meted out (the definitive privation of food and water being a weapon preferable to bullets), and the rats who ate the dead and the clothes of the living."[43]

But in the autocratic regime into which colonial society first falls, a result of the power vacuum left behind by colonialism and the impossibility of employing language to establish a democratic community, there is no place to despair at all these victims, all these losses. What this regime needs are heroes who can speak about their reclaimed freedom. Each time the narrator's father is obliged to at-tend one of the ostensibly therapeutic "Discussion Circles" compelled by the re-gime, he makes a "Friday face."[44] What the book presents here is quite obviously not the face of the "noble savage" in the sense of Robinson Crusoe, a figure sup-posedly untouched by decadent cultures, but that of a colonized subject already weighed down by the experience of European civilization. Authoritarian society

---

41 As, for instance, in a conversation with Bartholomäus Grill and myself at the *Haus der Kultu-ren der Welt* in Berlin on May 26, 2011.
42 Efoui, *The Shadow of Things to Come*, 7.
43 Efoui, *The Shadow of Things to Come*, 52.
44 Efoui, *The Shadow of Things to Come*, 69.

demands a mask of authenticity that hides absolute disillusionment. The one who is to learn is precisely the one who already knows. What promise can words still hold at all?

One can read this scene as an announcement that the society of victims is itself losing its innocence. The disconnect between language and lived reality gapes so wide here that the regime's New Speak now even abandons experience itself, eventually banning it altogether. Soon the society that has been liberated will itself become the master. To justify its repression of minorities, it resorts to the internalized mechanisms of a "false speech," a system of lies. This system perpetuates the modes of colonial language. In particular, it surreptitiously reestablishes the division between "civilized' and "uncivilized." It is as though language itself were contaminated, which leads to a loss of human expression that manifests itself in enigmatic signs Ikko draws during his military mission in the jungle.[45] The signs are difficult to interpret. Are they meant as a record of those who have fallen, a kind of body count? But then why are they broken into rhythmic lines? Ikko's world remains opaque. Indeed, if the marks *represent* anything at all, it can only be the impossibility of any signification.

---

45 Efoui, *The Shadow of Things to Come*, 89–90.

How could one escape such a hopeless situation? Events come to a head when the protagonist himself deserts from military service. Those who help him come, like the shadows cast by the future, from another world. They are crocodile-men.

Kossi Efoui heard of these *hommes-crocodiles* in the heart of the African continent, in Burkina Faso, where he was told of a community that lives alongside these dangerous creatures without suffering any harm. The fact that these people might belong to the realm of legend is not important for Efoui. What counts is the idea of them as a people who are completely at one with nature, who have not erected any symbolic order separating themselves from their environment. Efoui sets their home in an archipelago that has been spared the grip of colonialism and dictatorship. Their knowledge of the water, which allows them to avoid the dangerous surf, means the crocodile-men are the only ones who know the way through the reefs:

> I've long known there's no magic formula against the roaring of storms, that there's no prayer that will calm the furious sea. There's just the intelligence of mind of an expert at the helm, who is master, at every second, not of the wind but of his art of tacking, master at every second, and amazed too at each of these seconds that he was not smashed to pieces long ago.[46]

In these sentences—in which the diction of the narrative merges with the activity of the helmsman, and in which the French text enters the ups and downs of the waves—Efoui reveals the ambition of his writing: the writer must be a *homo faber*, a master of expression. It falls to him to create a language that gives access to this other way of listening to the world. His mission is to undertake a symbolic journey to the archipelago of crocodiles. Yet his aim is not to find fantasies of healing in a return to nature's bosom. Kitsch is not part of Efoui's repertoire. His language is unique: rhythmic, playful, but clear. For Efoui, the writer is a language worker in the face of danger; he must escape the emptying out of meaning that has beset words. Into the rationalistic language of modernity, whose designations rob speech of the energy it has to create a life world, i.e., of its poetic power, he must press a new way of structuring what is given to the senses: a way of speaking that produces astonishment, an opening up—a resensitization to the world. In this text, this narrative function falls to the recurring speaker, the *orateur*, whose voice is a *dire vrai*, a truthful speaking, amid the noise of the "great rumors." Efoui thus unfolds a poetics in which writing resembles a "perpetual revolution,"[47] a never-ending reworking of language in which possibilities of a new community emerge and survival becomes possible. For Efoui, the point of writing is to guide readers through the surf to a different imagination of the world. The quotation attributed by the

---

46 Efoui, *The Shadow of Things to Come*, 145–146.
47 The French is "Révolution interminable." English from Derrida, *Learning to Live Finally*, 31.

narrator to the fictional author of an account of the "unimaginable" crimes committed at the plantation can be understood in an autopoetic sense: "So 'novel,' then, seems the right word for the hope that 'readers will use their imagination.'"[48]

Like Alexis Jenni, Kossi Efoui turns against a powerful French tradition of linguistic rationalism, without which the particular characteristics of French imperialism cannot be understood. Efoui, however, is not concerned with defending his own—supposedly national—language or even with a conceptual battle between languages. Rather, his aim is to cast doubt on language in general, because of the violence with which it has been used as a medium of reconciliation. To both authors, speaking and writing seem equivalent in the sense that they risk historical contamination. Yet despite this fundamental skepticism, their writing is simultaneously an immense performative contradiction. Their intention in the resulting texts is not simply to tell history in a different way, but to reveal the ways in which history has been conditioned by the historical use of language.

In my view, attacking language itself as a problem appears to go beyond the historical-political strategy of postcolonial literatures, and not only because this way of grasping language sheds light on the specific violence of the French imperial regime. It aims instead at the fundamental emptying out of human expression one finds in a rationalist modernity that has produced not only moments of emancipation but also imperialism—and with imperialism, the experience and practice of total domination. Despite all the ways in which these accounts differ historically,[49] one can detect a quiet shift here comparable to that taking place in recent literature written in French about the Shoah: the realism of history is now giving way to the realism of survival. Boualem Sansal offers one such example, with his book *Le Village de l'Allemand*, which links the history of the Nazi era with the colonial history of Algeria;[50] or Ivan Jablonka, with his memory of his grandparents murdered by the Nazis, as an event he never experienced.[51] In their own way, both of

---

48 Efoui, *The Shadow of Things to Come*, 54.
49 Robert Stockhammer has attempted to balance these differences against each other in *Ruanda: Über einen anderen Genozid schreiben* (Frankfurt am Main: Suhrkamp, 2005); see also the discussion in Isaac Bazié, "Violences postcoloniales: Enjeux de la représentation et défis de la lecture," in *Violences postcoloniales: Représentations littéraires et perceptions médiatiques*, ed. Isaac Bazié and Hans-Jürgen Lüsebrink (Berlin: Münster Lit, 2011), 15–28.
50 Boualem Sansal, *Le Village de l'Allemand* (Paris: Gallimard, 2008); translated into German as *Das Dorf des Deutschen oder Das Tagebuch der Brüder Schiller* (Gifkendorf: Merlin, 2009) and into English by Frank Wynne as *An Unfinished Business* (New York: Bloomsbury, 2011).
51 Ivan Jablonka, *Histoire des grands-parents que je n'ai pas eus: Une enquête* (Paris: Editions du Seuil, 2012).

these authors pose the question of how one might confront the obsessions of history in order to escape their continuing domination.[52] Can we free ourselves from the traumas history has left in its wake?

Wajdi Mouawad—The Explosion of Silence

"Something that's true makes no noise but explodes in silence," the brother says urgently to his sister.[53] Both of them are huddled among trees, somewhere outside the village where the brother has dragged his sister so they can talk. A mob is raging in the village square, dancing uncontrollably around a mass grave—a scene from Lebanon during the civil war, probably in the latter half of the 1970s. In revenge for previous massacres, incited perhaps by Bachir Pierre Gemayel's Falangists, the mostly Christian inhabitants of a village are murdering the Muslim citizens of the country they all share. The houses in the village with all their belongings are being burned to the ground, twenty-three of the community's children are slaughtered before their parents' eyes: just one more immeasurable abyss of the twentieth century with its never-ending ethnonational, religious obsessions. "You're young, so be a hero and don't listen to anyone!" the brother shouts to his sister. "The truth is always hiding; its silence it what you have to follow and if you hear it whispering, speaking to you, murmuring advice, then beware that it's probably not the truth." He implores his sister to stay, to remain as a witness, and then he runs off, "returns to the place where the children's bodies are still piled up, and begins to cry and pray and sing in their own language, in their own prayers, in their own songs!" The others in the square try to silence him, but he takes the children one by one in his arms, kisses them, weeps for them, and curses the murderers. He is thrown to the ground. His own father rips the son's teeth out with pliers, one by one. To speak again, he would now have to relearn the words of his kind, his kin, his "race."

---

52 On contemporary forms with which novels work through history, see the essays in *Le savoir historique du roman contemporain*, ed. Wolfgang Asholt and Ursula Bähler, *Revue des Sciences Humaines* 321, no. 1 (2016).

53 Wajdi Mouawad, "L'Amour," unpublished manuscript and introduction. All quotes in the following paragraph are from this manuscript. I am grateful to Paul de Sinety, Commissaire général de la présence française à la Foire de Francfort, who had the brilliant idea of opening the book fair with Wajdi Mouawad's performance, and who kindly provided me with the texts in French and German. I thank Wajdi Mouawad himself for his generous permission to quote from these texts here.

But rather than scream, he laughed and laughed, with his mouth bleeding, and after it was all over he stood up, wilder than a beast out of the depths of the earth, and snatching the pliers from his father's hand, spewing, vomiting great gulps of blood, still laughing, he thrust them into his mouth to cut out his own tongue, threw it in his father's face, and through the incoherence of his voice we all heard him screaming words that were quite clear: "I am no longer your son!"

The murderers then finish him off with shots from their guns. The sister, though, whom he had held tight to keep her from dancing with the mob, bears the burden of the survivors. She is the one who assumes the responsibility toward history, the responsibility of witnessing. She takes the humanity of her brother upon herself— as the truth that all who were there know what happened, that no one can deny these events. "As if, by joining [the dead children], he was offering me the gift of their solidarity, their friendship, and the fathomless injustice of their death."

The truth must not allow itself to be warped by screams that drown it out, by stories that would make things right, by appeasing whispers. It survives only in the silence carrying the hush of those who were murdered, until it is witnessed as utterly unbearable and explodes. It creates justice. And though this may seem meager in the face of horrors, narrative is what makes survival possible in the first place: "Because power crushes everything and those who feel powerless are left with no possibility except to tell a story."[54] Narrating the truth enables a symbolic reparation to history that makes it possible to even bear humanity's past at all.

Is not the loss of the teeth, of the tongue, the sign of the impossibility of being human under such cruel circumstances, of joining the dead rather than incurring the culpability of becoming a beast? It is this tongue, the language of the fathers, the connection between generations, that is also torn as the son tears out his own tongue. And did not one of the fathers go mad with pain? "His three children lying at his feet, his mind, his heart destroyed, he began to run in circles around the pit, tearing off his clothes, barking, barking, yelping, I don't remember, he certainly had no words left, that man, he had no language left, nothing left to curse those who had done this to him."[55]

The great need to recover language, to be human, is what is told in this story "L'Amour" (Love) by Wajdi Mouawad. Within it lies the glowing core of his entire oeuvre. Born in 1968 in Deir al-Qamar in the Shuf district of Lebanon, Wajdi Mouawad grew up as a child in France and then in Canada, where his parents had emigrated. Today, he once again lives in France, where he directs the Théâtre

---

54 This is how the leader of the chorus responds to Oedipus's question of why this story of failure and death should be told at all for posterity; Wajdi Mouawad, *Les Larmes d'Œdipe* (Montréal, Arles: Actes Sud-Papiers, 2016), 20.
55 Mouawad, "L'Amour."

National de la Colline in Paris. The film adaptation of *Incendies* by Denis Ville-neuve,[56] the second volume of Mouawad's drama tetralogy *Le Sang des promesses*,[57] has also introduced him to audiences beyond the theater. His novels and plays are nonetheless still waiting to be discovered, especially in the context of German and European discourses on memory, as appropriations of history that paradigmatically express the dilemma of the twentieth century. How can the claim to humanity have any legitimacy if it cannot find language to express its utterly denuded, animalistic core, to regain this very thing, language, in the same way that a child uses language to gain an awareness of its existence? Language and lineage are closely connected; tearing out one's tongue, putting an end to speech, also breaks the chain of life. The dehumanization inherent in pain and violence requires the truthfulness of narration—of poetic language, one might even say, with reference to Adorno's question about the possibility of poetry after Auschwitz—for any possibility of being human at all:

> I understand where this idea comes from, of no longer being able to tell any *histoire*. But I'm not sure how to say this to you . . . ok, sure. But I'm sorry, I've got to go because I have an *histoire* to write! . . . Maybe it's also because I was born in Lebanon and grew up in Québec, where they don't have this guilt about the concentration camps. Or in any case we don't carry it the same way. Above all, we have not intellectualized it in the same way. We have not con-structed a Cartesian argument that says you can't give testimony about what happened in the gas chambers, and therefore one can't tell *histoires* anymore. This I understand completely. But to be frank, I don't carry that guilt around. My country needs to tell *histoires*. It's abso-lutely crucial. Because otherwise it will never cope. This is the only way it can preserve its memory and free itself from the pain in which it finds itself. Just imagine taking away the *histoires*! This is a culture made from *histoires* . . . it's impossible. . . . I think that this ques-tion of *histoire*, of the possibility of fiction, is a very Franco-German one.[58]

It seemed that the silence in the hall was about to explode when Wajdi Mouawad opened the 2017 Frankfurt Book Fair with his story "L'Amour." Mouawad had

---

56 Denis Villeneuve, *Incendies*, DVD, Paris 2014.

57 Wajdi Mouawad, *Le Sang des promesses*: 1. *Littoral* (1999); 2. *Incendies* (2003); 3. *Forêts* (2006); 4. *Ciels* (2009) (Montréal, Arles: Actes Sud, 2009). Published in English as *Tideline*, trans. Shelley Tepperman (2010); *Scorched*, trans. Linda Gaboriau (2009); *Forests*, trans. Linda Gaboriau (2011); *Heavens*, trans. Linda Gaboriau (2014) (all Toronto: Playwrights Canada Press). "*Tideline, Scorched, Forests, Heavens*—like the desire to recreate the elements, to respond to their loss. *Tideline*, for instance, is wrested from the sea; *Scorched* springs from desire, while the *Forests* come from the mountains and *Heavens* have been snatched from the birds." Wajdi Mouawad, *Le Sang des promesses: Puzzle, racines et rhizomes* (Montréal, Arles: Acte Sud, 2009), 6.

58 Lise Lenne, "Autour de Littoral, Incendies et Forêts," *Littoral, Incendies* et *Forêts*," interview with Wajdi Mouawad, in *Agôn: Revue des arts de la scène* (ENSLyon), paragraph 43, www.agon. ens-lyon.fr/index.php?id=290, accessed March 15, 2018.

concluded his text montage by briefly recounting the story of the mythical figure Hecabe, the last queen of Troy, wife of Priam. Of Priam it is told that when she saw her daughter Polyxene, who had been murdered by the Greeks, she lost her speech, began barking, and turned into a dog.[59] This transformation points to the goddess Hecate, the demonic mediator between the living and the realm of the dead, a ghostly mistress who is sometimes accompanied in depictions by packs of howling dogs representing the souls of those who have died, and especially the souls of childless women.[60] Of course, this refers to the myth, to the universal narrative, of the suffering of parents bereft of their children.[61] But it also refers to the fact that the murder will never escape the claims of justice, that it will not go unpunished. Like Hecate, it too moves through the twilight and lays claim on those born after it, on those who try but fail to flee from the ties of their past. Their entanglement with history remains preserved in silence.

Here, the complexity of the text-video montage with which Mouawad confronted the auditorium becomes apparent. The story of the murder of these twenty-three children was told to him by an old woman who was the same sister who had witnessed her brother's act of despair. She took from this witnessing an obligation to heal the wound inflicted by this infanticide upon the world. She devoted herself to love. Her life as a prostitute gives birth to twenty-three children whom she raises as a mother. She responds with love to counter the boundless hate. But what she also tells Wajdi Mouawad is that his mother's family was involved in the massacre.

He is speechless:

> Behind every word there is a why. And the answer to these whys is always the same: the Lebanese civil war, the exile of my parents. The child who loses his mother tongue does not know that he is losing it in the very moment of its loss; and as an adult, far from the shore where he was born, he will only have the taste of blood in his mouth. The taste of his lost tongue. As an adult, he will say: I remember that I spoke Arabic, and I remember that I spoke French, but I don't remember the transition from one to the other. It's like a knife in your throat.[62]

Whereas the protagonist of the story "L'Amour" tears out his tongue out of love for these victims, so as to interrupt the power of genealogy, Mouawad is left with

---

59 See Ruth E. Harder, "Hekabe," *Der neue Pauly: Enzyklopädie der Antike*, ed. Hubert Cancik and Helmuth Schneider, vol. 5 (Stuttgart: J.B. Metzler, 1998), 261–262.

60 Sarah Iles Johnston, "Hekate," in Cancik and Schneider, *Der neue Pauly*, 267–270.

61 See Lisa Evertz, "Mythos und Gewalt im (post)dramatischen Theater bei Wajdi Mouawad und Olivier Py" (PhD dissertation, Ludwig Maximilian University of Munich, 2018).

62 Mouawad, "L'Amour." Opening of the Frankfurt Book Fair 2017. In French, "langue" means both tongue and language.

the "taste of blood" in his mouth that forces him to take responsibility toward his own family history, but without the tongue he needs to do so. The Arabic language of his mother is the language of his own entanglement with the history of violence, the trace of his own sense of guilt. Yet this sentiment cannot be put into words because Wajdi Mouawad does not speak Arabic, a language that was erased in exile within his immediate, Christian family. He thus continues to write (his own) history as the insecurity of his own existence. Charlotte Farcet points out that in his younger years as an artist, Mouawad identified with Gregor Samsa, Kafka's alter ego from *The Metamorphosis*, who wakes up one morning to find himself transformed into an enormous, ungainly insect, unable to interact in any adequate way with the world.[63]

His salvation is the "language of hospitality": French. It is in French that Wajdi Mouawad told his story to those in the audience at the book fair, and to us. The French language has taken him in, it has become the language he has to give voice to history and thus to maintain that claim to humanity that the brother in this story imposes on his sister as a responsibility. But in doing so, Mouawad inscribes his own history, and this entire history, into French; it becomes part of the francophone community of speakers. But is this inscription not uncanny to this community? This is where Mouawad unfolds a final narrative layer.

> At a moment when the question of who is welcome is being so violently posed at Europe's gates, you have asked an Asian to speak at the opening night of the Frankfurt Book Fair, with France as its guest of honor. It is as though the Greeks were to ask a Trojan to open one of their great dramatic competitions. To ask the enemy. Because if the migrant is the threat today, then you have invited that threat to speak.[64]

The story of the murder of these twenty-three children was followed by a video showing an unchanging, frontal view of Wajdi Mouawad's face for several minutes as it appeared before the door of a house. In its characteristics and colors, the film was reminiscent of Pasolini's *Edipo Re*, the superb adaptation of the Oedipus myth from the period of Pasolini's work in the late 1960s, which was influenced by psychoanalysis. Mouawad then began to bark, and he kept barking, deep and hard, until he was drooling at the mouth and his voice had been rubbed raw and his face distorted, so that he lost his human countenance and became an animal creature. The hall was gripped by the scene. Emmanuel Macron, expected to speak next and give the evening a grand political opening, momentarily found himself at a loss for words before expressing how troubled he felt.

---

63 See Charlotte Farcet, "Postface" to *Littoral* (= *Le Sang des promesses* 1) (Arles: Actes Sud, 2009), 154.

64 Mouawad, "L'Amour," opening of the Frankfurt Book Fair 2017.

Wajdi Mouawad had taken on the role of the Trojan. His barking was meant to express the pain of Lebanon, the pain of infinite loss that has come from the immeasurable violence narrated by "L'Amour." But the narration in French blurs the boundaries of identity, as though the French language itself were to offer a space of resonance for this pain. This assemblage thus infiltrated the language of hospitality, smuggling into its discourse that part of history that lies in the combination of Arabic with French in the colonial past, that is still embodied by Wajdi Mouawad himself. French was the language of Lebanon because Lebanon had been a French mandate following the Sykes-Picot Agreement of 1916 and the League of Nations settlement of 1920. Lebanon's national independence in 1943, which was above all an independence from Syria, and the long dominance of the Maronites in its complex state structure can still be traced back to French policy. This prehistory holds some of the reasons for the country's sorrowful past. Hence once again, as a colonial language possessing its own entanglement with the ethnoreligious background of the Lebanese civil war, French itself is called upon to express this history. Wajdi Mouawad has only this one language; it is his exile and where he begins his reappropriation.[65] In it, silence and a coming to awareness find articulation in ghostly form.

Fate strikes us blind(ly), just as it did Oedipus in his ignorance, or in the same way that the sister from "L'Amour" grasps her history only across the span of a lifetime. In a Lebanese milieu where militias are preparing for war, the omnipresence of weapons conjures up fantasies of power in little Wajdi. He dreams of later becoming a fighter with the Maronite units. In an interview with Josyane Savigneau for *Le Monde*, Mouawad comments on these entanglements as follows:

> What shocks me about Sophocles is his obsession with showing how tragedy befalls the one who has blinded themselves and so fails to see their own hubris. This pushed me to ask about what I did not see of myself, what the world does not see of itself, this blind spot that could rend the fabric of my life by revealing itself. Revealing the fool that I am. What would have become of me if I had stayed in Lebanon?[66]

Would Mouawad have been involved in the Sabra and Shatila massacres if his family had not left the country shortly before? The drama exposes us to the peripeteias of life, the unpredictable turn of fate into happiness and misfortune.

---

65 See Françoise Coissard, *Wajdi Mouawad: Incendies* (Paris: H. Champion, 2014), 10.

66 Josyane Savigneau, "Raconter la manière avec laquelle je regarde le monde," interview with Wajdi Mouawad, in *Le Monde*, June 24, 2011, www.lemonde.fr/idees/article/2011/06/24/wajdi-mouawad-raconter-la-maniere-avec-laquelle-je-regarde-le-monde_1540516_3232.html, accessed April 30, 2021.

In his 2011 autobiographical essay *Le Poisson soi* (roughly: The fish-self), Mouawad generalizes the experience of being blindly at the mercy of war, which he understands as an aspect of his life that has accompanied him from the time of his birth during the Vietnam War to the killings in Yugoslavia, Rwanda, and Algeria.[67] His self, he says, is a dung beetle, a ball-rolling insect that draws its life from animal scat, from the "shit" of the world, which it "metabolizes" and transforms into a mirror.[68] Life beneath the sign of war is performatively transformed into a trace. Mouawad's partial sentences dissolve into a great flow without periods or commas; the spaces disappear and give way to a string of words; upper- and lowercase dissolve into one another; it is only the places of events that still stand out, capitalized; the I who would be tasked with developing a critical self-awareness in history dissolves amid the great, never-ending war:

> jesuisnépendantlaguerreduVietnamquelquessemainesaprèslesévénementsdeMai68. . .
>
> —
>
> iwasbornduringtheVietnamwarafewweeksaftertheeventsofMay1968. . .

War is universal; it is the great scene of existence. The tragedies of humanity are played out here, in those passions that incessantly return: obsessions with origin and descent, revenge and hubris, fratricide and patricide, incest, abduction, and separation—along with new bonds of kinship and belonging, unimagined magnificence and generosity. Herein lies for Wajdi Mouawad the importance of the Greeks' mythic understanding of the world, the universal status of epos and of tragedy.[69] "The world thinks it sees and keeps poking its eyes out when it's too late. Always the same story."[70] The tetralogy *Le Sang des promesses* is to be read as a longing for catharsis, for a liberation from those inner forces that blanket humanity with war. Mouawad's work is first and foremost a work of theater; it draws its pulse from the embodiment of drama, from the presence of human beings on stage.[71] At the same time, his way of writing is itself part of the dramaturgy. He has repeatedly revealed this dramaturgical process, and he has illustrated its preconditions in his book *Le Sang des promesses: Puzzle, racines et rhizomes.*[72]

---

67 Wajdi Mouawad, *Le Poisson soi (Version quarante-deux ans)* (Montréal: Boréal, 2011), 44–45.
68 Mouawad, *Le Poisson soi*, 42–43.
69 See Coissard, *Wajdi Mouawad: Incendies*, 25–29.
70 As spoken by the chorus to Oedipus and Antigone in Wajdi Mouawad, *Les Larmes d'Œdipe*, 18.
71 This dramatic potential, however, also influences his novelistic works, from psychological and poetological points of view. See especially Wajdi Mouawad, *Anima: A Novel* (Vancouver: Talonbooks, 2017).
72 Wajdi Mouawad, *Le Sang des promesses: Puzzle, racines et rhizomes* (Montréal, Arles: Actes Sud, 2009), 6.

In contrast to classical tragedy, the protagonists in *Le Sang des promesses* are not noble heroes. It is as our contemporaries that they are subject to fate. Nor are there any gods who could restore social or moral order. "What gods? Where are the gods?" asks Antigone in *Les Larmes d'Œdipe*, Mouawad's adaptation of the Oedipus myth. The gods are like children, Oedipus replies; we must be like parents to them. Human beings themselves bear responsibility for the worlds that remain untouched; only humans can protect them. Mouawad's reimagining and continuation of Sophocles's drama leads the blinded figure of Oedipus to modern-day Greece, where he has come to die; there, in the ruins of a theater, a coryphaeus tells him the real-life story of fifteen-year-old Alexandros Grigoropoulos, who was shot by police in 2008 while participating in a youth uprising in the Exarchia neighborhood of Athens. Every year since then, the death has been commemorated, leading to riots in many European cities. The boy had run to his death completely unawares. Just as the language of the oracle remains incomprehensible for the mythical Oedipus until he has committed his crimes, so too in the play the "monstrosity" of our time remains incomprehensible until it devours its children:

CORYPHAEUS. There is a monstrosity at the entrance of Athens that devours life.

ANTIGONE. What monstrosity?

CORYPHAEUS. It has no form, other than that of crushed lives.

OEDIPE. What is its name.

CORYPHAEUS. Crisis, austerity, corruption, liberalism, profit, who knows, no one sees it clearly and that is its principle. Error that cannot be spoken. Cannot be named. When it speaks, we suffer its devastation without understanding anything that it says. The thing that devours us cannot be traced.

OEDIPE. Tell everything anyway. What is the tribute it is demanding from you?

CORYPHAEUS. Dreams. Joy. Life.

OEDIPE. Any monstrosity can be defeated.

CORYPHAEUS. It devours even this hope.[73]

In this discussion between these three characters, Oedipus tells how he answered the riddle of the Sphinx at the gates of Thebes to free the city from this monster. As we know, Oedipus's answer to the Sphinx's complicated question was "man," the human being. And so it is that this is also Mouawad's answer to the monstrosity of the present. To recognize the human being, to take responsibility for it: this is the task of our

---

73 Mouawad, *Les Larmes d'Œdipe*, 33.

time. In finally lying down to die in the ruins of the theater, Mouawad's Oedipus refers to our fate and to the drama, the narrating of destiny, that holds the power of knowledge and catharsis. It is not the gods who can restore order, but only the will of human beings—the will to make possible something new by understanding history, by putting it into language.

Here, catharsis means liberation through the power of narration. In a first, unpublished version of *Le Poisson soi*, Mouawad writes that for him this power is not at all merely symbolic but existentially significant: "Theater is also about finding the militia that I dreamed of as a child. What would have become of me with a gun in my hand? . . . For me, dropping my pencil means once again picking up the Kalashnikov."[74] The function of writing is to articulate one's own *histoire*, one's own (hi)story, and its inherent violence, to retrieve it without repeating it. Writing thus follows the logic of both an unavoidable injury—those "bruises of memory"—and their treatment through the application of "disinfecting words."[75] And there is nothing to be taken for granted about the path to language. It is rather something imposed, compelled. History is a painful pressure point in that it permanently raises the question of the self: "I wish I didn't have to say / I / To worry about anything anymore / I just wish someone would say / HE / For me / To be free of it."[76] The question of the I leads to the sediments of one's existence, to those "living fossils," the "fish-self" that carries a heavy weight as a fossilization of identity but offers no access allowing its recovery.[77] The Arabic language has been buried with this self. But French, the language in which all of this is captured as metaphors, is itself a displacement that can put its lack into language but not suspend it. Hence language is the resistance in that classical interpretation of an odyssey as a search for identity, a return to oneself, that pulls Wajdi Mouawad toward the journey to Lebanon.

In this context, the report that Wajdi Mouawad submitted to the Canada Council for the Arts, which had awarded him a grant for a stay in Lebanon in 1992 that enabled his first return to the country of his violent early childhood, is extremely telling.[78] Mouawad asks for understanding for the fact that he was not able to realize his writing project, explaining that the encounter was nevertheless fundamental and he is sure it will determine his further writing. Under the weight of his impressions

---

74 Quoted from Coissard, *Wajdi Mouawad: Incendies*, 27.

75 "Les Mots mercurochrome / Sur les ecchymoses de la mémoire"; Mouawad, *Le Poisson soi*, 16.

76 Mouawad, *Le Poisson soi*, 16.

77 Mouawad, *Le Poisson soi*, 19.

78 Wajdi Mouawad, "Rapport écrit en mai 1995 pour le Conseil des arts du Canada," in *Le Sang des promesses: Puzzle, racines, rhizomes*, 15–20.

in Lebanon, he writes, his language was broken: "Over there, I didn't write a word. I couldn't write a word. I didn't want to write a single word about this subject. I wrote other things. Letters, yes, words, sentences, but that's all, there was nothing to be done, no point in insisting."[79] There was something "abysmal, uncontrollable" about this journey planned as a homecoming, or at least a return. The images flooded him; he burned them by the hundreds onto color film. And he attached one of them to his report: a photo of a house in Beirut from whose roof he had himself witnessed with his own eyes, as a seven-year-old boy, what is now known as the Ain el-Rammaneh incident or bus massacre, in which all the Palestinian occupants of a bus were shot dead on April 13, 1975, presumably by Falangists, and which is generally considered to have ignited the Lebanese civil war.

In Mouawad's work, then, the psychological relief that comes from acting out inner conflicts is not a suddenly triggered, cathartic excitement; it occurs via a laborious, yet highly inventive process of finding language for what must be said. This can certainly be understood in a therapeutic sense and reveals a modern anthropology that would employ narrative to bring to consciousness what escapes the self—to articulate what is unknown, unconscious. *Le Poisson soi* reveals the self as the problem of the stranger within oneself, which can be retraced in Wajdi Mouawad's writing in the anthropological sense as that which has been repressed, as an unknown aspect of biography or something that has been buried by history. In their protagonists' unexpected encounter with Lebanon, *Littoral* and *Incendies* play with a complex interweaving of these metaphors. Here, self-awareness is nothing fixed or familiar but rather a movement, a process that must first be established in narration.[80] In *Incendies*, this process is simultaneously the work's shaping poetic principle, which gradually reveals the story as an investigative gesture in which two siblings, Jeanne and Simon Marwan, track down the Lebanese backstory of their mother Narwal. The narrative unfolding of identity begins with circumstantial evidence as clues for a multifaceted diagnosis—a method that Carlo Ginzburg has shown to be a basic principle for the modern construction of human knowledge.[81] Modern social pathologies develop their theories for the overall condition of the world by beginning with local signs or circumstantial evidence. When the protagonists in *Incendies* become

---

79 Mouawad, "Rapport," 16.
80 See Lise Lenne, "*Le poisson-soi*: de l'aquarium du moi au littoral de la scène . . .," in *Agôn: Revue des arts de la scène* (= En), paragraph 3, https://doi.org/10.4000/agon.328, accessed May 28, 2021.
81 Carlo Ginzburg and Anna Davin, "Morelli, Freud and Sherlock Holmes: Clues and Scientific Method," *History Workshop*, no. 9 (Spring 1980): 5–36.

detectives on the case of their own lives, they are also pursuing the trail to discover the constitution of our own time. They are participating observers, speculating about the construction of the self and of society, acting on a stage of existential drama and genocidal modernity. They find themselves, blind, on both stages and strive to wrest understanding from the deep layers they encounter.[82] This is the task in a chaos-world:

> To take a risk. To get wet, to attach myself to a point of view on the world. To be stained by existence like a glass of wine forever stains a white tablecloth.[83]

Precisely because *Le Sang des promesses* does not—because it cannot—follow a classical logic of the Odyssey as a homecoming, the tetralogy tells of the new beginning within narration. This is most clearly made manifest in the first play, *Tideline*. The plot can be easily summarized: Wilfrid, a man who grew up and lives in Québec, learns of the death of his father, who had never denied his paternity but had not fully embraced it, either. From the reaction of the mother's family, Wilfrid suspects that something is lurking in the deep layers of his family, something about which he knows nothing. He thus opens letters that his father had written to him but never sent. The letters reveal two facts that upend his life. First, that his mother died during his birth. Either the mother or the child could have survived; his father was faced with a choice; and he followed the will of Wilfrid's mother in choosing the child. For his family, this made his father a murderer. And second, Wilfrid learns that his father is from Lebanon and never truly felt at home in exile. Wilfrid decides to bring his father's body to Lebanon in order to bury him in his homeland. And here begins Wilfrid's encounter with his own buried childhood.

Wilfrid's encounter with the village where his father grew up is an encounter with a haunting silence. The elders are unable to move beyond the war. They are epitomized in the figure of Hakim, a former militia chief who still delights with boundless sadism in the atrocities of the past;[84] and in Issam, who calls out in reply to the dreams of a young woman, Simone, who will not stop singing: "What were you hoping for? To bring the dead back to life? It's over! Everything's over!"[85] Wazâân, the blind man who sees what those with vision no longer can, is the only character who senses that the arrival of Wilfrid and the return of the dead father will bring a change. His first dialogue with Wilfrid points the way:

---

82 See also Lise Lenne, "*Le poisson-soi*," paragraphs 4–9.
83 As Wajdi Mouawad notes in Jean-François Côté, *Architecture d'un marcheur: Entretiens avec Wajdi Mouawad* (Montréal: Leméac, 2005), 15.
84 See Mouawad, *Tideline*, 73–77.
85 Mouawad, *Tideline*, 72.

WAZÂÂN Listen to what the star says, to what your merciless star is telling you.

WILFRID What is it saying?

WAZÂÂN Keep moving forward, even if you no longer believe. Keep going even when you've lost sight of your goal, keep going even when reason paralyzes you, even when you discover the futility of what going forward really means. Keep going even if you've lost all pride, all ability to hope. Keep moving forward.[86]

Since the village cemetery is overcrowded and the older generation seems incapable of accepting the history that comes with this corpse, Wilfrid follows Wazâân's advice and sets off at dawn into the unknown, seeking a place to bury his father. His is accompanied by Simone. She represents the younger generation who cannot make themselves heard under the laws of their elders. The song of these youth is the longing to tell their own story, to finally speak with truth, to arrive in reality, to exist. En route, they meet other young men and women whom they invite to join with them, among them, Sabbé.

SIMONE Do you want to leave?

SABBÉ Leave! That's a strange word. This country has turned into a real joke, everyone wants to leave. Everyone. And you, you're looking for a place to bury your father.[87]

Just as Simone can't stop singing, Sabbé can't stop laughing. Both can be interpreted as dissociative disorders stemming from traumatic experiences in childhood, as evidence of a strong rejection of these figures' social surroundings. All the young adults who gradually join them along the way have had horrific experiences of war: Sabbé's hysterical laughter set in when militiamen first chopped off his father's arms—"Since you know how to write," they tell him—and then they cut out his tongue and finally "slice off his head" and hand it to little Sabbé. Massi, who no longer has a family, laughs too. Amé, who had been taught to kill during the civil war, brutally murdered his own father out of fear when he encountered him at night without recognizing him. Since then, Amé has been turning a light bulb on and off every night, like a Morse code repeated incessantly, a compulsive action of psychological resistance and defense. In the same way that Wilfrid carries his father's body, Josephine carries around phone books in which she records the names of the missing that she has sought out. Simone, Amé, Sabbé, Massi, Josephine—what they all share is that they have lost their language. The horror Mouawad recounts in "L'Amour" is their fate. The society of the older generation makes it impossible for them to speak, because with its language this generation already conveys a

---

86 Mouawad, *Tideline*, 81–82.
87 Mouawad, *Tideline*, 91.

continuation of the horror. The younger generation counters this silence with a sign system of emotions, "a resistance cell made of shouts, singing and messages thrown into the river."[88]

Slowly they come together, village by village, and each tells their story to the others. To tell their story is to exist; to listen is to be in solidarity. And it is thus, in mutual respect for each other's personal telling, that they slowly weave a new community. Narrating the drama is how humanity survives. This is not only to be understood as an overcoming of pain, but also more concretely in the sense of the new generation speaking. Their narration can once again offer hope to the principles of humanity that are the aim of their liberation: recognition, solidarity, love.

Their speaking, though, does not emerge into a vacuum. There is no neutral ground. And herein lies the resistance to the truth. The truth cannot simply be swallowed. Those who experience it must change themselves, and this is why asserting the truth is a difficult task:

> AMÉ During the war I planted bombs.
>
> SIMONE The bomb I want to plant is worse than the worst bomb that ever exploded in this country.
>
> AMÉ We'll plant them in buses, in restaurants . . .
>
> SIMON No no, this bomb can only explode in a single place. In people's minds.
>
> AMÉ What do you mean?
>
> SIMON We'll go tell stories. Everything they want to make us forget, we'll invent, we'll say it! They'll be forced to smash our heads in!
>
> AMÉ What kind of stories?
>
> SIMONE Your story, my story. Everything we've never said out loud.[89]

This is why there is no homecoming. The so-called origins offer no paradise to be recovered. Wilfrid will not bury his father. He decides to give him over to the sea. As a ritual act, both father and son are set free: in ablutions at the edge of the ocean, attended by all these traveling companions, the father acknowledges that his journey is not an end point but a departure that will carry history on indefinitely. He speaks in the imagination of his son, as one who is dead, into the human dimension of the drama that appears before the reader: "the open sea, / That carries everything away / And that's now taking me, / That's taking me, taking me,

---

88 Mouawad, *Tideline*, 114.
89 Mouawad, *Tideline*, 84.

taking me . . ."[90]—words that continue on and on, across multiple lines, like the course of the waves, the eternal course of the world. For the son, however, the coast opens up to become a new horizon; the son recovers language and thus regains the principle of reality. Here, the imaginary knight Giromelans takes his leave, as a figure embodying Wilfrid's childish fantasies of omnipotence, as one who had constantly defended Wilfrid in his own imagination against the unbearable incursions of Wilfrid's repressed childhood memories, and against his origins in violence.

All of this can be read autobiographically. Wajdi Mouawad's writing cannot be separated from his own history, even as it transcends this origin toward a universal form of tragedy. His francophone theater provided him with a language that came to him in exile like a sound might come to a cat perched at the edge of a roof, forcing it to stop and listen.[91] This is not a language that can be taken for granted or understood simply, transparently. It bears a wound. It offers no healing through a transfigured, childlike unity. But this form of French has taken up, absorbed the silence. As with the cat that continues to scamper along because the sound has turned out to be harmless, here a moment of liberation sets in:

> This is proof that I didn't know how to read and understand Sophocles well enough, to read the affirmation he offers on every page that while hubris brings violence, for the Greeks there is always a moment of dazzling light that shines forth from this misfortune, as with Oedipus; that after the pain and suffering, something subsides, a tension, an inflammation that no longer needs to exist.[92]

---

90 Mouawad, *Tideline*, 144.

91 This is a reference to the painting *Le chat* (The cat) by François Vincent, which hangs in Wajdi Mouawad's apartment, and which he evokes in his collection of materials for *Le Sang des promesses* in precisely this sense: "I absolutely recognize myself in this cat, which for a moment was drawn to a noise that distracted him from his original destination. In my life, this noise was the theater. It appeared quite suddenly, with my exile." Wajdi Mouawad, *Le Sang des promesses. Puzzle, racines et rhizomes*, 4 (for the image), 6 (for the text).

92 Mouawad, *Les Larmes d'Œdipe*, 8–9.

Fraternité—Possibilities of a New We

Published in France in 2011, Shumona Sinha's novel *Assommons les pauvres!*—or "Beat Up the Poor"—scandalously burst into the debate about the treatment of migrants and asylum seekers.[1] It relentlessly exposes the inhumanity of an asylum system in which refugees are managed according to principles that cannot respond to their misery. As a symbol of the system's crisis, the background to the novel is the "Jungle of Calais," the illegal tent camps that had formed in the port area of the city and near the entrance to the Channel Tunnel, and which the state has cleared and razed to the ground several times since 2009. During the so-called refugee crisis of 2015, the camps sprung up once again. Then in 2016 they were supposed to be closed for good. A nature reserve now occupies the land where the "jungle" once stood, but camps still pop up in the region. The Jungle of Calais thus represents the hopeless situation of refugees who can neither pass through nor truly arrive, who dwell in an in-between world of illegality; it represents the failure of European refugee and immigration policies. And yet the target of Shumona Sinha's indictment is not only immigration and European asylum systems but Europe's relationship to the non-European world overall. "It would be wrong to think that the rich like to perpetuate poverty. Because they don't. They prefer to see the world evolve, not too ugly, not too sad, especially not half dead like an abandoned dog dying on their doorstep."[2] Where does Europe stand when there is a call for *fraternité*—for human solidarity?

Shumona Sinha's Farewell to the Other

When Shumona Sinha's book was published in 2011, she had been working for two years as an interpreter for the French migration authority; she promptly lost her job. At times verging toward reportage, her depictions had gone too far in hitting a nerve of failure. Told from the narrative perspective of a translator, *Assommons les pauvres!* describes the inner workings of an asylum system that accepts people through a restrictive filter—in this case, proof of political or ethnic persecution and threat to life and limb. The scores of individuals whose fates the narrator translates into French come mainly from Bengal and Bangladesh, and they come for the most part to escape the misery and lack of a future in their lives. This means they have to invent their stories, at least in part, and it becomes

---

1 Shumona Sinha, *Assommons les pauvres* (Paris: Édition de l'Olivier, 2011).
2 Sinha, *Assommons les pauvres*, 120.

increasingly clear that the role of translator is no neutral one. Sometimes nuances determine whether what is being said fits into the horizon of expectation embedded within in the system's administrative language. Should a translator convey the fabrications of men—the same men whom the narrator ironically exposes—by participating in proceedings that are at times grotesque?

> Some of the experts and magistrates needed a quarter of an hour before they were able to locate, on their maps, the applicants' countries of origin. With eyes wide open, they swallowed the fables of crimes told to them by the lawyers. All of it was popular, chaotic, shrill theater made for the crowds. Stories made up from scratch.[3]

Should she give herself over to a deeply felt solidarity with a "Chechen Eve"?

> I listen to their stories with tears in my eyes. Tears of distress and shame. Their lies make me blush. Yet I try to find the alleyways and exits between their words. If only I could—if only I could clear a path, could mark the way to save them amid the confusion, amid the sentences jumbled like entangled, entwined roots of trees on a riverbank.[4]

Caught between these refugees and the French authorities, the translator's position becomes increasingly untenable. Herself an immigrant from India, she is faced with a conflict tearing her apart that is structurally unresolvable: her own rise in French society catapults her to the "other side of things," where she becomes part of, and complicit in, the system of those who have privilege. For her, solidarity with these unfortunate refugees means acting without loyalty. "Loving Is Betraying" is Sinha's title for one chapter,[5] which presents the narrator's severing of old ties as a brutal leap into her new life, at the cost of incomprehension and loss: "I no longer recognize them, my parents."[6]

How is it possible here to be at peace with oneself? The narrator experiences a physicality with men whose presence brings her to feel her own vitality and vigor. But she is bereft of devotion and love; she is unable to embrace these other men because betrayal is always lurking nearby: "I'm the one smiling, radiant, after coitus."[7] And: "This is my own personal nihilism. Nothingness is a lavish celebration."[8] Eventually the situation falls apart; a conflict in the metro escalates; an asylum seeker recognizes her, shouts at her; and she strikes him with a bottle of wine. "Attacking him becomes the best defense of myself. It's a way to get out of myself and turn toward the other. It's worse than selfishness. It's better

---

3 Sinha, *Assommons les pauvres*, 118–119.
4 Sinha, *Assommons les pauvres*, 101.
5 Sinha, *Assommons les pauvres*, 103.
6 Sinha, *Assommons les pauvres*, 107.
7 Sinha, *Assommons les pauvres*, 94.
8 Sinha, *Assommons les pauvres*, 93.

than selfishness. At least it means taking an interest in the other."[9] She finds herself in a police cell. This is how the novel starts. This is the place from which she must justify herself.

Narrating from the aftermath is always subject to the presumption of wanting, of being able, to have a therapeutic effect. It makes it possible to find language for what has been survived, to process it. But doesn't Shumona Sinha seem to be telling us just the opposite? There's nothing to be saved here. Moving to the other side, to the side of wealth, leads at the same time to liberation and self-negation. "Crossing the border is irreversible," the narrator says. "It resembles mourning, the secret crime, loss of self, loss of reference, loss of life," she continues, speaking of this violent act in the same way she does of her own path.[10] It is from Baudelaire's collection of short prose poems *Paris Spleen* that Shumona Sinha takes the title of her novel. In Baudelaire's poem "Beat Up the Poor," the narrator attacks a beggar who fights back with the same brutal blows he received, giving the narrator a black eye and knocking out four teeth. "Thus it was," the narrator proclaims, "that my energetic treatment had restored his pride and given him new life."[11] In Sinha's telling, at least, the victim remains silent. The perpetrator is trapped. Is there no escape from a world of class segregation and racialization?

As an author, Sinha vents the rage in her soul through writing. With a view that is at times ironic, at times poetic, she wrests a bit of independence and hope from a brutal reality. The representation of misery does not remain fettered to its object. Rather, it renders its characters with sympathy and humor; it portrays their absurd situations with poetry and a vital spirit. It is only in her language that the bitter reality of misery comes to be expressed—because in this language a contrast, another possibility, appears.

It is no coincidence that this book is written by a translator. Translation in a broader sense is one of the great paradigms of contemporary cultural theory. It presupposes that others are different, that we thus cannot wholly understand them; but that we can still translate their thinking into our language, since they too are human beings. Shumona Sinha centers her novel on this problem. With her narrator, we witness the rooms of the asylum office, where understanding becomes a serious matter. We sit at the tables of a world in which some are already "inside" and others want to find a way "in." Taking on the dangerous journey is not enough; the endeavor must be explained, as well. The fact that we are

---

9 Sinha, *Assommons les pauvres*, 149.
10 Sinha, *Assommons les pauvres*, 149.
11 Charles Baudelaire, "Beat Up the Poor," in *Paris Spleen*, trans. Louise Varese (New York: New Directions 1970), 102.

forced to give an account of ourselves tragically reveals the existential situation of the asylum seekers. Narrating means legitimizing oneself as someone. But in the novel, translation becomes a betrayal of other human beings insofar as it exposes the incompatibility of horizons of expectation. At the same time, it also shows that other people come from a world that is not absolutely alien to ours. In her subsequent novel *Calcutta*, Shumona Sinha sends a narrator on a journey to attend the funeral of her father in Kolkata, in the Indian state of West Bengal where she herself comes from, as do the narrator and numerous characters in *Assommons les pauvres!*[12] In her memories and winding thoughts, an India of the 1970s unfolds before us, caught amid the violence erupting between communism and Hindu nationalism, and not so far removed from the social processes and terror of 1970s Europe. Modernity does not happen here, in Europe, while others live there, out of reach, in another world.

Sinha's latest novel, *Apatride* (Stateless), portrays the intersecting worlds of three women who fail, in Paris as in Kolkata, to live happy lives.[13] Their homelessness is universal, immeasurable. In *Calcutta*, mother and daughter wait for a deceased father who will never return. The poetic phenomenology of waiting uncovers an emptiness, a loneliness, a longing to embrace.

> The night becoming as thick as the ink at the bottom of his pot. We keep talking, exhausting ourselves and waiting. Minutes go by, then hours. No one comes out and no one can open the garden gate, the gravel in the driveway stands still, the silent darkness slowly swallows us up, swallows the house, the garden, me, and mother, it's getting late, no one is going anywhere, no one is coming back from anywhere.[14]

It is from this shared homelessness that Shumona Sinha's trilogy of novels turns to look upon humanity, with solidarity. Against a thinking of hardened alterity that has torn the world apart, imposing boundaries, she presents the perspective, gained from those different worlds, that is found in the in-between space of the novels. We must not forget that the emphasis on particularity had an emancipatory force in processes of decolonization; yet it also ultimately reinforced and repeated imperialistic structures of knowing the world.[15] With her poetics, Sinha aims at something else: a universality of the human being that no longer presupposes a universalistic centering, but that rather grows out of the particularistic narratives cast off by the centrifugal forces of reality.

---

12 Shumona Sinha, *Calcutta* (Paris: Éditions de l'Olivier, 2014).
13 Shumona Sinha, *Apatride* (Paris: Éditions de l'Olivier, 2017).
14 Sinha, *Calcutta*, 205.
15 See Achille Mbembe, *Critique of Black Reason*, trans. Laurent Dubois (Durham: Duke University Press, 2017).

Apatride ends with the first-person narrator Esha dying in a fire in her Paris apartment; her friend Mina, impregnated by the landlord's son, is drowned by a gang of men in India. There is no hope for these protagonists. "The body of the Woman, here or elsewhere, veiled or unveiled, always aroused equally vehement reactions. A few centimeters of fabric—here it was too much, elsewhere not enough."[16] Yet even if the plots of these novels do not themselves confer any hope, the interplay between the three books points to an outside point of view toward which the trilogy is oriented. This enables a view of differences and a skepticism towards a "flaccid globalism" that naively advocates for borderless cultural exchange stemming from the worldwide movement of goods.[17] But it also allows for a deeper understanding of "untranslatability," which only becomes comprehensible in the interpenetration of two spheres of life.[18] In recognizing, namely, that individual and collective languages are not absolutely transparent, that they cannot be entirely translated into each other, I refer to a standpoint of knowledge that indicates something beyond monolingualism.[19] But this standpoint does not exist from the outset; it is only created in the situation of translation, because it grows out of the permanent questioning that attends each respectively different language practice. In the process, I recognize that each way of using language grasps something that the other does not, and vice versa. It thus becomes clear that while neither way of speaking can represent the whole, both revolve around something in common. Souleymane Bachir Diagne speaks in this context of a "lateral universality of translation."[20] It is this understanding of translation that operates as a principle of Sinha's realist poetics. In the experience of the fatally closed life worlds of the novel's plots, the reader's gaze and its presuppositions are permanently and inescapably called into question. And in the opposition of these worlds, we experience the limits of a world that only seems to be open, just as in seeking out alignment between them, we also find what all humans share. The normative power of this experience lies in solidarity.

---

16 Sinha, *Apatride*, 144.

17 Emily Apter, *Against World Literature: On the Politics of Untranslatability* (London: Verso, 2013), 7.

18 Barbara Cassin et al., ed., *Dictionary of Untranslatables: A Philosophical Lexicon* (Princeton University Press, 2014).

19 Barbara Cassin, ed., *Après Babel, traduire*, catalogue of the exhibition of the same name at the *Musée des civilisations de l'Europe et de la Méditerranée* (MuCEM Marseille) (Arles: Actes Sud, 2016), 9.

20 Souleymane Bachir Diagne and Jean-Loup Amselle, *En quête d'Afrique(s): Universalisme et pensée décoloniale*, 76; see also Souleymane Bachir Diagne, "L'universel latéral comme traduction," in *Les Pluriels de Barbara Cassin ou le partage des équivoques*, ed. Philippe Büttgen, Michèle Gendreau-Massaloux, and Xavier North (Lormont: Le Bord de L'Eau 2014), 243–256.

Shumona Sinha's trilogy of novels thus points to a dilemma imposing itself on our present with increasing clarity. Today, the catastrophe of the imperialistic universalization of the Western model stands opposed by the diversity of what exists, as it is appearing in the literatures of the world.[21] These manifold representations of the world were initially subversive messengers for the freedom of human imagination—one thinks of the trenchant book title *The Empire Writes Back* by Ashcroft, Griffiths, and Tiffin from 1989.[22] But these representations were quickly othered to such a degree as expressions of culture that they seemed to lose any kind of universal horizon. The others became the Other. The importance of the other, and of its singular world poetics, has at times been so essentialized that Huntington's clash of civilizations appears to be merely a cynical twist to this historical movement. Today we are faced with the dilemma of how we might give individual narratives their due, without abandoning a universal perspectivization of the world that is fundamental for organizing world society according to principles of law and justice.

Édouard Glissant's Chaos-World

With his *Introduction to a Poetics of Diversity*, the writer, literary theorist, and philosopher Édouard Glissant (who moved back and forth between Martinique and Paris throughout his life) has proposed one important model for expanding diversity to encompass a teleology of openness to a new universal consciousness.[23]

In the sense of a grand theory of narration, he considers the poetic constitution of the reference texts that belong to cultural communities to manifest a consciousness of the world: he argues that these texts represent the world in a specific constitution that can solidify into social reality, can "become real." Glissant explicitly takes recourse here to Hegel's philosophy of spirit, according to which these forms of representation express the consciousness of historical

---

21 See Ottmar Ette, *TransArea: Eine literarische Globalisierungsgeschichte*; Ottmar Ette and Gesine Müller, eds., *Worldwide: Archipels de la mondialisation/Archipiélagos de la globalización* (Madrid: Iberoamericana and Frankfurt am Main: Vervuert Verlagsgesellschaft, 2012).

22 Bill Ashcroft, Gareth Griffiths, and Helen Tiffin, eds., *The Empire Writes Back: Theory and Practice in Post-colonial Literatures* (London: Routledge, 2002).

23 Édouard Glissant, *Introduction to a Poetics of Diversity*, trans. Celia Britton (Liverpool: Liverpool University Press, 2020). See Souleymane Bachir Diagne, "Édouard Glissant: l'infinie passion de tramer," *Littérature*, vol. 174 (June 2014): 88–91. For a historical contextualization, see Gesine Müller, "J.-M. G. Le Clézio, Glissant, Epeli Hau'ofa: Avantgarden in Ozeanien," in *Avantgarde und Modernismus: Dezentrierung, Subversion und Transformation im literarisch-künstlerischen Feld*, ed. Wolfgang Asholt (Berlin: De Gruyter, 2014), 169–180.

collectives. In his view, however, Hegel's "foundational books" (for Glissant: "li-vres fondateurs") on which European culture is based—that is, the Old Testa-ment, the *Iliad* and the *Odyssey*, and even "other, more imperial epics," such as the *Aeneid* or the *Divina Commedia*—are narratives of finding a home and thus of establishing order: "These communities that are beginning to take shape formu-late and project a poetic cry that gathers together the home, the place and the nature of community and by the same token excludes from the community every-thing that is not the community."[24] What emerges from this for Glissant are grand narratives of the "whole-world," forms of world poetics, in the sense used by Erich Auerbach, that aim for unity. This is a systemic thinking whose most powerful expression in the nineteenth century, at the height of European appro-priation and assimilation of the world, was Hegel's philosophy of history itself.

What is interesting about Glissant's interpretation is that he sees these grand narratives not as triumphal gestures, but as sublimations of an anxiety—an anxiety producing the very obsessions with rootedness, purity, and monolingualism that have repeatedly led to violence and genocide. Glissant calls this consciousness of the world "continental" because it is based on isolation and self-referentiality. In con-trast, he attempts to formulate what he calls "archipelagic thinking,"[25] a thinking of diverse and permanent relationality that does not systematically conflate everything in the unity of a concept, but rather comes to terms with the incompatibility and nonsimultaneity—in short, the cacophony and chaos—of the world, because it understands culture as a constant process of exchange and creolization. This think-ing starts out from what is concrete, from individualized life worlds and diverse practices of speaking.[26] In his *Philosophie de la relation*, Glissant characterizes this consciousness as an acknowledgments of the opacity of the "whole-world," as some-thing that must be accepted, in its facets and its entirety, as impervious to penetra-tion or recognition.[27] For Glissant, this notion of opacity, of an impenetrability and

---

24 Glissant, *Introduction to a Poetics of Diversity*, 21. In the translation of Glissant's *Poetics of Relation*, "livres fondateurs" is rendered as "founding books"; see *Poetics of Relation*, trans. Betsy Wing (Ann Arbor: University of Michigan Press, 2010), 15.

25 Glissant, *Introduction to a Poetics of Diversity*, 26.

26 See Édouard Glissant, *Tout-monde* (Paris: Gallimard, 1993), as well as *Treatise on the Whole-World*, trans. Celia Britton (Liverpool: Liverpool University Press, 2020). Pointing to the dual ef-fect of sublation and totalizing that emerges from the fixation on everyday figures and their lan-guage games, Buata B. Malela has identified a shift from Aimé Césaire, who placed the historical heroes of the Caribbean archipelago at the center of his critique of colonialism; see Buata B. Malela, "Colonialité, subjectivité, et déconstruction dans la pensée d'Édouard Glissant," in "Lit-erature and Globalism: A Tribute to Theo D'haen," special issue, *Canadian Review of Comparative Literature/Revue Canadienne de Littérature Comparée* 43, no. 3 (2016): 414–425, on 416.

27 See Édouard Glissant, *Philosophie de la relation: poésie en étendue* (Paris: Gallimard, 2009), 70.

idiosyncrasy of speaking and narrating, derives essentially from the experience of poetry, the literary genre in which the individual use of language and world-creation are practically identical.[28]

In this sense, "archipelagic thinking" is indeed a way of thinking that gives rise once again to a grand world narrative, to an epic of a new community. But this generalizes the trace of insecurity that Glissant argues had already been laid down in the "great foundational books of humanity":

> And if one examines the Old Testament, the *Iliad*, the sagas, the *Aeneid*, one sees straight away that these books are "complete" because even within their calling for rootedness, they are also, directly, a call to wandering. And it seems to me that a new, contemporary, epic literature will start to appear as soon as the totality-world begins to be perceived as a new kind of community. . . . The new epic literature will establish relation and not exclusion.[29]

For Glissant, the new awareness of the world can thus no longer be universalistic, but only a consciousness of what he calls the "tout-monde," an "all-world" in which everything occurs, and must be thought, alongside everything else. The goal of history is for Glissant accordingly a consciousness of absolute openness in which everything can be thought, everything can be lived. Engendering this kind of consciousness is the task of contemporary literature, of narration in the broader sense, which is able to deploy an infinite complexity in multiple languages without having to create a hierarchy among the complexity of its relationalities and references, of its stances and models of life. The new global consciousness is thus an "esthétique de la relation," an "aesthetic of relation" that reshapes our perception of the sensuous world.[30] The power this "all-world" has to send a signal is clear: without needing to predetermine the future, that is to say, without needing to assert one narrative against all others, it preserves an openness in the development of history, which unfolds of its own accord out of these infinite relations. Global, planetary consciousness takes shape here "from below" and constitutes itself as a consciousness of complexity. One difficulty in this context is defining the limits that this consciousness can have vis-à-vis the dynamics of globalization itself, which tend to entail a boundless interchangeability of everything with everything else. Glissant is not simply aiming for a world

---

28 See Gisela Febel, "Poesie und Denken: Lyrische Form, kreolisierte Erinnerung und Erkenntnis bei Édouard Glissant," in *Kreolisierung revisited: Debatten um ein weltweites Kulturkonzept*, ed. Gesine Müller and Natascha Ueckmann (Bielefeld: transcript Verlag, 2013), 163–180.
29 Glissant, *Introduction to a Poetics of Diversity*, 42–43.
30 This is the subtitle of the fourth chapter of Glissant, *Introduction to a Poetics of Diversity*, "The Chaos-World: Towards an Aesthetic of Relation." Like the English word "to relate," the French term "relation" can mean both "relationship" and a "report/representation."

consciousness that would basically contain everything that occurs; would be, in other words, the set of all world narratives.

Glissant is well aware that world narratives are beset by conflict. Inasmuch as it is no longer possible to systematize the multiplicity of phenomena, we live in a time of *choc* (shock), *répulsion* (repulsion), *attirances* (attractions), *connivences* (complicities), *oppositions* (oppositions) and *conflits* (conflicts)—in short, in a *chaos-monde*. If the reaction to this is not to be violence, Glissant continues, then we must live with and in this excess of the world *(démesure)*; we must endure these tensions and develop an awareness for the possibility and openness posed by the unforeseen.

Glissant's poetics of multiplicity is thus more than a rejection of binary thinking made by reference to relationality. A directionality of history enters the picture here, in which individual consciousness encounters the multirelational constitution of the world to then attain—dialectically, one is tempted to say—a higher level of consciousness. Glissant's world poetics accordingly attempts a philosophy of history that seeks to grasp a new consciousness of the world in the "chaos-world" and to emphatically turn this consciousness toward itself. In this, it resembles Hegel's project to a certain extent, except that the goal of history is no longer the coming-to-itself of (European) philosophical reason as a consciousness of freedom, but the coming-to-itself of a consciousness of the diversity in the phenomenal world.

The problem of this world poetics lies in the question of violence: how does such a consciousness relate to narratives of violence that dissolve their own boundaries?

Glissant's response to this question consists of self-restraint: the only possibility of establishing peace rests in the consciousness that every individual can have of their own particularity in relation to an "all-world." All human beings would need to internalize this excessiveness of the world and ultimately acknowledge that maintaining their own form of life requires them to adhere to rules of relationality, in the sense of a *poetics of diversity*. What Glissant ultimately proposes is a stoic stance of self-restraint that remains open toward the course of the world. Hegel, it is worth noting, had described the Stoic attitude toward the world as the compensation for a surrendered consciousness of freedom.

Glissant's *Poetics of Diversity*, whose great merit lies in the political weight it accords to singular world narratives and their permanent relationality in times marked by cultural clashes, is paradoxical: it can offer little to oppose the violence it sets out to defeat. Lest it appear cynical about these violations of humanity, it must set borders to openness. But it cannot do so by attaining normativity. We are faced here with the problem to which the narratological theorist Albrecht Koschorke has explicitly pointed: "Like thinking and speaking in general, narration does not have a sufficient intrinsic truth-sign at its disposal."[31] In other words: relying on the coexistence of narratives does not obviate the question of their legitimacy, validity, and universality.

In his *Critique of Black Reason,* a critical reading of the tradition of anticolonial counterdiscourse that draws on the *négritude* movement from Fanon and Senghor to Césaire and Glissant, the Cameroonian historian and philosopher Achille Mbembe has for this reason emphasized that the idea of the *tout-monde* can only be invoked without restriction if this "all-world" appears as a whole in which everyone participates equally, and which can thus be asserted as a general human horizon. But, he continues, colonial history has meant an unequal distribution of world goods, which first needs to be compensated by symbolic and material reparations. Mbembe's conception goes beyond postcolonial counteressentializations in that it aims to enable a new universal claim to humanity:

> Restitution and reparation, then, are at the heart of the very possibility of the construction of a common consciousness of the world, which is the basis for the fulfillment of universal justice. The two concepts of restitution and reparation are based on the idea that each person is a repository of a portion of intrinsic humanity. This irreducible share belongs to all of us. Its effect is that we are both different from one another and alike. The ethic of restitution and reparation implies the recognition of what we might call the other's share, which is not ours, but for which we are nevertheless the guarantor, whether we want to be or not. This share of the other cannot be usurped without consequences with regard to how we think about ourselves, justice, law, or humanity itself, or indeed about the project of the universal, if that is in fact the ultimate goal.[32]

What is interesting about Mbembe's position is the refounding of humanity at its imperial margins. Since the early modern slave trade, Mbembe argues, the European powers had subordinated the universalist fundamental rights they formulated to capitalist premises, leading to forms of racist relativism that could be economically instrumentalized, and to what Mbembe calls a necropolitics.[33] In Mbembe's view, this capitalist appropriation of values is today catching up with European societies themselves. And this means Europe needs the knowledge of the former colonies of the "all-world" in order to defend its own emancipatory heritage. Mbembe here ultimately calls into question the center-periphery power structure in the representation of universality.

Universality can no longer be postulated from a center—in the same way this was done by the ideology of European universalism, as it was articulated by Hegel's

---

31 Albrecht Koschorke, *Fact and Fiction: Elements of a General Theory of Narrative,* trans. Joel Golb (Berlin: De Gruyter 2018), 4.

32 Mbembe, *Critique of Black Reason,* 182–183.

33 Achille Mbembe, *Necropolitics,* trans. Steven Corcoran (Durham: Duke University Press, 2019).

idea of the "coming-to-itself" of spirit as a European process; rather, it must arise from and be embodied in concrete contexts, whose intrinsic right and complexity Glissant has rightly emphasized. One way of avoiding totalizing forms of world poetics in the sense of the European model, while at the same time maintaining the validity of universal claims, is to take seriously the fact that narration must always vest the general toward which it aims with a form drawn from the singular; this is its basic anthropological premise.[34] This process generates and grounds new perspectives on universality—perspectives that, as Orhan Pamuk writes in his Norton Lectures on poetics, are essentially based on similarities between singular human behavior and on the recognizability of affects and intensities.[35] Can this provide a foundation for fundamental principles of human coexistence?

Léonora Miano's (Hi)story of Solidarity

Léonora Miano, a Cameroonian writer, has ventured one shrewd approach to this problem in her novel *Season of the Shadow*.[36] Her book is a distinctive work of narration that uses the model of the novel in order to reshape it, by appropriating French with the force of voices and ways of speaking that have been inscribed into it by other linguistic cultures.[37] "I write jazz (a mixing), soul (a cry), and

---

34 Various preconditions are necessary for this to work; see, for example, Jurij M. Lotman, *Die Innenwelt des Denkens: Eine semiotische Theorie der Kultur*, ed. S. K. Frank, C. Ruhe, and A. Schmitz (Berlin: Suhrkamp, 2010), especially 163–173.

35 Orhan Pamuk, *The Naive and Sentimental Novelist*, trans. Nazim Dikbas (Cambridge, MA: Harvard University Press, 2010), 49. *Similarity* as a concept that connects one particular with another and thereby points toward generality—that is to say, as a concept that can point beyond the antagonism between universalist and relativist schemas—has also been championed from the perspective of cultural theory by Anil Bhatti and Dorothee Kimmich; see Anil Bhatti and Dorothee Kimmich, eds., *Ähnlichkeit: Ein kulturtheoretisches Paradigma* (Paderborn: Konstanz University Press, 2015).

36 Léonora Miano, *Season of the Shadow*, trans. Gila Walker (London: Seagull Books, 2018 [2013]).

37 In her discussion "Habiter la frontière" (literally: "inhabiting the border," or "settling in the inbetween") at the Journée internationale de la Francophonie in Copenhagen in 2009, Léonora Miano highlighted two basic structuring principles for this program: her own polyphony, by which she means not only multilingualism per se, but also a linguistic "multi appartenance," a belonging to different linguistic cultures (African, European, Afro-American, and Caribbean); and jazz, as a structure that mixes rhythms, motifs, and styles; see Léonora Miano, *Habiter la frontière: Conférences* (Paris: L'Arche, 2012), 28–30. The interweaving of linguistic styles and intralinguistic differences, genres, and modes of narration, of other media and art forms, is what Bruno Blanckeman and Barbara Havercroft fundamentally identify as a characteristic of the contemporary novel. See Blanckeman

blues (reality). I write what I am. I write how I am."[38] This is true not only lexically, in her use of dozens of words from Duala that are explained to the reader in a glossary provided in an appendix to the novel. It is even more apparent in how a network of protagonists unfolds in the book, consisting of the female characters Ebeise, Ebusi, Eleke, and Eyabe as well as the male characters Mukano, Mutango, Mundene, Mukate, Musima, and Mutimbo, of the Mulongo tribe. Readers must continually remind themselves of the relationships between these figures, along with their social functions—who in their sheer abundance are unavoidably reminiscent of the large casts of characters found in the Russian novels of the nineteenth century. This alone points to a narrative structure that emphasizes a complex interweaving of perspectives toward an epic whole. This particular narrative construction is further reinforced by the fact that direct speech is not placed within quotation marks but inscribed into the text using italics. The result is an unusual typographical design, combined with a reading flow that is left unimpeded by signs. Things coexist; they resonate with each other as if coinciding in a "long chorus"[39]—the dead with the living, political discourse with spiritual providence. Everything is in flux, as though the narrative were the unfolding of history itself. The novel performatively demonstrates the interweaving of all sediments of life:

> The woman answers that their forbearers are within them. They are in the drum rolls, in the way [food] is prepared, in beliefs that endure and are transmitted. The people who came before them in the land of the living inhabit the language they are speaking. It will be transformed through contact with other languages that it will infuse as much as the other will permeate it. The ancestors are here. Neither time or space limits them. They reside wherever their descendants are. *A great many of ours have perished*, she adds, *but not all are dead. Where they have been taken, they are doing as we do.*
>
> *Even in hushed tones, they speak our language. When they cannot speak, it remains the vehicle of their thoughts, the rhythm of their emotions.* The woman says that you cannot dispossess people of what they have received, learnt, experienced. They themselves could not do so, even if they wanted to. Human beings are not empty calabashes.[40]

That is to say: individual speech exists in concrete situations, but it is always caught up in an overall process generated by an overarching narrative principle. The text thus makes tangible a fundamental experience of the Mulongo, who

---

and Havercroft, eds., *Narrations d'un nouveau siècle: Romans et récits français (2001–2010)*, Colloque de Cerisy (Paris: Presses Sorbonne nouvelle, 2012), 7–9.

38 Miano, *Habiter la frontière*, 30.

39 Here, too, see Miano, *Habiter la frontière*, for a discussion of this sound-image of slightly divergent tone of equal vibration.

40 Miano, *Season of the Shadow*, 235.

"had found themselves implicated in something that went beyond them."[41] The formative principle is thereby neither omniscient in the sense of our present nor neutral in the sense of a representation of purely external processes. Rather, it establishes a context that follows the protagonists' knowledge of the world. As readers, then, we are transported into an event that shifts almost imperceptibly from an authorial to a personal perspective:

> The motives of the assailants may still be unknown to her but the woman is now sure of their identity. She will have to lead Ebusi down a different road.
>
> Maybe in walking to jedu, they will find Mukano and his men. Maybe if they go that way they will see Eyabe. Maybe, by misfortune, they will encounter the Bwele warriors face to face.[42]

This "maybe" that recurs persistently at the beginning of the sentence is a word that belongs more to spoken language: it colors the narrative, giving it a perspective, or even a stance; almost imperceptibly, the reading slides into an inner experience. This is reinforced in what follows by a play on the grammatical ambiguity of the French impersonal pronoun "il," "one," which can refer to both "they" and "we": "Quoi qu'il en soit, il faut partir. Il n'y a plus rien ici."[43] (The published English translation is forced to make a choice in rendering this as "they": "Whatever may be, they must leave. There is nothing left here anymore."[44]) The general narrative process thus converges with a stance that no longer entails only a coloring through perspective but could instead constitute an inner commentary, even an exclamation. Only the final word "ici," "here," provides surety that in this place a standpoint emerges, that we encounter the character's world.

This narrative process makes it possible to experience a change in the world as a change in the consciousness of human beings. We experience the opening of a horizon of understanding. Miano, for instance, narrates the emerging slave trade not only from the perspective of our contemporary consciousness of the world, or from a new retelling "from Africa." Rather, she transports readers into the consummation of a vast change in the world that unfolds as a consciousness within ourselves, like a great stream of composite voices and storylines. We are not necessarily drawn into this current. Rather, we must read our way into its foreign diction. But en route we are not able to free ourselves from its forces. The novel thereby fundamentally shifts our view of events. Miano narrates an odyssey that is disturbingly structured by the Hegelian narrative of Africa's entry into history; but at the same

---

41 Miano, *Season of the Shadow*, 194.
42 Miano, *Season of the Shadow*, 216.
43 Léonora Miano, *La Saison de l'ombre* (Paris: Bernard Grasset, 2013), 222.
44 Miano, *Season of the Shadow*, 216.

time she decisively retells the central questions of arriving in modernity, and of our knowledge of it.

A village in the African bush is attacked during the night. Twelve firstborn Mulongo men vanish. The tribe cannot understand what has happened: the structure of their world does not allow it. There are no enemies to explain it. So the reason must lie in the world of demons. The mothers of the sons who have disappeared are therefore confined in a hut apart from the others in the village. A dark shadow hangs over the building, portending calamity.

From this point on, the novel tells the story of this mysterious vanishing from the perspective of various Mulongo. This search leads the tribe into history—which is here the history of slavery. The neighboring Bwele have kidnapped the twelve men to deliver them to the Isedu, the powerful and cruel coastal tribe to whom the Bwele pay tribute. The Isedu trade with the Whites, at the "brink of the world" where the infinite ocean begins—the inexplicable expanse of power possessed by the "hommes aux pieds de poule," the "men with hen feet," meaning the Portuguese men wearing Turkish trousers.

Léonora Miano presents two ways of responding to events: one that corresponds to the traditional male-centered power structure of knowledge and authority, and a female way that belongs to the traditional care of ensuring survival. The male way of responding leads to ruin. Mukano, the chief of the village, sets out with his bodyguard to search for the missing men of the tribe. The troop perishes in the mangrove swamps because none of the men can swim. Left defenseless, the village is again raided by the Bwele; its villagers are captured or killed. Neither might nor strength can triumph against the supremacy of these historical forces.

Success, rather, is promised by the way of women. The women initially stand for love, for care that ensures survival—a perspective that is not entirely unproblematic when viewed from contemporary notions of gender. Eyabe, for instance, sets out for the ocean with the placenta of her first-born son Mukate, one of the twelve captured men, in order to allow him to pass on into the realm of the dead. She is discovered by the Isedu but manages to flee, escaping into the mangroves where she is able to take refuge in the village of Bebayedi. There she meets Ebeise, the matron and midwife of the Mulongo, along with Ebeise's companion Ebusi. These two women, who had survived the attack on the village, felt compelled to venture to the ocean in order to preserve the tribe's history. It is this ability to escape inflexibility, not remain with oneself, but to set out and face the unknown, that opens up new knowledge for the women and allows them to survive. Along the way, classic gender roles change: "I generally like to produce female bodies inhabited by a masculine (authoritarian, cold, courageous . . .) energy," Miano writes in her lecture "Habiter la frontière," with an intention equally grounded in poetology and identity politics.[45]

The women's paths thus function as odysseys across the boundaries of the familiar into new forms of coexistence. They neither follow the genealogical idea of returning to an origin nor merge into a teleology of history. Their trek to the sea is indeed the trek from being-in-itself to being-for-itself. This certainly follows the logic of a new confrontation of consciousness with the world: a new realization gives rise to a sense of freedom; new possible worlds emerge at the edge of the ocean. But it is not the Europeans who open up these worlds—not in any moral sense, not by their values or conduct, or by their relationality, which Miano identifies as a link in the chain of human striving for power. Rather, it is the massive upheaval of history itself that opens up a new history. This leads to Bebayedi: the village of refugees on the coast, hidden in the mangroves, protected by the high tides, where a diversity of destinies, generations, and tribes can be found. This is a community that must first negotiate a new world and its language in order to survive:

> The woman says this land is called Bebayedi. It is the country that those who escaped capture found for themselves. Here, the memories of the different peoples join to weave a story. . . . The ancestors are here and they are not a confinement. They conceived a world. This is their most precious legacy: the obligation to invent in order to survive.[46]

Arriving here means freedom, but it also means never returning home. The genealogical story of the Odyssey is cut off here. The refugees *give* themselves a new country; they *invent* a new community out of their needs for freedom. Léonora Miano's rewriting of history brings forth a consciousness of the world that, to use the language of Ernst Tugendhat, opens up a "we" which we as readers can join because we want to—or not.[47] This is no abstract "we." It is conditioned by specific memories: those of direct human experience of enslavement and objectification. These experiences are unique and yet, as memories of loss, death, and exile, also fundamental experiences of modernity. "The border reminds us of relations," Léonora Miano writes in "Habiter la frontière":

> She says that peoples have met, sometimes in violence, hatred, contempt, and that despite this, they have given birth to meaning. My *multibelonging* itself has meaning. It reminds

---

45 Léonora Miano, "Habiter la frontière," lecture held at the Journée internationale de la francophonie in 2009 at the University of Copenhagen, published in Léonora Miano, *Habiter la frontière*, 25–32, on 31.

46 Miano, *Season of the Shadow*, 235–236.

47 Ernst Tugendhat, *Vorlesungen über Ethik*, 8th ed. (Frankfurt am Main: Suhrkamp, 2012), 29–30.

those who believe in the permanence of things, and of identities in particular: it is not only that the plant cannot be reduced to its roots, but that these roots can be repotted, can blossom in new soil.[48]

The "we" that arises in Bebayedi is one that turns against modernity's obsessions with rootedness and purity. It must accept the driving back of what is supposedly its own, accept a specific homelessness; and in return, it experiences in this opening the chance to preserve humanity. This is a "we" of solidarity that embraces both the critique of modernity's destructive power and modernity's emancipatory possibilities.

Liberty, equality, and solidarity—the principles of a nongenealogical time— acquire a different status here than that which results from fusing the idea of liberty with European intellectuality. These ideals do not come ashore with the Europeans and their functionalist rationality. For Miano, however, this does not mean that there are no universals—only that we have to seek them out in concrete contexts, to invent their power anew: "Totalizing the thinkable is not the only way to universalize it."[49] Born of need and solidarity, ideals of humanity stretch from the local context to the potentially global horizon of the ocean. Here, reality takes on a new tension compared to its grand narrative—signifying the emergence of a new world poetics.

---

48 Léonora Miano, "Habiter la frontière," 25.
49 Étienne Balibar, *On Universals: Constructing and Deconstructing Community*, trans. Joshua David Jordan (New York: Fordham University Press, 2020), viii. Balibar has proposed the concept of the "multiverse" to indicate that universality can henceforth be thought exclusively as a multiplicity of differences; see Balibar, *On Universals*, viii–ix; 96–119.

Bibliography

Adichie, Chimamanda Ngozi. "The Danger of a Single Story." Lecture at the TED Global Talks 2009. https://ted.com/talks/chimamanda_adichie_the_danger_of_a_single_story/details, accessed August 10, 2021.

——. *We Should All Be Feminists*. New York: Anchor Books, 2014.

al-Azm, Sadik. "What's in a name? 'Naher Osten,' 'Vorderasien' und die Macht der Bezeichnung." In *Fluchtpunkt*, edited by Franck Hofmann and Markus Messling, 27–35. Berlin: Kulturverlag Kadmos, 2017.

Appadurai, Arjun. *The Future as Cultural Fact*: *Essays on the Global Condition*. New York: Verso Books, 2013.

Apter, Emily. *Against World Literature: On the Politics of Untranslatability*. London: Verso, 2013.

Arendt, Hannah. *The Origins of Totalitarianism*. New York: Schocken, 1951.

Ashcroft, Bill, Gareth Griffiths, and Helen Tiffin, eds. *The Empire Writes Back*: *Theory and Practice in Post-colonial Literatures*. London: Routledge, 2002.

Asholt, Wolfgang. "Der romantische Durchbruch." In *Französische Literatur des 19. Jahrhunderts*, edited by Wolfgang Asholt, 88–108. Stuttgart: J.B. Metzler, 2006.

——. "Un renouveau du 'réalisme' dans la littérature contemporaine?" *Lendemains* 38, no. 150/151 (2013): 22–35.

Asholt, Wolfgang and Ursula Bähler, eds. "Le savoir historique du roman contemporain." Special issue, *Revue des Sciences Humaines* 321, no. 1 (2016).

Auerbach, Erich. "Philology and Weltliteratur." Translated by Maire and Edward Said. *The Centennial Review* 13, no. 1 (Winter 1969): 1–17.

——. *Mimesis*: *The Representation of Reality in Western Literature*. Translated by Willard R. Trask. Princeton: Princeton University Press, 2003.

Bachmann-Medick, Doris. *Cultural Turns: New Orientations in the Study of Culture*. Berlin: De Gruyter, 2016.

Bailly, Jean-Christophe. *Le Dépaysement*: *Voyages en France*. Paris: Seuil, 2011.

Balibar, Étienne. *Equaliberty*. Translated by James Ingram. Durham: Duke University Press, 2014.

——. *Des Universels: Essais et conferences*. Paris: Editions Galilée, 2016.

——. *On Universals: Constructing and Deconstructing Community*. Translated by Joshua David Jordan. New York: Fordham University Press, 2020.

Barthes, Roland. *How to Live Together: Novelistic Simulations of Some Everyday Spaces; Notes for a Lecture Course and Seminar at the Collège de France (1976–1977)*. Translated by Kate Briggs, edited by Claude Coste. New York: Columbia University Press, 2013.

Baudelaire, Charles. "Beat Up the Poor." In *Paris Spleen*, translated by Louise Varese, 101–103. New York: New Directions, 1970.

Bazié, Isaac. "Violences postcoloniales: Enjeux de la représentation et défis de la lecture." In *Violences postcoloniales*: *Représentations littéraires et perceptions médiatiques*, edited by Isaac Bazié and Hans-Jürgen Lüsebrink, 15–28. Berlin: Münster Lit, 2011.

Beck, Ulrich, and Edgar Grande. "Varieties of Second Modernity: Extra-European and European Experiences and Perspectives." *The British Journal of Sociology* 61, no. 3 (2010): 409–638.

Beercroft, Alexander. *An Ecology of World Literature*: *From Antiquity to the Present Day*. New York: Verso, 2015.

Bellay, Joachim du. *La Deffence, et Illustration de la langue Francoyse*. Edited by Henri Chamard. Paris: Fontemoing, 1904.

Bender, Niklas. "Die Lehre des Scheitern III: Das Ende der Möglichkeiten." In *Verpasste und erfasste Möglichkeiten: Lesen als Lebenskunst*, edited by Niklas Bender, 63–75. Basel: Schwabe, 2018.

——. "Angst als literarisches Lebenselixier." *Frankfurter Allgemeine Zeitung*, January 12, 2019, 18.

Benjamin, Walter. *Charles Baudelaire: Ein Lyriker im Zeitalter des Hochkapitalismus*. Frankfurt am Main: Suhrkamp, 1974.

——. *Charles Baudelaire: A Lyric Poet in the Era of High Capitalism*, in *Walter Benjamin; Selected Writings*. Translated by Harry Zohn. London: Verso, 1997.

——. "The Paris of the Second Empire in Baudelaire." In *Selected Writings*, vol. 4, 1938–1940, edited by Howard Eiland and Michael W. Jennings, 3–92. Cambridge, MA: Belknap Press, 2003.

Bertina, Arno. *Mona Lisa in Bangoulap*: *Die Fabel vom Weltmuseum*. Berlin: Matthes & Seitz, 2016.

Bhatti, Anil, and Dorothee Kimmich, eds. *Ähnlichkeit*: *Ein kulturtheoretisches Paradigma*. Paderborn: Konstanz University Press, 2015.

Blanckeman, Bruno, and Barbara Havercroft, eds. *Narrations d'un nouveau siècle: Romans et récits français (2001–2010)*. Colloque de Cerisy. Paris: Presses Sorbonne nouvelle, 2013.

Bossong, George. *Das maurische Spanien: Geschichte und Kultur*. 3rd ed. Munich: C.H. Beck, 2016.

Branche, Raphaëlle. *Papa, qu'as-tu fait en Algérie?* Paris: La Découverte, 2020.

Brändle, Stefan. "Michel Houellebecq: Der Prophet der 'Gelbwesten.'" *Frankfurter Rundschau*, January 1, 2019. https://fr.de/kultur/literatur/michel-houellebecq-der-prophet-der-gelbwesten-a-1646182, accessed August 11, 2021.

Brinkmann, Reinhold. "Musikalische Lyrik, politische Allegorie und die 'heil'ge Kunst': Zur Landschaft von Schuberts Winterreise." *Archiv für Musikwissenschaft* 62, no 2 (2005): 75–97.

[Bruno, G.] Fouillée, Augustine. *Le Tour de la France par deux enfants: Devoir et Patrie. Livre de lecture courante. Avec 212 gravures instructives pour les leçons de choses et 19 cartes géographiques. Entièrement revue et augmentée d'un epilogue*. 338th ed. Paris: Belin, 1907.

Buck-Morss, Susan. "Hegel and Haiti." *Critical Inquiry* 26, no. 4 (2000): 821–865.

——. *Hegel, Haiti, and Universal History*. Pittsburgh: University of Pittsburgh Press, 2009.

Calvino, Italo. *If on a Winter's Night a Traveler*. London: Picador, 1982.

Calvet, Louis-Jean. *Linguistique et colonialisme: Petit traité de glottophagie*. Paris: Payot, 1974.

Camus, Albert. *The Rebel: An Essay on Man in Revolt*. Translated by Anthony Bower. New York: Vintage Books, 1991.

Casanova, Pascale. *The World Republic of Letters*. Translated by M. B. DeBevoise. Cambridge, MA: Harvard University Press, 2004.

Cassin, Barbara et al., eds. *Dictionary of Untranslatables: A Philosophical Lexicon*. Princeton University Press, 2014.

Cassin, Barbara, et al. *Après Babel, traduire*. Catalogue of the exhibition of the same name at the Musée des civilisations de l'Europe et de la Méditerranée (MuCEM Marseille). Arles: Actes Sud, 2016.

Centre Marc Bloch and Literarisches Colloquium Berlin (lcb). "Europe and its borders/L'Europe et ses frontiers – international writers conference." Discussion panel with Priya Basil, Camille de Toledo, and Jürgen Trabant, moderated by Maike Albath, November 15, 2018.

Certeau, Michel de, Dominique Julia, and Jacques Revel, eds. *Une politique de la langue: La Révolution française et les patois; L'Enquête de Grégoire*. Paris: Gallimard, 1975.

Cohn-Bendit, Daniel, and Romain Goupil. *La Traversée/On the Road in France*, documentary, March 16, 2018, Paris. https://www.imdb.com/title/tt7543794/.

Coissard, Françoise. *Wajdi Mouawad: Incendies*. Paris: H. Champion, 2014.

Chakrabarty, Dipesh. *Provincializing Europe*: *Postcolonial Thought and Historical Difference*. Princeton: Princeton University Press, 2000.

——. "The Climate of History: Four Theses." *Critical Inquiry* 35, no. 2 (2009): 197–222.

——. *Europa als Provinz: Perspektiven globaler Geschichtsschreibung*. Frankfurt am Main: Campus Verlag, 2010.

Chakravorty Spivak, Gayatri. *Death of a Discipline*. New York: Columbia University Press, 2003.

Cheah, Pheng. *What Is a World? On Postcolonial Literature as World Literature*. Durham: Duke University Press, 2016.

Compagnon, Antoine. "L'Épuisement de la littérature et son éternel recommencement," in the chapter "XXe siècle." In *La littérature française: dynamique & histoire*, vol. 2, edited by Jean-Yves Tadié, 783–787. Paris: Gallimard, 2007.

Conrad, Sebastian. *Globalgeschichte: Eine Einführung*. Munich: C.H. Beck, 2013.

Côté, Jean-François. *Architecture d'un marcheur: Entretiens avec Wajdi Mouawad*. Montréal: Leméac, 2005.

Dakhli, Leyla. "Accolade for Mathias Énard." Translated by Holger Fock and Sabine Müller. In *Leipziger Buchpreis zur Europäischen Verständigung/Leipzig Book Award for European Understanding 2017: An Mathias Enard*, edited by City of Leipzig, 69–74. Leipzig: Leipzig Book Award, 2017.

Damrosch, David. *What Is World Literature?* Princeton: Princeton University Press, 2003.

Deleuze, Gilles, and Félix Guattari. *Toward a Minor Literature*. Translated by Dana Polan. Minneapolis: University of Minnesota Press, 1986.

Derrida, Jacques. *The Other Heading: Reflection on Today's Europe*. Translated by Pascale-Anne Brault and Michael Naas. Bloomington: Indiana University Press, 1992.

——. *The Monolingualism of the Other: The Prosthesis of Origin*. Translated by Patrick Mensah. Stanford: Stanford University Press, 1998.

——. *Learning to Live Finally: The Last Interview*. Translated by Pascale-Anne Brault and Michael Naas. New York: Palgrave Macmillan, 2007.

Descola, Philippe. *Beyond Nature and Culture*. Translated by Janet Lloyd. Chicago: University of Chicago Press, 2013.

Diagne, Souleymane Bachir. "On the Postcolonial and the Universal?" *Rue Descartes* (Collège international de Philosophie) 18, no. 2 (2013): 7–18.

——. "L'universel latéral comme traduction." In *Les Pluriels de Barbara Cassin ou le partage des équivoques*, edited by Philippe Büttgen, Michèle Gendreau-Massaloux, and Xavier North, 243–256. Lormont: Le Bord de L'Eau, 2014.

——. "Édouard Glissant: l'infinie passion de tramer." *Littérature* 174 (June 2014): 88–91.

——. "Penser l'universel avec Étienne Balibar." *Raison publique* 19, no. 2 (2014): 15–21.

Diagne, Souleymane Bachir, and Jean-Loup Amselle. *En quête d'Afrique(s): Universalisme et pensée décoloniale*. Paris: Albin Michel, 2018.

——. "Rhinoceros Asks . . . Souleymane Bachir Diagne: What Is Reparation?" https://www.rhinozeros-projekt.de/zeitschrift/das-projekt, accessed March 29, 2021.

Dorlin, Elsa. *Se défendre:Une philosophie de la violence*. Paris: La Découverte, 2017.

Duden Onlinewörterbuch. Entry on "Wehmut." https://duden.de/rechtschreibung/Wehmut, accessed August 11, 2021.

Efoui, Kossi. *Solo d'un revenant*. Paris: Editions du Seuil, 2008.

——. *The Shadow of Things to Come*. Translated by Chris Turner. London: Seagull Books, 2013. Originally published as *L'ombre des choses à venir* (Paris: Éditions du Seuil, 2011).

El Feki, Shereen. *Sex and the Citadel: Intimate Life in a Changing Arab World*. New York: Pantheon Books, 2012.

Énard, Mathias. *L'alcool et la nostalgie*. Paris: Inculte, 2011.

——. *Street of Thieves*. Translated by Charlotte Mandell. Rochester, NY: Open Letter, 2014. Originally published as *Rue des voleurs* (Arles: Actes Sud, 2012).

——. *Zone.* Translated by Charlotte Mandell. London: Fitzcarraldo Editions, 2014. Originally published as *Zone* (Arles: Actes Sud, 2008).

——. *Der Alkohol und die Wehmut.* Translated by Claudia Hamm. Berlin: Matthes and Seitz, 2016.

——. *Compass.* Translated by Charlotte Mandell. New York: New Directions Publishing, 2017. Originally published as *Boussole* (Arles: Actes Sud, 2015).

——. "Prize Winner's Acceptance Speech." Translated by Holger Fock and Sabine Müller. In *Leipziger Buchpreis zur Europäischen Verständigung/Leipzig Book Award for European Understanding*, edited by City of Leipzig, 77–81. Leipzig: Leipzig Book Award, 2017.

Éribon, Didier. *Returning to Reims.* Translated by Michael Lucey. Los Angeles: Semiotext(e), 2013.

Erfurt, Jürgen. Frankophonie: *Sprache – Diskurs – Politik.* Tübingen: Francke, 2005.

Ette, Ottmar. *Weltbewußtsein*: *Alexander von Humboldt und das unvollendete Projekt einer anderen Moderne.* Weilerswist: Velbrück, 2002.

——. *ÜberLebenswissen*: *Die Aufgabe der Philologie.* Berlin: Kulturverlag Kadmos, 2004.

——. "Wege des Wissens: Fünf Thesen zum Weltbewusstsein und den Literaturen der Welt." In *Lateinamerika: Orte und Ordnungen des Wissens*, edited by Sabine Hofmann and Monika Wehrheim, 169–184. Tübingen: Narr, 2004.

——. "European Literature(s) in the Global Context." In *Literature for Europe?*, edited by Theo D'haen and Iannis Goerlandt, 123–160. Amsterdam: Rodopi, 2009.

——. *List, Last und Lust literarischer Konvivenz im globalen Maßstab.* Berlin: Kulturverlag Kadmos, 2010.

——. *TransArea: Eine literarische Globalisierungsgeschichte.* Berlin: De Gruyter, 2012.

——. *Konvivenz: Literatur und Leben nach dem Paradies.* Berlin: Kulturverlag Kadmos, 2012.

——. *WeltFraktale*: *Wege durch die Literaturen der Welt.* Stuttgart: J.B. Metzler, 2017.

Ette, Ottmar, and Judith Kasper. *Unfälle der Sprache: Literarische und philologische Erkundungen der Katastrophe.* Vienna: Turia + Kant, 2014.

Ette, Ottmar, and Gesine Müller, eds. *Worldwide: Archipels de la mondialisation/Archipiélagos de la globalización.* Madrid: Iberoamericana and Frankfurt am Main: Vervuert Verlagsgesellschaft, 2012.

Evertz, Lisa. "Mythos und Gewalt im (post)dramatischen Theater bei Wajdi Mouawad und Olivier Py." PhD dissertation, Ludwig Maximilian University of Munich, 2018.

Faerber, Johan. "Camille de Toledo: à livre ouvert (Le Livre de la Faim et de la Soif)." *Diacritik*, February 8, 2017. https://diacritik.com/2017/02/08/camille-de-toledo-a-livre-ouvert-le-livre-de-la-faim-et-de-la-soif/, accessed August 11, 2021.

Fanon, Frantz. *The Wretched of the Earth.* Translated by Richard Philcox. New York: Grove Press, 2004.

——. *Black Skin, White Masks.* London: Penguin Classics, 2020.

Farcet, Charlotte. "Postface" to *Littoral* (= *Le Sang des promesses* 1). Arles: Actes Sud, 2009.

Febel, Gisela. "Poesie und Denken: Lyrische Form, kreolisierte Erinnerung und Erkenntnis bei Édouard Glissant." In *Kreolisierung revisited*: *Debatten um ein weltweites Kulturkonzept*, edited by Gesine Müller and Natascha Ueckmann, 163–180. Bielefeld: transcript Verlag, 2013.

Forsdick, Charles, and David Murphy, eds. *Postcolonial Thought in the French Speaking World.* Liverpool: Liverpool University Press, 2009.

Fuhrig, Dirk im Gespräch mit Gabi Wuttke. "Warten auf den neuen Houellebecq: Prophet der 'Gelbwesten'-Proteste." *Deutschlandfunk Kultur*, January 3, 2019. https://deutschlandfunkkultur. de/warten-auf-den-neuen-houellebecq-prophet-der-gelbwesten.1013.de.html?dram: article_id=437421, accessed August 11, 2021.

Fukuyama, Francis. *The End of History and the Last Man.* New York: Free Press, 1992.

Garcia, Tristan. "Frankreich wird gewaltsamer, aber auch ehrlicher." Interview with Stephanie von Hayek, *Kulturaustausch: Zeitschrift für internationale Perspektiven* 4 (2017): 19–21.

——. *Wir*. Suhrkamp: Berlin, 2018.

Gehrmann, Susanne. "Afropolitanism and Afro/euro/peanism: New Identity Concepts in the Era of Globalization." *Ibadan Journal of Humanistic Studies* 26, no. 2 (2016): 177–191.

——. "Cosmopolitanism with African Roots: Afropolitanism's Ambivalent Mobilities." *Journal of African Cultural Studies* 28, no 1 (2016): 61–72.

Gilroy, Paul. "Planetarity and Cosmopolitics." *The British Journal of Sociology* 61, no. 3 (2010): 620–626.

Ginzburg, Carlo. *Clues, Myths, and the Historical Method*. Translated by John and Anne C. Tedeschi. Berkeley: University of California Press, 2012.

Ginzburg, Carlo, and Anna Davin. "Morelli, Freud and Sherlock Holmes: Clues and Scientific Method." *History Workshop* 9 (Spring 1980): 5–36.

Glissant, Édouard. *Tout-monde*. Paris: Gallimard, 1993.

——. *Poetics of Relation*. Translated by Betsy Wing. Ann Arbor: University of Michigan Press, 1997.

——. *Philosophie de la relation: poésie en étendue*. Paris: Gallimard, 2009.

——. *Introduction to a Poetics of Diversity*. Liverpool: Liverpool University Press, 2020.

——. *Treatise on the Whole-World*. Translated by Celia Britton. Liverpool: Liverpool University Press, 2020.

——. *Introduction to a Poetics of Diversity*. Translated by Celia Britton. Liverpool: Liverpool University Press, 2020.

Gobineau, Comte de. "Essai sur l'inégalité des races humaines." In *Oeuvres I*, edited by J. Gaulmier, 133–1174. Paris: Gallimard, 1987.

Godard, Jean-Luc. *Film Socialisme: La liberté coûte cher*. Paris 2010. https://imdb.com/title/tt1438535/, accessed August 11, 2021.

Habermas, Jürgen. "Der interkultureller Diskurs über Menschenrechte." In *Recht auf Menschenrechte: Menschenrechte, Demokratie und internationale Politik*, edited by Hauke Brunkhorst, Wolfgang R. Köhler, and Matthias Lutz Bachmann, 216–227. Frankfurt am Main: Suhrkamp, 1999.

Hacks, Peter. *Zur Romantik*. Hamburg: Konkret Literatur, 2008.

Harder, Ruth E. "Hekabe." In *Der neue Pauly: Enzyklopädie der Antike*, edited by Hubert Cancik and Helmuth Schneider, vol. 5, 261–262. Stuttgart: J.B. Metzler, 1998.

Haym, Rudolf. *Wilhelm von Humboldt: Lebensbild und Charakteristik*. Berlin: R. Gaertner, 1856.

Hegel, Georg Wilhelm Friedrich. *Lectures on the Philosophy of World History*. Translated by H. B. Nisbet. Cambridge: Cambridge University Press, 1975.

Helgesson, Stefan, and Pieter Vermeulen. *Institutions of World Literature: Writing, Translation, Markets*. London: Routledge, 2016.

Helgesson, Stefan, Helena Bodin, and Annika Mörte Alling, eds. *Literature and the Making of the World: Cosmopolitan Texts, Vernacular Practices*. New York, London: Bloomsbury, 2022.

Hofmann, Franck, and Markus Messling. *Leeres Zentrum: Das Mittelmeer und die literarische Moderne. Eine Anthologie*. Berlin: Kulturverlag Kadmos, 2015.

——. *Fluchtpunkt: Das Mittelmeer und die europäische Krise*. Berlin: Kulturverlag Kadmos, 2017.

——, ed. *The Epoch of Universalism/L'époque de l'universalisme (1769–1989)*. Berlin: De Gruyter, 2021.

Horkheimer, Max, and Theodor W. Adorno. *Dialectic of the Enlightenment: Philosophical Fragments*. Translated by Edmund Jephcott. Stanford: Stanford University Press, 2002.

Houellebecq, Michel. Interview in *Art Press* 199 (1995): 37–48. Reprinted in Michel Houellebecq. *Interventions*. Paris: Flammarion, 1998.

——. *Whatever*. Translated by Paul Hammond. Burnaby, B.C.: University of Simon Fraser Library, 2014. Originally published as *Extension du domaine de la lutte* (Paris: Éditions Maurice Nadeau, 1994).

——. *Platform*. Translated by Frank Wynne. London: Vintage Books, 2003. Originally published as *Plateforme* (Paris: Flammarion, 2001).

——. *Atomised*. Translated by Frank Wynne. London: Vintage House, 2007. Originally published as *Les particules élémentaires* (Paris: Flammarion, 1998).

——. *The Map and the Territory*. Translated by Gavin Bowd. New York: Alfred A. Knopf, 2012. Originally published as *La carte et le territoire* (Paris: Flammarion, 2010).

——. *Submission*. Translated by Lorin Stein. London: W. Heinemann, 2015. Originally published as *Soumission* (Paris: Flammarion, 2015).

——. *Serotonin: A Novel*. Translated by Shaun Whiteside. New York: Farrar, Straus and Giroux, 2019. Originally published as *Sérotonine* (Paris: Flammarion, 2019).

——. "Donald Trump Is a Good President: One Foreigner's Perspective." Translated by John Cullen. *Harper's Magazine*, January 2019. https://harpers.org/archive/2019/01/donald-trump-is-a-good-president/, accessed August 11, 2021.

Hunt, Lynn. *Writing History in the Global Era*. New York: W.W. Norton and Company, 2014.

Inculte Collective. *Devenirs du roman*. Paris: Inculte/Naïve, 2007.

Inrockstv. "Michel Houellebecq: 'Je fais partie de l'élite mondialisée. J'ai perdu le contact.'" May 5, 2017. https://lesinrocks.com/inrocks.tv/michel-houellebecq-je-fais-partie-de-lelite-mondialisee-jai-perdu-le-contact/, accessed August 11, 2021.

Jablonka, Ivan. *Histoire des grands-parents que je n'ai pas eus: Une enquête*. Paris: Editions du Seuil, 2012.

Jameson, Fredric. *The Antinomies of Realism*. New York: Verso, 2015.

Jenni, Alexis. *The French Art of War*. Translated by Franck Wynne. London: Atlantic Books, 2017. Originally published as *L'art français de la guerre* (Paris: Gallimard, 2011).

Johnston, Sarah Iles. "Hekate." In *Der neue Pauly: Encyclopedia of Antiquity*, edited by Hubert Cancik and Helmut Schneider, vol. 5, 267–270. Stuttgart: J.B. Metzler, 1998.

Jullien, François. *Il n'y a pas d'identité culturelle*. Paris: L'Herne, 2017.

Kilani, Mondher. *Pour un universalisme critique: Essai d'anthropologie du contemporain*. Paris: La Découverte, 2014.

Klemperer, Victor. *LTI: The Language of the Third Reich*. London: Bloomsbury Academic, 2013.

Kojève, Alexandre. *Introduction to the Reading of Hegel; Lectures on the Phenomenology of Spirit*. Assembled by Raymond Queneau. Translated by James H. Nichols. Ithaca: Cornell University Press, 1980.

Koppenfels, Martin von. *Immune Erzähler: Flaubert und die Affektpolitik des modernen Romans*. Munich: Wilhelm Fink, 2007.

Koschorke, Albrecht. *Fact and Fiction: Elements of a General Theory of Narrative*. Translated by Joel Golb. Berlin: De Gruyter, 2018.

——. "Die akademische Linke hat sich selbst dekonstruiert: Es ist Zeit, die Begriffe neu zu justieren." *Neue Zürcher Zeitung*, April 18, 2018. https://nzz.ch/feuilleton/die-akademische-linke-hat-sich-selbst-dekonstruiert-es-ist-zeit-die-begriffe-neu-zu-justieren-ld.1376724, accessed August 11, 2021.

Krüger, Hans Peter. *Heroismus und Arbeit in der Entstehung der Hegelschen Philosophie (1793–1806)*. Berlin: Akademie Verlag, 2014.

Küpper, Joachim. *Approaches to World Literature*. Berlin: De Gruyter, 2013.

Le Monde. "Manifeste pour une littérature-monde." March 16, 2007. Republished with artists' statements as Michel Le Bris and Jean Rouaud, eds. *Pour une littérature-monde*. Paris: Gallimard, 2007.

Lenclud, Gérard. *L'Universalisme ou le pari de la raison: Anthropologie, Histoire, Psychologie*. Paris: Gallimard, 2013.

Lenne, Lise. "Autour de Littoral, Incendies et Forêts." *Littoral Incendies* et *Forêts*," Interview with Wajdi Mouawad, in *Agôn: Revue des arts de la scène* (ENSLyon), paragraph 43, www.agon.ens-lyon.fr/index.php?id=290, accessed March 15, 2018.

——. "*Le poisson-soi*: de l'aquarium du moi au littoral de la scène . . . ." In *Agôn: Revue des arts de la scène* (= En), paragraph 3, https://doi.org/10.4000/agon.328, accessed May 28, 2021.

Lepper, Marcel. *Goethes Euphrat: Philologie und Politik im "Westöstlichen Divan."* Göttingen: Wallstein Verlag, 2016.

Levi, Giovanni. "On Microhistory." In *New Perspectives on Historical Writing*, edited by Peter Burke, 93–113. Cambridge: Polity Press, 1991.

Lévi-Strauss, Claude. *Race and History*. Paris: UNESCO, 1952.

Lionnet, Françoise, and Shu-mei Shih. *The Creolization of Theory*. Durham: Duke University Press, 2011.

Lotman, Jurij M. *Die Innenwelt des Denkens*: *Eine semiotische Theorie der Kultur*. Edited by S. K. Frank, C. Ruhe, and A. Schmitz. Berlin: Suhrkamp, 2010.

Lukács, Georg. *The Theory of the Novel*: *A Historico-philosophical Essay on the Forms of Great Epic Literature*. Translated by Anna Bostock. Cambridge, MA: MIT Press, 1989.

Maalouf, Amin. "Lost Legitimacy." In *Disordered World: Setting a New Course for the Twenty-First Century*, edited by Amin Maalouf, 69–152. London: Bloomsbury, 2011.

Mabanckou, Alain. *Broken Glass*. Translated by Helen Stevenson Berkeley: Soft Skull Press, 2009.

——. *Le monde est mon langage*. Paris: Bernard Grasset, 2016.

——. "Introduction: Labourer de nouvelles terres." In *Penser et écrire l'Afrique aujourd'hui*, edited by Alain Mabanckou, 9. Paris: Éditions du Seuil, 2017.

——. "'Lettres noires': Afrikanische Literaturen heute." *Sinn und Form* 1 (January/February 2017).

Malela, Buata B. "Colonialité, subjectivité, et déconstruction dans la pensée d'Édouard Glissant." In "Literature and Globalism: A Tribute to Theo D'haen. Special issue, *Canadian Review of Comparative Literature/Revue Canadienne de Littérature Comparée* 43, no. 3 (2016): 414–425.

Malhotra, Rajiv. *Being Different: An Indian Challenge to Western Universalism*. Noida: HarperCollins Publishers India, 2011.

Mani, Venkat B. *Recoding World Literature*: *Libraries, Print Culture, and Germany's Pact with Books*. New York: Fordham University Press, 2017.

Martin, Nastassja. *Croire aux Fauves*. Paris: verticales/Gallimard, 2019.

Marx, William. *L'Adieu à la littérature: Histoire d'une dévalorisation, XVIIIe-XXe siècle*. Paris: Les Éditions de Minuit, 2005.

Mbembe, Achille. *Critique of Black Reason*. Translated by Laurent Dubois. Durham: Duke University Press, 2017.

——. "L'Afrique qui vient." In *Penser et écrire l'Afrique aujourd'hui*, edited by Alain Mabanckou, 17–31. Paris: Éditions du Seuil, 2017.

——. *Necropolitics*. Translated by Steven Corcoran. Durham: Duke University Press, 2019.

——. *Out of the Dark Night: Essays on Decolonization*. Translated by Daniela Ginsburg. New York: Columbia University Press, 2019.

——. "Le droit universel à la respiration." *Analyse Opinion Critique*, April 6, 2020, https://aoc.media/opinion/2020/04/05/le-droit-universel-a-la-respiration/, accessed May 2, 2021.

Menke, Christoph, and Arnd Pollmann. *Philosophie der Menschenrechte*. Hamburg: Junius, 2007.

Merlin-Kajman, Hélène. *La langue est-elle fasciste? Langue, pouvoir, enseignement*. Paris: Éditions du Seuil, 2003.

Messling, Markus. "Behauptung (in) der Schrift: Zur Problematik von Schrift und Individualität bei Wilhelm von Humboldt und Jacques Derrida." *KODIKAS/CODE: Ars semeiotica, An International Journal of Semiotics* 27, no. 3–4 (2004): 163–179.

——. "Ernüchtert ans Meer: Moderne Kritik und (anti)urbane Utopien bei Stendhal, Gobineau und Michelet." In *Literarische Stadtutopien zwischen totalitärer Gewalt und Ästhetisierung*, edited by Barbara Ventarola, 297–320. Munich: M. Meidenbauer, 2011.

——. "Von der Adelsranküne zur Rassentheorie: Gobineaus Sprach- und Kulturanthropologie." In *Rassedenken in der Sprach- und Textreflexion: Kommentierte Grundlagentexte des langen 19. Jahrhundert*, edited by Philipp Krämer, Markus A. Lenz, and Markus Messling, 189–209. Paderborn: Fink, 2015.

——. "Anthropologie du Mal et politique de la littérature: Michel Houellebecq et Roberto Bolaño." *Revue des Sciences Humaines* 321 (2016): 51–66.

——. *Gebeugter Geist: Rassismus und Erkenntnis in der modernen europäischen Philologie*. Göttingen: Wallstein Verlag, 2016.

——. "W. von Humboldt's Critique of a Hegelian Understanding of Modernity: A Contribution to the Debate on Postcolonialism." *Forum for Modern Language Studies* 53, no. 1 (2017): 35–46.

——. "Réalisme esthétique et cosmopolitisme littéraire: Poétiques de la perte chez Giorgos Seferis et Kossi Efoui." In *Décentrer le cosmopolitisme: Enjeux politiques et sociaux dans la littérature*, edited by Guillaume Bridet et al., 71–84. Dijon: Éditions Universitaires de Dijon, 2018.

——. *Philology and the Appropriation of the World: Champollion's Hieroglyphs*. Translated by Michael Thomas Taylor and Marko Pajević with the collaboration of Karina Berger. Cham: Palgram Macmillan/Springer, 2023.

Messling, Markus, and Jonas Tinius, eds. *Minor Universality: Rethinking Humanity after Western Universalism*. Berlin: De Gruyter, 2023.

Miano, Léonora. *Habiter la frontière: Conférences*. Paris: L'Arche, 2012.

——. *Season of the Shadow*. Translated by Gila Walker. London: Seagull Books, 2018. Originally published as *Saison de l'ombre* (Paris: Bernard Grasset, 2013).

Moretti, Franco. "Conjectures on World Literature." *New Left Review* 1 (January/February 2000): 54–68.

Moser, Christian, and Linda Simonis. "Einleitung: das globale Imaginäre." In *Figuren des Globalen: Weltbezug und Welterzeugug in Literatur, Kunst und Medien*, edited by Christian Moser, and Linda Simonis, 11–22. Bonn: Bonn University Press, 2014.

Mouawad, Wajdi. *Le Sang des promesses: Puzzle, racines et rhizomes*. 1. *Littoral* (1999); 2. *Incendies* (2003); 3. *Forêts* (2006); 4. *Ciels* (2009). Montréal, Arles: Acte Sud, 2009. English versions: *Tideline*, translated by Shelley Tepperman (Toronto: Playwrights Canada Press, 2010); *Scorched*, translated by Linda Gaboriau (Toronto: Playwrights Canada Press, 2009); *Forests*, translated by Linda Gaboriau (Toronto: Playwrights Canada Press, 2011); *Heavens*, translated by Linda Gaboriau (Toronto: Playwrights Canada Press, 2014).

——. *Le Poisson soi (Version quarante-deux ans)*. Montréal: Boréal, 2011.

——. *Les Larmes d'Œdipe*. Montréal, Arles: Actes Sud-Papiers, 2016.

——. *Anima: A Novel*. Vancouver: Talonbooks, 2017.

——. "L'Amour." Manuscript read at the opening of the Frankfurt Book Fair, 2017.

Moura, Jean-Marc. *Littératures francophones et théorie postcoloniale*. Paris: PUF, 2017.

Moyn, Samuel, and Andrew Sartori. "Approaches to Global Intellectual History." In *Global Intellectual History*, edited by Samuel Moyn and Andrew Sartori, 3–30. New York: Columbia University Press, 2013.

Moyn, Samuel. *The Last Utopia: Human Rights in History*. Cambridge, MA: Harvard University Press, 2012.

——. *Christian Human Rights*. Philadelphia: University of Pennsylvania Press, 2015.

Bibliography ━━ **139**

Müller, Gesine. "J.-M. G. Le Clézio, Glissant, Epeli Hau'ofa: Avantgarden in Ozeanien." In *Avantgarde und Modernismus*: *Dezentrierung, Subversion und Transformation im literarisch-künstlerischen Feld*, edited by Wolfgang Asholt, 169–180. Berlin: De Gruyter, 2014.

Müller, Gesine, and Dunia Gras. *América latina y la literatura mundial*: *Mercado editorial, redes globales y la invención de un continente*. Madrid: Iberoamericana, 2015.

Nussbaum, Martha. *Women and Human Development*: *The Capabilities Approach*. Cambridge: Cambridge University Press, 2000.

Onfray, Michel. "'Dieu vous entende, Michel': L'entretien entre Michel Houellebecq et Michel Onfray." In "La fin de l'Occident." Special issue, *Front Populaire: La revue des souverainistes*, November 29, 2022, 2–45.

Orsini, Francesca. "The Multilingual Local in World Literature." *Comparative Literature* 4, no. 67 (2015): 345–374.

Osterhammel, Jürgen. *The Transformation of the World*: *A Global History of the Nineteenth Century*. Princeton: Princeton University Press, 2014.

Pajević, Marko. *Poetisches Denken und die Frage nach dem Menschen: Grundzüge einer poetologischen Anthropologie*. Freiburg: Karl Alber, 2012.

Pamuk, Orhan. *The Naive and Sentimental Novelist*. Translated by Nazim Dikbas. Cambridge, MA: Harvard University Press, 2010.

Pasquier, Renaud. "Camille de Toledo, Le livre de la faim et de la soif." *La Nouvelle Revue Française* 624 (May 2017): 153–154.

Polaschegg, Andrea. *Der andere Orientalismus: Regeln deutsch-morgenländischer Imagination im 19. Jahrhundert*. Berlin: De Gruyter, 2005.

Rabaté, Dominique. "Extension ou liquidation de la lutte? Remarques sur le roman selon Houellebecq." In *Le Discours "néo-reactionnaire": Transgressions conservatrices*, edited by Pascal Durand and Sarah Sindaco, 265–279. Paris: CNRS Éditions, 2015.

Rabault-Feuerhahn, Pascale. *Théories intercontinentales: Voyages du comparatisme postcolonial*. Paris: Demopolis, 2014.

Rancière, Jacques. *The Politics of Aesthetics: The Distribution of the Sensible*. Translated by Gabriel Rockhill. New York: Continuum, 2004.

——. *The Politics of Literature*. Translated by Julie Rose. Cambridge: Polity Press, 2011.

——. "Auerbach and the Contradiction of Realism." *Critical Inquiry* 44 (Winter 2018): 227–241.

Remaud, Oliver. *Un monde étrange: Pour une autre approche du cosmopolitisme*. Paris: Puf, 2015.

——. "Le choc des cosmopolitismes?" Lecture, delivered at the Chair of European Philosophy at the University of Nantes, May 17, 2017. Extract published in *Le Monde des Idées*, May 6, 2017, page 7 ("Débat").

Revel, Jacques. *Jeux d'échelles*: *La micro-analyse à l'expérience*. Paris: Gallimard, 1996.

Ribéry, Fabien. "Tramways de porcelaine, pour clochettes, zarb, et bols tibétains." Interview with Mathias Énard in *le poulailler*, November 5, 2015. https://le-poulailler.fr/2015/11/tramways-de-porcelaine-pour-clochettes-zarb-et-bols-tibetains/, accessed August 11, 2021.

Ritte, Jürgen. "Michel Houellebecq: 'Serotonin.' Schlechtes Kabarett." https://deutschlandfunk.de/michel-houellebecq-serotonin-schlechtes-kabarett.700.de.html?dram:article_id=439318, accessed August 11, 2021.

Rivarol, Antoine de. "Discours sur l'universalité de la langue française." In *Académie de Berlin: De l'universalité européenne de la langue française*, edited by Pierre Pénisson. Paris: Fayard, 1995.

Rothberg, Michael. *Multidirectional Memory: Remembering the Holocaust in the Age of Decolonization*. Stanford: Stanford University Press, 2009.

Ruffel, Lionel. *Brouhaha: Worlds of the Contemporary.* Translated by Raymond N. MacKenzie. Minneapolis: University of Minnesota Press, 2018.

Rühle, Alex. "Interview with Michel Houellebecq: 'Das Leben ist ohne Religion über alle Maßen traurig.'" *Süddeutsche Zeitung,* January 22, 2015. https://sueddeutsche.de/kultur/interview-mit-michel-houellebecq-das-leben-ist-ohne-religion-ueber-alle-massen-traurig-1.2316339, accessed August 11, 2021.

——. "Der Prophet des Untergangs." *Süddeutsche Zeitung,* January 4, 2019. https://sueddeutsche.de/kultur/michel-houellebecq-serotonin-rezension-1.4274668, accessed August 11, 2021.

Said, Edward W. *Orientalism: Western Conceptions of the Orient.* 4th ed. London: Penguin Books, 1995.

——. *Humanism and Democratic Criticism.* New York: Columbia University Press, 2004.

—— *Music at the Limits.* With a foreword by Daniel Barenboim. New York: Columbia University Press, 2009.

Sansal, Boualem. *Poste restante; Alger: Lettre de colère et d'espoir à mes compatriotes.* Paris: Gallimard, 2006.

——. *Le Village de l'Allemand.* Paris: Gallimard, 2008. Translated into German as *Das Dorf des Deutschen oder Das Tagebuch der Brüder Schiller* (Gifkendorf: Merlin, 2009) and into English by Frank Wynne as *An Unfinished Business* (New York: Bloomsbury, 2011).

Sapiro, Gisèle. *Translatio: Le marché de la traduction en France à l'heure de la mondialisation.* Paris: CNRS Éditions, 2008.

——. "Notables, esthètes et polémistes: manière d'être un écrivain 'réactionnaire' des années 1930 à nos jours." In *Le Discours "néo-reactionnaire": Transgressions conservatrices,* edited by Pascal Durand and Sarah Sindaco, 23–46. Paris: CNRS Éditions, 2015.

Sarr, Felwine. *Afrotopia.* Translated by Drew S. Burk. Minneapolis: University of Minnesota Press, 2019.

Sarr, Felwine, and Bénédicte Savoy. *Restituer le patrimoine africain.* Paris: Philippe Rey/Édition du Seuil, 2018.

——. "Rapport sur la restitution du patrimoine culturel africain. Vers une nouvelle éthique relationnelle." November 2018, https://www.vie-publique.fr/sites/default/files/rapport/pdf/194000291.pdf, accessed May 2, 2021.

Savigneau, Josyane. "Raconter la manière avec laquelle je regarde le monde." Interview with Wajdi Mouawad, in *Le Monde,* June 24, 2011, www.lemonde.fr/idees/article/2011/06/24/wajdi-mouawad-raconter-la-maniere-avec-laquelle-je-regarde-le-monde_1540516_3232.html, accessed April 30, 2021.

Savoy, Bénédicte. *Die Provenienz der Kultur: Von der Trauer des Verlusts zum universalen Menschheitserbe.* Berlin: Matthes & Seitz, 2018.

Schaeffer, Jean-Marie. *Pourquoi la fiction?* Paris: Seuil, 1999.

Schlegel, Friedrich von. *Ueber die Sprache und Weisheit der Indier: Ein Beitrag zur Begründung der Alterthumskunde, Nebst metrischen Uebersetzungen indischer Gedichte.* Heidelberg: Mohr und Zimmer, 1808.

——. *The Philosophy of History in a Course of Lectures.* Translated by James Burton Robertson. London: Saunders and Otley, 1835.

——. *Philosophie der Geschichte: In achtzehn Vorlesungen gehalten zu Wien im Jahre 1828,* in *Kritische Friedrich-Schlegel-Ausgabe,* edited by Ernst Behler et al., vol. 9. Munich: Thomas, 1971.

——. *On the Language and Wisdom of the Indians.* Translated by H. H. Wilson. London: Ganesha Pub., 2001.

──. "On the Language and Philosophy of the Indians." In *The Aesthetic and Miscellaneous Works of Frederick von Schlegel*. Translated by E. J. Millington, 425–465. London: Henry G. Bohn, 1849, reissued Cambridge: Cambridge University Press, 2014.

Schober, Rita. *Auf dem Prüfstand: Zola – Houellebecq – Klemperer*. Berlin: Edition Tranvía, 2003.

Schor, Naomi. "The Crisis of French Universalism." *Yale French Studies* 100 (2001): 43–64.

Schwab, Raymond. *The Oriental Renaissance: Europe's Rediscovery of India and the East, 1680-1880*. Translated by Gene Patterson-King and Victor Reinking. New York: Columbia University Press, 1984.

Scott, David. *Refashioning Futures: Criticism after Postcoloniality*. Princeton: Princeton University Press, 1999.

──. *Conscripts of Modernity: The Tragedy of Colonial Enlightenment*. Durham: Duke University Press, 2004.

Sebald, W. G. *Vertigo*. Translated by Michael Hulse. New York: New Directions, 2016.

Selasi, Taiye. "African Literature Doesn't Exist." Opening speech at the internationales literaturfestival berlin 2013. Berlin: Berliner Festspiele, 2016.

Sinha, Shumona. *Assommons les pauvres*. Paris: Édition de l'Olivier, 2011.

──. *Calcutta*. Paris: Éditions de l'Olivier, 2014.

──. *Apatride*. Paris: Éditions de l'Olivier, 2017.

Stael, Madame de. *Germany*. London: C. Baldwin, 1813.

Staël, Madame de. *De l'Allemagne*. 2 vols. Paris: Garnier-Flammarion, 1968.

Starobinski, Jean. *Montaigne in Motion*. Chicago: University of Chicago Press, 2009.

Steinfeld, Thomas. *Das Phänomen Houellebecq*. Cologne: DuMont, 2001.

Stockhammer, Robert. "Welt oder Erde? Zwei Figuren des Globalen." In *Figuren des Globalen*: *Weltbezug und Welterzeugug in Literatur, Kunst und Medien*, edited by Christian Moser, and Linda Simonis, 47–72. Bonn: Bonn University Press, 2014.

──. *Ruanda: Über einen anderen Genozid schreiben*. Frankfurt am Main: Suhrkamp, 2005.

Stora, Benjamin. "Les questions mémorielles portant sur la colonization et la guerre d'Algérie." January 2021, https://www.elysee.fr/admin/upload/default/0001/09/0586b6b0ef1c2fc2540589c6 d56a1ae63a65d97c.pdf, accessed May 2, 2021.

Taylor, Charles. "Conditions on an Unforced Consensus on Human Rights." In *The East Asian Challenge for Human Rights*, edited by Joanne R. Bauer and Daniel A. Bell, 124–144. Cambridge: Cambridge University Press, 1999.

Thiong'o, Ngũgĩ wa. *Decolonizing the Mind*: *The Politics of Language in African Literature*. London: J. Currey, 1986.

Thomas-Fogiel, Isabelle. *Le Lieu de l'universel: Impasses du réalisme dans la philosophie contemporaine*. Paris: Édition du Seuil, 2015.

Toft, Lise. ed. *Une francophonie plurielle: langues, idées et cultures en mouvement*. Copenhagen: Museum Tusculanum Press, 2009.

Tötösy de Zepetnek, Steven and Tutun Mukherjee. *Companion to Comparative Literature, World Literatures, and Comparative Cultural Studies*. New Delhi: Foundation Books, 2013.

Toledo, Camille de. *Coming of Age at the End of History*. Translated by Blake Ferris. Brooklyn: Soft Skull Press, 2008. Originally published as *Archimondain jolipunk: Confession d'un jeune homme à contretemps* (Paris: Calmann-Lévy, 2002).

──. *Visiter le Flurkistan, ou les Illusions de la littérature-monde*. Paris: Presses universitaires de France, 2008.

──. *Le Hêtre et le bouleau: Essai sur la tristesse européenne, suivi de L'utopie linguistique ou la pédagogie du vertige*. Paris: Seuil, 2009.

──. *L'inquiétude d'être au monde*. Lagrasse: Verdier, 2010.

——. *Vies pøtentielles*. Paris: Seuil, 2011.

——. *Le livre de la faim et de la soif*. Paris: Gallimard, 2017.

——. "Pøtentielle Leben." In Jerôme Ferrari and Cornelia Ruhe, eds., "Den gegenwärtigen Zustand der Dinge festhalten: Zeitgenössische Literatur aus Frankreich." Special issue, *die horen: Zeitschrift für Literatur, Kunst und Kritik* 267 (2017).

——. *Herzl: une histoire européenne*. Paris: Denoël, 2018.

——. "La traduction ou comment émouvoir l'Europa." https://web.archive.org/web/20120312122309/http://www.seau.org/fr/about, accessed August 2, 2018. toledo-archives.net/biography/, accessed April 1, 2018.

——. *Thésée, sa vie nouvelle*. Lagrasse: Verdier, 2020.

Trabant, Jürgen. "Die Sprache der Freiheit und ihrer Feinde." *Zeitschrift für Literaturwissenschaft und Linguistik* 41 (1981) (= Sprache und Literatur in der Französischen Revolution): 70–89.

——. *Traditionen Humboldts*. Frankfurt am Main: Suhrkamp, 1990.

——. *Der Gallische Herkules: Über Sprache und Politik in Frankreich und Deutschland*. Tübingen/Basel: Francke, 2002.

——. *Mithridates im Paradies: Kleine Geschichte des Sprachdenkens*. Munich: C.H. Beck, 2003.

——. "Sprach-Passion: Derrida und die Anderssprachigkeit des Einsprachigen." In *Exophonie: Anders-Sprachigkeit (in) der Literatur*, edited by Susan Arndt, Dirk Naguschewski, and Robert Stockhammer. Berlin: Kulturverlag Kadmos, 2007.

Tugendhat, Ernst. *Vorlesungen über Ethik*. 8th ed. Frankfurt am Main: Suhrkamp, 2012.

Viard, Bruno. "La Carte et le Territoire, roman de la représentation: entre trash et tradition." In *Michel Houellebecq: questions du réalisme d'aujourd'hui*, edited by Jörn Steigerwald, and Agnieszka Komorowska, 87–95. Tübingen: Narr, 2011.

——. *Littérature et déchirure de Montaigne à Houellebecq: Étude anthropologique*. Paris: Classiques Garnier, 2013.

Viart, Dominique, and Bruno Vercier. *La littérature française au présent: Héritage, modernité, mutations*. 2nd ed. Paris: Bordas, 2008.

Villeneuve, Denis. *Incendies*. DVD. Paris 2014.

Vogl, Joseph. *The Specter of Capital*. Translated by Joachim Redner and Robert Savage. Stanford: Stanford University Press, 2015.

Wallerstein, Immanuel. "The Ideological Tensions of Capitalism: Universalism versus Racism and Sexism." In: *Race, Nation, Class: Ambiguous Identities*, edited by Étienne Balibar and Immanuel Wallerstein, 29–36. New York: Verso, 1991.

——. *European Universalism: The Rhetoric of Power*. New York: New Press, 2006.

Walter, Monika. *Der verschwundene Islam? Für eine andere Kulturgeschichte Westeuropas*. Munich: Wilhelm Fink, 2016.

Walzer, Michael. "Two Kinds of Universalism." In *Nation and Universe: The Tanner Lectures on Human Values*, delivered by Michael Walzer at Brasenose College, Oxford University, May 1 and 8, 1989, 509–532. https://tannerlectures.utah.edu/_documents/a-to-z/w/walzer90.pdf, accessed August 31, 2020.

ZDFheute. "Provokateur und Prophet: Houellebecqs neuer Roman." January 4, 2019. https://zdf.de/nachrichten/heute/houellebecqs-neuer-roman-ist-da-serotonin-100.html, accessed February 7, 2019.

Author and Translator

Markus Messling, born in 1975, is full professor of Romance literatures and comparative literary and cultural studies at Saarland University, where he currently directs the project "Minor Universality: Narrative World Productions after Western Universalism" funded by the European Research Council (ERC). Beginning in April 2024, he will codirect the Käte Hamburger Research Centre for Cultural Practices of Reparation (CURE) with Christiane Solte-Gresser, an institute for advanced study funded by the German Federal Ministry of Research and Education (BMBF). From 2015 to 2019, he was vice director of the Centre Marc Bloch, the Franco-German institute for research in the social sciences and humanities, and, beginning in 2018, also held a position as professor for Romance literatures at Humboldt University of Berlin. He holds a Dr. phil. in Romance philology from the Free University of Berlin (2007) and a habilitation in Romance philology and comparative literature from Potsdam University (2015). In 2007/2008, Markus Messling was program director for science & research at the private ZEIT Foundation in Hamburg; and in 2008/2009 he was a postdoctoral fellow at École des Hautes Études en Sciences Sociales (EHESS) in Paris, funded by a grant from the Fondation Maison des Sciences de l'Homme and the German Academic Exchange Service (DAAD). From 2009 to 2014, he directed an Emmy Noether Excellence Grant on "Philology and Racism in the 19th Century" funded by the German Research Foundation (DFG). During the same period, he held a position as an assistant professor at Potsdam University. He has been a fellow of the renowned German Academic Scholarship Foundation (Studienstiftung), was awarded the Tiburtius Prize by the universities of Berlin in 2008, and received the Brandenburg Science Award in the Humanities in 2010. Markus Messling has held fellowships and visiting professorships at EHESS Paris (2011, 2015), the School of Advanced Study at the University of London and at Cambridge University (both 2014), and at Kobe University in Japan (2016).

Publications (selected): *Pariser Orientlektüren: Zu Wilhelm von Humboldts Theorie der Schrift* (Paderborn: Schöningh, 2008); *Gebeugter Geist: Rassismus und Erkenntnis in der modernen europäischen Philologie* (Wallstein: Göttingen, 2016); ed. with I. Dayeh, T. Hever, and E. E. Johnston, *Formations of the Semitic: Race, Religion, and Language in Modern European Scholarship* (Leiden/Boston: Brill, 2017) = Philological Encounters 2, no. 3–4; ed. with F. Hofmann, *Point de fuite: La Méditerranée et la crise européenne* (Paris: Éditions Hermann, 2019); ed. with C. Ruhe, L. Seauve, and V. de Senarclens, *Mathias Enard et l'érudition du roman* (Leiden/Boston: Brill Rodopi 2020); ed. with I. Dayeh, *Early Modern "New Sciences": Inquiries into Ibn Khaldūn and Giambattista Vico* (Leiden/Boston: Brill, 2020) = Philological Encounters 5, no. 1; ed. with F. Hofmann, *The Epoch of Universalism/L'Époque de l'universalisme (1769–1989)* (Berlin/Boston: De Gruyter, 2022); *Philology and the Appropriation of the World: Champollion's Hieroglyphs*, revised edition, trans. Michael Thomas Taylor and Marko Pajević (Cham: Palgrave Macmillan, 2023); ed. with J. Tinius, *Minor Universality: Rethinking Humanity after Western Universalism/Universalité mineure: Penser l'humanité après l'universalisme occidental* (Berlin/Boston: De Gruyter, 2023).

Michael Thomas Taylor, born in 1977, works as a Berlin-based editor and translator and as a research scholar at the Max Planck Institute for the History of Science in Berlin. He received a PhD from Princeton University in 2007 and has held assistant and associate professorships in German studies and humanities at the University of Calgary (Alberta, Canada), and Reed College (Portland, Oregon, USA). He also teaches at Bard College Berlin and has cocurated several exhibitions (in Berlin, Munich, and Calgary) on the history of sexuality and transgender history. He is one of the authors of the 2020 book *Others of My Kind: Transatlantic Transgender Histories* (Calgary: Calgary University Press), selected as a Choice Outstanding Academic Title in 2021. Other publications include *Not Straight from Germany: Sexual Publics and Sexual Citizenship since Magnus Hirschfeld*, ed. Michael Thomas Taylor, Annette F. Timm, and Rainer Herrn (Ann Arbor: University of Michigan Press, 2017) and *Vor der Familie: Grenzbedingungen einer modernen Institution*, with Albrecht Koschorke, Nacim Ghanbari, Eva Eßlinger, and Sebastian Susteck (Konstanz: Konstanz University Press, 2010). Recent academic translations, in addition to Markus Messling's *Philology and the Appropriation of the World*, include Juliane Vogel, *Making an Entrance: Appearing on the Stage from Racine to Nietzsche*, with Benjamin R. Trivers (Berlin: De Gruyter, 2022), with a translator's introduction; Florian Sprenger and Gottfried Schnödl, *Uexküll's Surroundings: Nazi Entanglements of Umwelt Theory*, cotranslated with Wayne Yung (Lüneburg: Meson Press, 2022); and Susanne Rau, *History, Space, and Place* (Abingdon: Taylor & Francis, 2019). Recent translations of trade books include Katrin Richter, *Else's Story: The Life of the World's First Woman Stockbroker* (LUCIA Verlag: Weimar, 2023); Gerda Breuer, *HerStories in Graphic Design* (Berlin: jovis Verlag, 2023); Zara Pfeifer, *ICC Berlin* (Berlin: jovis Verlag, 2022); and Peter Ortner, *The Essence of Berlin-Tegel* (Berlin: jovis Verlag, 2020).

Index

www.ingramcontent.com/pod-product-compliance
Lightning Source LLC
Chambersburg PA
CBHW051426090426

42737CB00014B/2849